Sweet Lou:

WHEN THE GAME CHANGED

An Oral History of Baseball's True Golden Age: 1969-1979

Only 3 pages for

GEORGE CASTLE

you ... weren't you a wild Seventies child!

LYONS PRESS
Guilford, Connecticut
An imprint of Globe Pequot Press

— George B. Castle

Lyons Press is an imprint of Globe Pequot Press.

Text design: Sheryl P. Kober
Project editor: Julie Marsh
Layout: Kevin Mak

Library of Congress Cataloging-in-Publication Data

Castle, George.
  When the game changed : an oral history of baseball's true golden age, 1969-1979 / George Castle.
      p. cm.
  Includes index.
  ISBN 978-1-59921-933-2
  1. Baseball--United States--History--20th century. 2. Nineteen seventies. 3. Oral history. I. Title.
  GV863.A1C376 2011
  796.357'6409047--dc22

                              2010030531

Printed in the United States of America

10 9 8 7 6 5 4 3 2 1

NATIONAL LEAGUE PITCHERS

EAST

MONTREAL
1 Carrithers
2 Fryman
3 Granger
4 Kirby
5 Murray
6 Renko
7 Rogers
8 Scherman
9 Stanhouse
10 Warthen

NEW YORK
1 Apodaca
2 T. Hall
3 Koosman
4 Lockwood
5 Lolich
6 Matlack
7 Sanders
8 Seaver
9 Swan
10 Webb

...DELPHIA
...rlton
...ristenson
...rber
...at
...nborg
...cGraw
...eed
...chueler
...itchell
...nderwood

PITTSBURGH
1 Candelaria
2 Demery
3 Giusti
4 R. Hernandez
5 Kison
6 Medich
7 Moose
8 Reuss
9 Rooker
10 Tekulve

ST. LOUIS
1 Curtis
2 Denny
3 B. Forsch
4 Frisella
5 Hrabosky
6 McGlothen
7 Proly
9 Rasmussen
10 M. Wallace

WEST

...ANTA
...Capra
...Dal Canton
...Devine
...Messersmith
...Moret
...Morton
...P. Niekro
...Quintana
...Ruthven
...Sosa
...Torrealba

CINCINNATI
1 Alcala
2 Billingham
3 Borbon
4 Darcy
5 Eastwick
6 Gullett
7 McEnaney
8 Nolan
9 Norman
10 Zachry

HOUSTON
1 Andujar
2 Barlow
3 Cosgrove
4 Dierker
5 K. Forsch
6 T. Griffin
7 Hardy
8 McIntosh
9 J. Niekro
10 Pentz
11 J.R. Richard
12 Rondon
13 J. Sosa

LOS ANGELES
1 Downing
2 Hooton
3 Hough
4 John
5 M. Marshall
6 Rau
7 Rhoden
8 Sutton
9 Wall

SAN DIEGO
1 Dupree
2 Folkers
3 A. Foster
4 Greif
5 R. Jones
6 B. Metzger
7 Spillner
8 Strom
9 Tomlin
10 Wehrmeister

SAN FRANCISCO
1 J. Barr
2 Caldwell
3 D'Acquisto
4 Halicki
5 Heaverlo
6 Lavelle
7 Minton
8 Moffitt
9 Montefusco
10 C. Williams

1976 UMPIRES NUMERICAL LISTING

...Colosi	9 McSherry	17 Stello	
...Dale	10 Montague	18 Sudol	
...Davidson	11 Olsen	19 Tata	
...Engel	12 Pryor	20 Vargo	
...Froemming	13 Pulli	21 Wendelstedt	
...German	14 Quick	22 Weyer	
...Harvey	15 Rennert	23 A. Williams	
...Kibler	16 Runge	24 B. Williams	

Ticket Information

Box Seats	$4.50
Reserved Grandstand	3.50
General Grandstand (Adults)	2.50
General Grandstand (Children under 14)	1.25
Bleachers	1.25

To make sure of getting the location you want, buy your reserve box seat tickets well in advance at Wrigley Field, or Bonds Store at State and Jackson. Orders for box seat tickets are being accepted now for games through the end of the season.

Mail orders receive prompt attention. Just forward the check or money order to Ticket Office, Wrigley Field, Chicago, Illinois 60613.

TIME OF GAMES

Single Games Mon. thru Fri.	1:30 P.M.
Single Games Sat. and Sun.	1:15 P.M.
All Doubleheaders	12:00 Noon

All fans expecting emergency calls are asked to register your seat location before the game in the Information and Services Office on the ground level near the Clark Street entrance. An usher will contact you at your seat if a call is received. We thank you for your cooperation.

Games Coming Up

SUN	APRIL 18	**PHILADELPHIA**
MON	APRIL 19	MONTREAL
TUE	APRIL 20	MONTREAL
WED	APRIL 21	MONTREAL
THUR	APRIL 22	LOS ANGELES
TUE	May 4	LOS ANGELES
WED	MAY 5	LOS ANGELES
THUR	MAY 6	CINCINNATI
FRI	MAY 7	CINCINNATI
SAT	MAY 8	CINCINNATI
SUN	MAY 9	**CINCINNATI**

Sundays, Holidays and Doubleheaders in Bold face.

Your complete home schedule is as close as the inside back cover of Chicago's Yellow Pages.

R—Indicates game has been interrupted because of rain.

THE NATIONAL ANTHEM

O say, can you see by the dawn's early light, What so proudly we hailed at the twi-light's last gleaming, Whose broad stripes and bright stars, through the perilous fight. O'er the ramparts we watched, were so gallantly streaming? And the rockets' red glare, the bombs bursting in air, Gave proof through the night that our flag was still there. O say does that star-spangled banner yet wave, O'er the land of the free and the home of the brave!

AMERICAN LEAGUE PITCHERS

EAST

BALTIMORE
1 D. Alexander
2 Cuellar
3 Flanagan
4 Garland
5 Grimsley
6 Holtzman
7 G. Jackson
8 D. Miller
9 J. Palmer
10 M. Smith
11 Willis

Boston
1 Burton
2 Cleveland
3 House
4 Jenkins
5 T. Jones
6 B. Lee
7 Pole
8 Tiant
9 Willoughby
10 Wise

CLEVELAND
1 Bibby
2 J. Brown
3 Buskey
4 P. Dobson
5 Eckersley
6 Hood
7 Kern
8 LaRoche
9 Peterson
10 Raich
11 S. Thomas
12 Waits

DETROIT
1 Bare
2 Coleman
3 J. Crawford
4 Fidrych
5 Grilli
6 Hiller
7 Laxton
8 D. Roberts
9 Ruhle
10 B. Taylor

MILWAUKEE
1 Broberg
2 Castro
3 Champion
4 Colborn
5 Hausman
6 T. Murphy
7 E. Rodriguez
8 Slaton
9 Travers

NEW YORK
1 K. Brett
2 Ellis
3 Figueroa
4 Gura
5 C. Hunter
6 S. Lyle
7 T. Martinez
8 R. May
9 Pagan
10 Tidrow

WEST

CALIFORNIA
1 Brewer
2 Drago
3 Dunning
4 Hartzell
5 Hassler
6 Kirkwood
7 Monge
8 G. Ross
9 N. Ryan
10 M. Scott
11 Tanana

CHICAGO
1 Barrios
2 C. Carroll
3 Forster
4 Gossage
5 D. Hamilton
6 Jefferson
7 B. Johnson
8 Kucek
9 Vuckovich
10 Wood

KANSAS CITY
1 Bird
2 Busby
3 Fitzmorris
4 Leonard
5 Littell
6 McClure
7 Mingori
8 Pattin
9 Sadecki
10 Splittorff

MINNESOTA
1 Albury
2 Blyleven
3 Burgmeier
4 B. Campbell
5 Decker
6 Goltz
7 J. Hughes
8 Luebber
9 Pazik

OAKLAND
1 Abbott
2 Bahnsen
3 Blue
4 D. Bosman
5 Fingers
6 Lindblad
7 P. Mitchell
8 Norris
9 Todd
10 M. Torrez

TEXAS
1 S. Barr
2 Briles
3 Foucault
4 Hargan
5 Hoerner
6 G. Perry
7 Perzanowski
8 Singer
9 Terpko
10 Umbarger

Official infield tractor used at Wrigley Field is an International Harvester Cub Cadet.

The organ music at Wrigley Field is provided by a Lowery organ and a Gibson amplification system.

Lunch Well—and Economically

You'll enjoy a snack at Wrigley Field, where we serve only the best of food and drinks, and at prices lower than you'll pay elsewhere. Pay no more than these listed prices.

Oscar Mayer Hot Dog	50c	Taffy Apple	30c
Corned Beef Sandwich	80c	Cigars	20c, 25c, 30c
Hamburger Sandwich	50c	Cigarettes	65c
Bratwurst Sandwich	55c	Wrigley's Gum (7-stick pkg.)	15c
Barbecued Beef Sandwich	60c	Wrigley Field Program	20c
Smokie Link Sandwich	65c	Cubs Program Pencil	10c
Ham Sandwich	45c	1976 Cubs Roster Book	75c
Cheese Sandwich	80c	Pennant (All N.L. Teams)	75c
Italian Beef Sandwich	35c	1976 Cubs Color Team Picture	$1.00
French Fries	50c	Cub Rings (Round or Square)	$1.00
Teen-Rite Cheese Pizza	60c	Ballpoint Pen Set	$1.75
Teen-Rite Sausage Pizza	20c	12 Miniature N.L. Pennants	$2.00
Borden's Frostick	40c	Cubs Plastic Helmet	$2.50
Borden's Frosty Malt	20c	Caps 'n Bats Kit	$2.25
Coffee	30c	Bobble Head Mascot Doll	$3.50 & $2.50
Milk	30c	Souvenir Caps	$3.00 & $2.50
Coca Cola or Fresca	25c	Cub T-Shirts	$3.25
Home Juice Lemonade	25c	Autographed Baseballs	$2.00
Home Juice Orangeade	25c	Plastic Autograph Ball Holder	$4.00
Heileman's Old Style Beer	65c	Cubs Sweatshirts (Childrens)	$4.75
Schlitz Beer	15c & 25c	Cubs Sweatshirts (Adults)	$9.00
Salted-In-Shell Peanuts	20c	Cubs Windbreaker (Childrens)	$10.00
Popcorn		Cubs Windbreaker (Adults)	

Contents

Prologue: Taking the Measure of a Decade iv

1: Baseball, the Lazarus Sport 1

2: Return of Leo the Lip,
    the Splendid Splinter, and Joltin' Joe 11

3: The Greatest Collection of Talent Ever? 35

4: Batsmen in Business Again 40

5: Duels to a Standstill,
    Complete Games, and Rubber Arms 74

6: Immortalized by a Ligament 106

7: Everyday Men, Splitters, and Setting It Up 111

8: Centerpieces 123

9: Would-Be Dynasties 141

10: Collapses, Should-Have-Beens, and Wannabes 182

11: Throwing Off the Shackles 214

12: Baseball Finally in Living Color 225

13: Characters 253

14: Bread and Circuses;
    Hot Dogs, Hair, and High Jinks 283

15: 1979 and Beyond 313

Acknowledgments 319

Index 322

About the Author 328

Prologue:
Taking the Measure of a Decade

We prefer to gauge history in 10-year intervals. It's a tidy way to bring order to the chaos of modern existence—separate world-turning events, social mores, trends, culture, and political change into decade-long chunks, and put labels on the time periods, too.

There was the Roaring Twenties, the Fabulous Fifties, the Swinging Sixties. History will have to put an appellation on the decade ending at this writing, but it's not going to be a pleasant description no matter how hard the pundits try.

The most common moniker for the 1970s is the "Me Decade," named for an emphasis on individualism and even self-centeredness, the latter a quality that really roared to the forefront in the 1980s and hasn't abated yet.

When we peg a decade as belonging to a certain style or flow of news, we really force the issue. We identify the Great Depression with the 1930s, but in reality the economic downfall began with agriculture, then equities back in the "booming" 1920s. We can't say the 1950s were quiet and serene as they opened with a hot war in Korea that cost more than 50,000 American lives and had more than a few envisioning a nuclear conflict with the Soviet Union. The 1960s were revolutionary from the get-go, but the relative peace of the previous decade crossed over to the assassination of John F. Kennedy and lasted into 1966 or there-abouts. The actual '60s of protest and upheaval, of defrocked presidents Lyndon Johnson and Richard Nixon, probably faded out for good around 1975, after the last helicopter fled the U.S. Embassy grounds in Saigon.

Culturally defined decades follow the same pattern, especially rock 'n' roll decades. The '50s of Elvis, doo-wop, and girl groups commingled with the British Invasion for about two years after the Beatles hit New York and *The Ed Sullivan Show* before finally fading. The all-time peak of rock, complete with its core of deceased pacemakers like Jim Morrison and Janis Joplin, stretched from the mid-1960s to the mid-1970s, when the glitter of the disco culture set in.

But if you want to start in year zero and end on December 31 of a year concluding in "9," enough decades will satisfy you with a logical beginning, middle, and end.

The 1940s started with the United States finally entering World War II, were divided in half by the V-E and V-J Days along with the start of the nuclear age in 1945, and ended with the spreading Red menace—the Soviet A-bomb and Mao's takeover of China—turning the United States into the world's policeman.

The 2000s began with the tech bust and a recession, both events paling in comparison with the modern-day Pearl Harbor of 9/11. The new millennium soon degenerated into war in Iraq and a misdirection from the original effort to hunt down Osama bin Laden. The 2000s were bisected by the reelection of a president who soon would be among the most unpopular in history presiding over another contrivance: an unsustainable housing boom bubble. The inevitable economic collapse teetered perilously close to another Great Depression, and the electorate reacted by breaching the greatest color line of all, that in the White House.

And the 1970s, which some call a "slum of a decade" for all its low-water marks, shaped life as it is now as much as any decade. In reality it was packed with news and technological and social advancements that had been talked about for decades, that are now second nature. It was not all sex, drugs, and rock 'n' roll, as popularly depicted on TV shows like *Swingtown*. Don't believe everything portrayed on *That Seventies Show*. Hollywood exaggerates historical popular culture and ends up wildly inaccurate in many instances.

The 1970s began with an unexpected escalation in Vietnam via the invasion of Cambodia and the deaths of student protestors at Kent State, the rise of embedded inflation, and the first serious incidents of international terrorism, especially at the Munich Olympics. The decade was bisected by the quintet of Nixon's Watergate, the Arab oil embargo bringing an end to the carefree era of the U.S. economy, a nasty recession that then stood as the worst since the Great Depression, the final retreat from Vietnam, and the Bicentennial celebration. Then, after a short breather, the dizzying windup: Three Mile Island, a "national malaise" proclaimed by Jimmy Carter, near-hyperinflation and double-digit interest rates, the Iran hostage crisis, and the Soviet invasion of Afghanistan, which would have a domino effect—as Vietnam never proved to be—two decades down the line as an incubator for 9/11.

But no matter how troubled an American decade is, one traditional lift to the national psyche is baseball. James Earl Jones's speech near the end of *Field of Dreams* about baseball's comforting continuity amid armies of steamrollers changing America was no celluloid fantasy. The game can always be depended upon to play above itself for the greater good.

Franklin D. Roosevelt wrote his "green light" letter to Kenesaw Mountain Landis early in 1942, giving his blessing for baseball's continuation during World War II as entertainment for war workers and stateside servicemen. The Tigers' World Series title in 1968 was credited with soothing wounds and forging a temporary sense of civic unity from the devastating Detroit riots of the previous year. Cubs TV announcer Jack Brickhouse, a master of homilies, often urged the 1950s viewer to forget his troubles "and let [managers] Bob Scheffing and Danny Murtaugh do the worrying for you." Twenty years later, in the late 1970s, the Cubs and Pirates managers were named Herman Franks and Chuck Tanner, but Brickhouse's message still rang.

But as hard as it tries, baseball can't always play foil to society's evolution. The 1970s version of the game featured more radical changes that shaped baseball into what is played today than any other decade-long period in its history. Always more conservative than the outside world it served due to the macho creed of its players and the exclusive old-boys network of owners, baseball in the 1970s was forced by various circumstances to alter its somewhat languid, pastoral, but always profit-motivated personality. Its typical pace of glacial change dramatically sped up.

The period of advancements actually lasted more than a decade. It began in 1968 when the day's pitching-oriented game—reminiscent of the early 1900s—drew fire from football-loving critics and turned off fans, who began filtering out of ballparks toward an increasing array of entertainment options. The timeline concluded late in 1979 when fireballing Nolan Ryan corralled the first $1 million annual contract. Ballplayers would thereafter be compensated at the market level they had never before achieved despite ranking as some of the country's most famous celebrities. They no longer were bound to their original teams via the age-old reserve clause—the ultimate restraint-of-trade. The well-compensated players put on a good enough show to start a salary escalation, fueled by eager TV networks thrusting billions of dollars in rights fees baseball's way. The teams spent the windfall as fast as they collected it.

In between the offensive-minded changes baseball mandated to prevent itself from slipping as "America's national pastime" and Ryan's payday, the game of the 1970s instituted free agency, arbitration, the designated hitter, divisions, league championship playoffs, night World Series games, the specialization of the bullpen, the breaking of the color line for managers and general managers, national cable TV coverage, far-out facial hair, double-knit uniforms, and, taking advantage of advances in orthopedics, Tommy John surgery to salvage and even enhance pitchers' careers. Like society, the game became more inclusionary. With a couple of exceptions, informal racial quotas on roster makeup ended while recruiting of talent from Latin America dramatically increased.

Amid garishly colored uniforms and disco-world Afros, ugly cookie-cutter stadiums built to also serve NFL teams, Astroturf, and some rudimentary drug use, the era may have truly been baseball's greatest of modern times. Forget the 1950s—that was generally a New York–driven memoir to the exclusion of the rest of baseball. The bevy of talent who made their debuts in the 1950s were still mainstays in the 1970s, if not in their primes. And they were now supplemented by a new crop of Hall of Fame–bound players. After some run-producing adjustments, baseball would exist in a fine balance of hitting and pitching.

Nirvana it wasn't, to be sure. Labor strife broke out in earnest with a 1972 strike. Owners could not hold back the charge led by Players Association impresario Marvin Miller. Three more labor strikes and ownership collusion to hold the line on salaries would mar the game in the 1980s and 1990s before a labor-management détente was finally achieved. The flip side of maximum rights and pay for players was the ebbing of the game as the most affordable of the major pro sports. The $1 bleacher seat of 1972 has ballooned to $60 today—with the same hard wooden bench, and you aren't even allowed in the gate three hours early to watch all of home batting practice. In most markets you must subscribe to cable TV to watch the majority of televised games. The days of exclusively over-the-air, free telecasts are over, with cable now the predominant carrier of baseball. All the while, the NFL Colossus and the innovative NBA seem to stay one step ahead of baseball in marketing, negating the 1970s gains in minority players. Football and basketball appear more attractive financially and aesthetically for the African-American athlete than the often-frustrating climb through the minor leagues to "the Show."

Romanticism and realism exist side by side in baseball. There is plenty of room for both. That is the gamut of emotions included here for a time-trip into baseball's first true era of living color, mimicking the by-then established method of TV transmission in the 1970s.

The game stops for nobody, and tomorrow is never promised. But yesterday is forever. And as NBA Commissioner David Stern has admitted, basketball would die for a history like baseball's.

1

Baseball, the Lazarus Sport

Our eternal game, baseball survives everything thrown at it.

A widespread, embedded gambling culture culminated in the Black Sox Scandal of 1919–21 and required an imperious commissioner and a larger-than-life Bambino to save it. Strikes and almost constant labor acrimony grew in intensity until the World Series was canceled in 1994, sandwiched between two truncated seasons. Only future Supreme Court Justice Sonia Sotomayor's intervention in the spring of 1995 prevented an even longer strike. Recreational-drug scandals of the 1980s morphed into the culture of steroids as the 1990s got under way, first uplifting the poststrike game, then dragging it into the muck and congressional committee rooms.

All the while, the media pundits were tougher on baseball than any other sport. Football could have been first to pump itself up with steroids, basketball had point-shaving scandals and corrupt referees, and the Olympics were fraught with low politics, including an anti-American bias in the 1972 basketball championship game. But when baseball makes a mistake, it is pilloried like no other athletic enterprise.

Commissioner Bud Selig picked up on the trend when he was a relatively new owner of the Milwaukee Brewers.

"This was in the mid-1970s. . . . I remember sitting with Bowie [Commissioner Kuhn] and John Fetzer of the Tigers, who was a great owner, and I sort of complained about the same thing," Selig said of baseball being trashed while football seemingly got a free pass. "Bowie had a theory that we were always held to a higher standard by the media, and we should regard that as a compliment. I do take it as a compliment."

The criticism the sport receives is often valid. Baseball needs to be knocked down before it institutes necessary changes. Selig's administration was slow to address steroids until its greatest stars, pushing the home-run record into science-fiction territory, were linked to juicing. Expansion of instant replay to rectify glaring umpiring mistakes is the next frontier. And back in the mid-20th century, major-league baseball was dragged kicking and screaming into the modern era of integrated rosters, at least a decade after African-Americans should have been allowed to play.

And baseball dodged a salvo of bullets in the 1960s. Pro football's spectacular and well-marketed rise, cultural changes in society, lack of innovation in baseball itself, and the game's own pitching excellence prompted mostly New York–based pundits, the most high profile being Howard Cosell, to proclaim that "baseball is dead."

They were exaggerating, of course. Yet perception is everything. Baseball always works best on a timeless level, the structure, rules, and presentation of the game the same as decades past. If you left a 2010 game and stepped back in time 50 years, much of what you'd witness would be the same, other than a quicker pace due to fewer pitching changes, baggy uniforms, and no piped-in stadium entertainment. And, sure enough, by the mid-1960s baseball had hardly changed since its post–World War II boom years. To be sure, natural evolution did occur: four expansion teams, several franchise shifts, the big move to the West Coast, and a few new stadiums.

Yet in an era when the pace of life dramatically quickened, baseball was chastened for its comparatively languid tempo. Jet planes, interstate highways, and instant, fast everything became staples in the 1960s. More important, a pro football league that only a decade earlier was one cut above the barnstorming level had become preeminent, led by a savvy young marketing genius named Pete Rozelle. And it didn't hurt that the pigskin first boomed in media capital New York via the perennially contending Giants, who were led by telegenic all-purpose back Frank Gifford.

When New York native Vince Lombardi quickly molded the Packers, playing in tiny Green Bay, into the NFL's second glamour team after the Giants, *Time* magazine proclaimed pro football "The Sport of the Sixties" in the cover story of its December 21, 1962, issue.

Chicago Sun-Times baseball writer Jerome Holtzman, a future inductee into the writers' wing of the Baseball Hall of Fame and the game's official historian before his death in 2008, detected the Big Apple–originated push for football as the new national pastime in the early 1960s.

"The skeptic from the Midwest or from the Far West can only wonder if the New York communication captains would have stirred to such a response if the Giants were dull and not winning [division] championships," Holtzman wrote in a four-part series in February 1963 that examined whether football had replaced baseball as the national pastime. "Not too long before, the Los Angeles Rams, the Cleveland Browns, and the Baltimore Colts were dominating the league. No such enthusiasm accompanied them and there were few, if any, words gushing and heralding professional football's reign."

TV by then had penetrated almost every home after its growth period in the 1950s. By the early 1960s, Rozelle's owners were still protective of their home gates blacking out local telecasts. However, new lucrative contracts with CBS provided that all road games in the 14-game schedule would be televised back to the originating markets. Even more pro football inventory became available when the upstart American Football League began in 1960. The AFL immediately landed a network contract with ABC, so the consuming public could enjoy their choice of games on most autumn Sundays. The American couch potato who blocked out Sunday afternoon quickly became an institution, even with the home-game blackout lasting until 1973.

In contrast, with the exception of the Chicago Cubs and the New York teams—who televised all or most of their home games—baseball owners rationed their TV exposure to protect their ticket sales. The Chicago White Sox shared WGN-TV with the Cubs, but until the mid-1960s only allowed home day games on the tube to protect the night games' gates. Owners also worried that the free telecasts had a big part in a steady decline in minor-league attendance that began in the early 1950s.

This was an era when regular Sunday doubleheaders made up for modest crowds on weekdays and 1 million annual attendance was a Holy Grail goal, as many teams operated with a 700,000 or 800,000 gate. When Walter O'Malley moved the Dodgers to Los Angeles, he permitted only games from San Francisco to be televised back home in LA. Gussie Busch of the Cardinals allowed just 40 road games on TV, with benefits accruing to Harry Caray and his exciting radio play-by-play. Baseball had a colorful, syntax-mangling character in Dizzy Dean fronting its Saturday afternoon *Game of the Week* telecasts on CBS, but barred the games from broadcast in major-league markets, again to protect the home gate and any local telecasts. Not until 1965, when ABC acquired the Saturday games and hired Jackie Robinson as the first African-American network sports color analyst, did the national game air throughout the entire country.

Baseball derived comparative chump change from its broadcast rights. In 1962 the White Sox pulled down about $1 million for radio and TV. But Cubs owner Phil Wrigley, in one of his eccentric, baseball-ignorant edicts, believed in virtually free publicity for his sagging product. Wrigley drew just $600,000 from WGN-TV and Radio, even though Cubs video ratings were higher than the Sox's, according to Vince Lloyd, who announced for both teams.

Meanwhile, the network *Game of the Week* revenue was unevenly divided among franchises, depending upon how frequently each appeared on Saturdays. Naturally, the Yankees pocketed the most dollars. Not until the 1965 ABC contract did baseball adopt a Rozelle-style revenue-sharing arrangement with the $5.7 million deal divided equally among all teams. NBC replaced the low-rated ABC in 1966 with a three-year contract, including the World Series and the All-Star Game, for $11.8 million per year. In contrast, CBS's deal with the NFL in 1964 netted the league $18.8 million annually. The AFL switched allegiance and acquired color telecasts via NBC for 1965 by way of a five-year deal for $35 million.

On TV, with the game presented in old ballparks with odd nooks and crannies, baseball seemed to stand still compared to football, which suited the small screen well. Despite stoppages in between plays, timeouts, and penalties, football action moved back and forth on a rectangular field with cameras at the 50-yard-line. The pass-happy AFL was especially made for TV.

Football backers nailed baseball for its seemingly pedestrian pace and frequent lack of action.

"Even baseball, the sportswriters' 'national pastime,' can be a slow-motion bore," wrote a *Time* correspondent in his 1962 ode to Lombardi. "Finger resin bag, touch cap, look for sign, shake head, shake again, check first, big sigh, wind up, finally pitch. Crack! Foul ball—and the fans could be halfway to Chicago by jet. Even a good thing palls when the games go on day after day for six months."

Throw in football's violence, its appeal to the public's bloodlust in an era when TV programs and movies became successively more gory, culminating in the massacre shot of *Bonnie and Clyde* in 1967. CBS even crafted a 1961 documentary, *The Violent World of Sam Huff*, a Giants linebacker, who was a latter-day Ray Lewis.

The *Saturday Evening Post* described pro football as "the ultimate test of man's strength and endurance and of his willingness to endure pain and risk and serious injury." The magazine even quoted Huff as some noble gladiator inflicting and receiving pain: "Once you've signed your contract, you don't even think about money for the rest of the year."

The Friday office pool, settled up on Monday, along with the weekly visit to the local bookie became a part of the American landscape. Football knowledge may not have been deep for the average fan, who was hard-pressed to name his team's entire offensive line or define a "red dog." But to the sports' backers, it didn't matter. The *Time* correspondent cited an anecdote of a man asking his wife at a Giants–Browns game at Yankee Stadium: "Honey, do you understand anything about this game?" She replied: "Not a thing, except I like it."

With pundit Howard Cosell adding his two cents via his nightly ABC Radio commentary and gaining more prominence with his advocacy of semirebellious Muhammad Ali, the drumbeat of baseball-as-boring gained momentum as the 1960s reached their midpoint, and some baseball announcers attempted to put up a defense. References to the steady flow of action unfolding before them were made by Joe Garagiola and Phil Rizzuto on the NBC Radio broadcast of Game 7 of the 1964 World Series between the Cardinals and Yankees. On April 12, 1965, Harry Caray counterpunched on his far-flung St. Louis radio network during the Opening Day broadcast between the Cardinals and Cubs at Wrigley Field in a game called on account of darkness in a 10–10 tie after 11 innings.

"I'd like to see those guys who write those stories about what's wrong with baseball, that there's no action to it," Caray crowed at midgame. "I'd like to see them watch this ball game today. Everything has happened."

But baseball's shortsighted TV policies hardly promoted the game. The average '60s owner was content to fling his gates open daily with little promotion besides the odd Bat Day. Season-ticket sales were only a small part of the typical franchise's attendance, which depended upon team performance, weather, and ballpark location, which was increasingly in tough urban neighborhoods by the mid-20th century. Teams missed a golden opportunity for self-promotion with a fantastic array of Hall of Fame–bound talent, particularly in the National League, all playing at once. The NL's early recruitment of African-American players led to some of the greatest players of all time taking five different teams to the pennant between 1960 and 1964. But the game did not do itself any favors by not producing consistent challengers to the New York Yankees, who won the AL pennant in all but two years between 1949 and 1964. Too many teams were out of the pennant race too early in the season, hurting the gate. AL attendance declined from 10.2 million in 1961 to 8.9 million in 1966. Without September drama to boost day-of-game ticket sales, the majority of AL teams yielded their markets to football as summer waned.

Baseball also may have lent credence to accusations that the game was too pedestrian and low-scoring via a 1963 decision to expand the strike zone to its literal limits, ranging between the batter's shoulders and knees. The action to cut down hitting was rivaled only in the early Depression-era move to deaden the ball (which was done to prevent gaudy home-run or batting-average numbers to influence players' contract talks). In his *Sun-Times* series, Holtzman speculated the strike-zone tactic was done to speed up the games to better compete with pro football.

Little did the Lords of the Game know they'd regret their decision in less than a half decade—and would never again actively jigger the game to aid pitching.

The expanded strike zone had an immediate impact, negating an offensive surge in 1961–62 partially caused by the dilution of talent associated with expanding by four teams, including some positively dreadful pitching by the 120-defeat '62 Mets. The Pirates led the NL in ERA in '62 with 3.37; the Dodgers paced the senior circuit with 2.85 in '63, a season in which the entire league's ERA was just 3.29. Amazingly, the Cubs were second with 3.08 with lefty Dick Ellsworth sporting a 2.11 ERA, which has never been matched in post–World War II Chicago history. Meanwhile, the Orioles led the AL in ERA with 3.69 in '62, compared to the White Sox's 2.97 in '63. Thanks to Sandy Koufax's otherworldly dominance, the Dodgers kept their team ERA under 3.00 through

1966, Koufax's final season, while the White Sox never sported an ERA over 3.00 until 1969. In fact, the White Sox outdid even the Dodgers in 1967 with a team ERA of just 2.45.

Despite the increasing dominance of pitching and low-run games, baseball attendance did stage a comeback in 1966. Close pennant races in the NL provided a modest attendance spark as the crowds reached a record 25 million in 1966. Then, despite a memorable four-team AL race to the season's final day in 1967, the pitchers totally took over and the crowd counts began to significantly drop.

The gate went backward in tandem with hitting. Some of the all-time greatest starting pitchers took full advantage of a high mound and big strike zone to dominate like never before. The 1968 season soon was branded the Year of the Pitcher. The American League composite batting average dropped to .230; the National League's was .243. Carl Yastrzemski won the AL batting title with just a .301 batting average, the only full-time hitter in the league to crack the .300 mark. Bob Gibson, great under any circumstances, far outdid anyone in history with a 1.12 ERA over 304⅔ innings. Luis Tiant of the Indians paced the AL with a 1.60 ERA. Tough-luck pitchers abounded with just 6.8 runs being scored per game. Fergie Jenkins of the Cubs lost five games by 1–0 scores—of which there were a total of 82 that season—while lefty Bob Veale of the Pirates had a 13–14 record despite just a 2.05 ERA. Tommy John of the White Sox was lucky: He was 10–5 with a 1.98 ERA on a bad team, a season after going 10–13 with a 2.47 ERA on a contender.

"Yaz led with .301 and Danny Cater was second at .288. It was like uh-oh, they better do something to bring hitting back into the game," John said. "I think that you just went through a cycle where hitters were down. I finished fifth in the AL with ERA. Usually 1.98 is going to win [the ERA title]. But Tiant won and Gibson won."

Worse yet, the lack of pennant races in the cumbersome 10-team leagues dampened interest while ceding September to pro football. The Tigers won the AL pennant by 12 games, while the Cardinals finished nine ahead in the NL. Pity the fans and ticket-takers of teams finishing 8th through 10th. Yes, the two leagues each had *10* teams. Win the pennant and you went directly to the World Series then. But if you finished last or even in the second division of a 10-team league, where was the hope late in the season?

Baseball had seemed rudderless under ineffectual commissioner William Eckert, a retired U.S. Army general dubbed the "unknown soldier" by critics during his term, which began in 1965. Interestingly, his biggest impact was in his last official act as commissioner at the winter meetings in San Francisco on December 3, 1968. Baseball's rules committee enacted, on Eckert's recommendation, three key rules changes.

Foremost was lowering the mound from 15 to 10 inches high, a compromise from an original recommendation of 8 inches. The mounds were mandated to be sloped gradually so that pitchers would not appear to be chucking off a steep cliff.

"To give perspective, if you're a hitter and I'm standing above you on a stepladder and I'm dropping a ball down on you vertically, that's virtually impossible to hit," said John. "So now if I am standing horizontally with you and I'm throwing horizontally, that ball is the easiest ball to hit. Let's say you're 6-foot-3 and now you're 7-foot-8 inches [on a 15-inch mound] and your hand is slightly above your head, so now you're 8 feet and you're throwing on an angle in a 2½-foot drop. [Lowering the mound] makes it easier as a hitter."

The rules committee also reversed the 1963 strike zone expansion. Now it would stretch only from the tops of the knees to the armpits, although its exact boundaries would vary from umpire to umpire.

The third mandate was the AL's first experiment with a designated hitter for the pitcher in spring training 1969. The seed thus planted, the idea was eventually adopted for the regular season in 1973, forever transforming the AL into an offense-oriented league.

Along with rules changes, the owners paved the way for new leadership by forcing out Eckert during the 1968 winter meetings. But they did not heed the storm warnings of a new, energized Players Association under the two-year-old leadership of Marvin Miller. A labor economist, Miller began transforming a house union into the most powerful labor association in the country by educating and unifying the players. Like a crafty control pitcher, Miller realized a blazing fastball down the middle would not work to strike down the etched-in-stone reserve clause that bound players to their teams into perpetuity. Instead, he methodically began working the corners to set up legal precedents.

The Players Association began rattling the chains in a demand for a beefed-up pension agreement at the 1968 winter meetings. But its biggest victories would be recorded, like other transformative changes begun in San Francisco, during the tumultuous decade to come.

Baseball had risen, albeit modestly, from the perceived dead. Football would continue to gain momentum, especially from "Broadway Joe" Namath's predicted New York Jets' win over the heavily favored Baltimore Colts in Super Bowl III just a month after the winter meetings concluded. Still, the battered national pastime would no longer stand still and take the barbs tossed at it. A game that only changed glacially now would move faster, saving itself in the process and laying the groundwork for renewed growth then and far into the future.

2

Return of Leo the Lip, the
Splendid Splinter, and Joltin' Joe

Baseball had nowhere to go but up after a tumultuous 1968 went down in history as one of the most critical and depressing years of the 20th century. No, the real world did not evolve into the "Age of Aquarius" promised in the popular *Hair* musical of the time. Yet somehow a course of spectacular events began to lift the spirits of an emotionally battered populace.

To be sure, there was the daily bad news of the Vietnam War, a military draft, and the massive protests that included a national "moratorium" in the fall for which even freshmen in high school simply walked out of classes. No quick end to the senseless conflict was at hand as newly inaugurated President Richard M. Nixon sought "peace with honor." Dissidents to Nixon's philosophy quickly racked up dossiers on his secret "enemies list."

But spirits were lifted by the midsummer extravaganzas of the *Apollo 11* moon landing and the Woodstock music festival. Neil Armstrong's first step on the moon moved TV news anchor Walter Cronkite in a manner not seen since he announced the death of President John F. Kennedy on November 22, 1963. Meanwhile, a city's worth of young people similarly journeyed sky-high in a spectacular demonstration of peaceful community and love of music on a farmer's field that became known as Woodstock.

The far more conservative world of baseball resumed its role as a distraction in troubled times as the changes mandated at the 1968 winter meetings took hold. "You tell me baseball is dead . . . hah!" harrumphed Cubs radio announcer Vince Lloyd, setting the scene as an SRO crowd of more than 40,000 streamed into Wrigley Field for Opening Day, April 8, 1969. Hitting reversed its massive downward trend of the mid-1960s, boosted further by the inept pitching of four expansion teams, including the 110-defeat San Diego Padres and Montreal Expos. Third-year Oakland A's slugger Reggie Jackson punctuated the hitting revival by taking aim at Babe Ruth's 60-homer mark, belting 37 by the All-Star break before cooling off. Meanwhile, the best pitchers still thrived despite the game's rules being tightened against them. The majority adjusted to the drop to a 10-inch mound as nine 20-game winners still dominated in the NL.

A new commissioner, Bowie Kuhn, former attorney for the NL, took office and began to plant seeds of a nascent marketing program. Baseball would celebrate its centennial as a pro sport in 1969, complete with the introduction of its traditional batter's symbol and the return of fan voting for the All-Star Game, absent since the infamous 1957 ballot-stuffing episode of Cincinnati Reds fans. The Mid-Summer Classic appropriately was held in Washington, D.C., where Nixon hosted the All-Stars in a gala White House reception.

Had the conspiratorial Nixon become an ink-stained wretch instead of a stained politician, he would have more than met his match in Leo Durocher, the lightning rod of the rivalry between the Chicago Cubs and the New York Mets, two formerly downtrodden franchises stirred to life in 1969. The Big Apple vs. the Second City, but more important in the eyes of fans and many baseball officials, good vs. evil—a miracle team vs. Durocher, perhaps the most despised man in the game in '69. The outcome of the duel would affect the fortunes of the Cubs and Mets for decades to come and, just as impactful, would emblazon themselves in the psyches of their fans forevermore.

The story of the 1969 Miracle Mets has been told and retold, probably puffed up to even more amazing heights than the real-life team achieved. However their story is angled, the Mets did usher in the 1970s on a wave of enthusiasm. And while the Mets' championship shelf life was confined to October 1969, they did represent the new taking over from the old. Manager Gil Hodges employed role players instead of a static, set lineup, used a five-man rotation to take pressure off his hard throwers, and even dabbled in bullpen roles—all standard parts of baseball in decades to come. Hodges's strategy was in stark contrast to the old-school ways of Cubs counterpart Leo Durocher, possessed of superior overall talent that he wore down throughout the dog days of August into September.

LEO THE LIP

Symbolically, the Hodges vs. Durocher duel represented other old-school standbys of prewar baseball dovetailing with the new generation—and not all in negative ways—as the 1960s waned. Nineteen sixty-nine was the only year that both Joe DiMaggio, voted the greatest living ballplayer that season, and rival Ted Williams donned uniforms at the same time in their post–playing career days. DiMaggio counseled young outfielders as a part-time coach for an Oakland Athletics franchise, which was just shaking off its decades-long doldrums that had started three cities earlier in Philadelphia. Williams took over as manager of the woeful Washington Senators, reviving them for one blessed season before they reverted to form.

The self-promoting Durocher, of course, enmeshed himself in controversy, taking center stage, compared to the more dignified DiMaggio and outspoken Williams. In October 1965 Cubs owner Phil Wrigley hired the brash, self-aggrandizing Leo Durocher as manager. He possessed the deserved nickname "the Lip" and was probably the most amoral man in baseball. He had not managed in a decade. But his past record piloting the previously comical Brooklyn Dodgers into contender status, then leading the New York Giants to two pennants in 1951 and 1954, winning it all the latter year, attracted Wrigley. Never mind that Durocher had been suspended from baseball for the entire 1947 season for his associations with gangland-related people.

Never mind that Durocher revealed his personal style to future *Boys of Summer* author Roger Kahn in 1954—when picking up a woman on a date, immediately put your hand on her crotch to test her lust factor. If she pushed your hand away, you had the entire evening to find another date. But if she didn't, Durocher reasoned, you were in like Flynn—and many famous women, he claimed, didn't swat his hand away.

Never mind that Durocher, once accused by roommate Babe Ruth of stealing his watch, fit all the classic definitions of a first-class jerk and admitted as much. His third wife, whom he married on June 19, 1969, in the Chicago social event of the summer, likely had a few opinions on the subject.

LYNN WALKER GOLDBLATT DUROCHER (Leo Durocher's third wife): They don't make up rules for guys like that. They make their own rules. I don't know if Leo considered himself a celebrity. He considered himself a good manager. He loved baseball. A "Damon Runyon" character was the best description for him.

After a halting 1966 season, when Durocher forecast the Cubs were not an 8th-place team and instead finished 10th—dead last—he spearheaded a spectacular revival. The 1967 Cubs zoomed to first place on several occasions in July before a more talented Cardinals club overwhelmed them. They took a step back early in 1968 but were revived in the second half of the season. When April 8, 1969, arrived, pennant talk abounded in Chicago with the two-time defending NL champion Cardinals the chief obstacle. The Mets weren't on anyone's radar. The two top Cubs baseball officials crowed their optimism on the radio pregame show on Opening Day, explaining they were not going to tinker with their strong nucleus of regulars.

LEO DUROCHER (manager, Cubs, Astros, 1969–73): They want all our frontline players. Give them four or five for one. We didn't tear this club down and start from the bottom and build it up to where we have it now to give these players away.

JOHN HOLLAND (general manager, Cubs, 1969–75): It's the best front line we've ever had during the period I've been here. Back in 1960, we brought up Santo and Williams—they were just babies then. They are ready to contend for the championship. Take [Adolfo] Phillips. He has all the ability in the world. If we can just get it out of him, he's ready now to come. With Phillips in there, he does settle the club down.

But the GM inadvertently expressed a harbinger of things to come with his next broadcast thought.

HOLLAND: Making a deal with another ball club is the most difficult thing in the world. We have worked constantly since the expansion draft last November. We knew we would be short in some positions, especially on the bench. Trying to fill those spots has been very tough. Expansion clubs do have some ballplayers who we feel in time will be available. Right now they're holding up everyone, asking too much for them. And we don't intend to break up our front line.

Cubs players felt ready to win, too, and the fans picked up on their confidence.

BILLY WILLIAMS (Cubs, Athletics, 1969–76): The Cubs hadn't won a World Series in some time. Leo put a team together. People hadn't seen a winner in so many years. We had played together so long. We were household names to the fans who came out. People took a liking to us. We signed autographs. The situation with the ballpark, the clubhouse, and the dugout, all these things became a factor in why people accepted us and loved us so much. We had to walk from the clubhouse [in the left-field corner] to the dugout. There were many, many times when we saw the same people on the rail. When we started, there were only 5,000 or 6,000 fans, and we knew them.

A spectacular Opening Day win over the Phillies on Willie Smith's walk-off two-run pinch homer in the 11th sparked an 11–1 start and Cubs mania throughout Chicago. Meanwhile, the Mets lurched through the first two months, their record just 18–23 at one point. Their ambitions were upbeat but far more modest than the Cubs, according to outfielder Ron Swoboda, now a broadcaster for his hometown Triple-A New Orleans Pelicans but then a grizzled four-year Mets veteran.

RON SWOBODA (Mets, Expos, Yankees, 1969–73): We thought the next step would be .500, maybe a little above. We thought we were more competitive. We didn't feel like the doormats any more. We didn't set the world on fire. We sensed we were a better team, but we didn't have anything together yet. We'll improve, and we'll be the pumpkin in somebody else's Cinderella story. We turned out to be the princes.

The Cubs zoomed to a 40–18 record and an eventual nine-game lead by mid-June as the favored Cardinals wallowed in a poor start, while the Pirates could not get a full head of steam. Back in the pack in the new National League East, something unusual was percolating. The Mets won 11 in a row in late May and into June—the final seven games of a Shea Stadium home stand, all against the Padres, Dodgers, and Giants, then four more on the West Coast. Later, in August, the New Yorkers would go 14–2 against these same teams. It was like a spiritual transfer from their Big Apple baseball ancestors.

As the Cubs were high-flying at midseason, "Cub Power" buttons and even a record made by players proliferated through the better part of Chicago. Players were fixtures at postgame appearances at car dealers and grocery stores. Durocher himself starred in a popular TV commercial for Schlitz beer. "Have another *Slitz*," the Lip implored while recounting how he kicked dirt on umpire Jocko Conlan: "He kicked me, and I kicked him."

Almost out of sight of the Bums and other parts of the growing Cubs Universe, Durocher steadily added enemies. Although he justifiably gave breaks to young players in 1966–67, in many cases out of necessity on the previously talent-bereft Cubs, Durocher suddenly developed impatience with the kids. He became reliant and overly loyal to his core of lineup regulars and rotation centerpieces. Any player on the outside had to be a sensational standout to earn Durocher's patronage, but he put them in a catch-22 situation by not giving them legitimate chances to succeed. He was cantankerous, condescending, contradictory, crude, and cruel.

No wonder a 1969 rookie like pitcher Jim Colborn privately questioned Durocher's style. Colborn was a product of Whittier College, alma mater of Richard Nixon, signed for just $400 in 1967. He later went on to be a prominent big-league pitching coach starting in the 1990s.

JIM COLBORN (Cubs, Brewers, Royals, Mariners, 1969–78): I always thought he was on the cusp of two generations. He was from an era when no one questioned authority and no explanations were needed for subordinates. I had a theory that Leo didn't like college graduates, young people, or extra men.

We were pretty much scared to death of what Leo might do. You were trying to learn desperately. But the expectations were that you know it already. Do it or you were out—no explanations. We were like puppies that were being whipped.

But Durocher couldn't help himself. His third wife said he was a product of his times.

LYNN WALKER GOLDBLATT DUROCHER: Leo was outraged by a bunch of things in baseball. One thing he said was that younger players were making too much money. He felt they were a bunch of sissies out there. They're overpaid, not hungry enough. Today, it's like they were doing you a favor. He believed they don't appreciate the game like he did [in the 1920s and 1930s].

But Durocher went beyond personal outrage. He abused his young players. Upset because rookie starter Gary Ross wasn't hiding pitches to his manager's satisfaction in a 1968 game, Durocher hollered to the opposing Giants the pitches Ross planned to throw. He upbraided 6-foot-3 rookie catcher John Felske, a future Phillies manager, because he could not crouch low enough to get "underneath" the hitter. Capable starter Ray Culp, 26 in 1967, went to too many 3-and-2 counts, so Durocher banished him to Boston, where he won 51 games the next three seasons. Joe Niekro, another future baseball achiever, drove Durocher nuts by fiddling with his cap after every pitch, so away Niekro went, eventually to learn the knuckleball mastered by brother Phil Niekro. Durocher warned second-year pitcher Bill Stoneman to keep throwing his fastball till it was banged off the scoreboard clock instead of a crackling curve that Stoneman later used to good success in Montreal. The Expos also ended up the destination for center fielder Adolfo Phillips, whose skittishness at the plate on close pitches ruined his confidence, while his complaints of a legitimate stomach ailment gave him an image of a hypochondriac. Phillips thus fell out of favor with the Lip, the two being in conflict. When Durocher forced Phillips out of Chicago two months into the '69 season, it opened up a gaping hole in center field for three seasons. Eventually, the disgust with Durocher spread to key veterans—"half a dozen guys," in the estimation of ace Fergie Jenkins. Unreported in Chicago media when it was uttered in June 1969—not long before the Cubs were nearing their apogee—was a comment from what the *Sun-Times'* Tom Fitzpatrick would attribute to a "prominent player" in a September 7 Sunday magazine profile on Durocher. The player said a team revolt was imminent: "Something has to be done because we can't win the pennant with Durocher. He just doesn't know how to handle pitchers."

Longest suffering of the media mob covering Leo the Lip was future Hall of Famer Lou Boudreau, who had to deal with the raging ego of Durocher for all 162 games during the pre-game radio show. Fortunately, the former shortstop had good use for his fast hands, pulling the mic away when Durocher's potty mouth got the best of him. Here is his recollection from 1994, seven years before his death at 84.

LOU BOUDREAU (Cubs announcer, 1969–79): There were a lot of bleeps in my interview. Sometimes it took about five takes. They were three-minute shows. Vince [Lloyd] helped me out in Philadelphia one day. I went to the ballpark. I wasn't feeling good. I had to do the Durocher show. Whenever there were several sportswriters around, Durocher was at his best, but not for the interview. We got through several attempts for the interview and I decided I'd had enough. I told Vince I'd had it and he'll have to do it. I always thought Leo liked me. He always had to use those [profane] words.

Vince and I were flying to California once. Milton Berle was on the plane and we talked sports. I got the idea— why not have Milton on for the show? I completed the first Durocher show and put it on tape. Something happened with it being relayed to Chicago. Vince called me and told me I'd have to do it live, that we had no tape of the *Durocher in the Dugout* show. I told Milton to meet me at the dugout. He didn't realize we were doing the show live.

Milton said, "Do you think you can keep the Cubs in the first division?" Leo's first words were *bleep* and I threw the microphone into the other hand, worried now that answer got over the air. I called Vince from the dugout, and we received several calls in Chicago—they wanted to know what Durocher's answer was.

One contemporary got the best of Durocher in 1969. Former arch-rival Gil Hodges from the Brooklyn Dodgers–New York Giants rivalry was a 1970s manager going up against a 1930s manager in Durocher. Leo the Lip was a "hunch" manager who believed in playing the hot hand. "Back up the truck" was his byword for dumping nonproductive players back to Triple-A. Durocher had a set lineup of stars and a multiple 20-win pitcher in Fergie Jenkins. Three future Hall of Famers played for him in 1969. That lineup would be set in stone every day, barring injuries, through the brutal all day-game schedule at Wrigley Field, which in future decades was medically and scientifically proven to tire out teams. Meanwhile, Hodges maneuvered around his lack of lineup stars and platooned his role players, using their strengths. He did not overpitch aces Tom Seaver and Jerry Koosman. They occasionally got extra rest with one of the first uses of a five-man rotation.

RON SWOBODA: Hodges was a smart guy who was all about winning and doing the best. Leo was always about looking good. Leo always had to look good and you knew it and he made you know it. Flashy women. Like he was smarter than the game. But there was nobody smarter about the game than Hodges. He was just an interesting baseball man. You understood why he did it, but we said, "That's interesting."

Hodges used to monkey with Leo. They'd have the Saturday *Game of the Week.* After that game they always left technical stuff in the dugout. Hodges took one of the headsets and put it on—you could see one another from each dugout. He put it on like he was talking to somebody out in center field. I know it was related to that whole business where the Giants got the signals from [a spy in] the scoreboard in the Polo Grounds. He got a towel and made a big splash with it—like he was secretive with it. He was playing with Leo. Those guys had to have a little history together. We're talking pretty good egos here.

Hodges began outmanaging Durocher in two midseason series in which the Mets took four of six—July 8 to 10 at Shea Stadium and July 14 to 16 at Wrigley Field. In cutting the Cubs' lead to four games and establishing themselves as legit contenders, the New Yorkers started flashing their miracle magic in front of packed houses in both cities. After being held to one hit by Fergie Jenkins through eight innings on July 8, the Mets rallied for three runs in the bottom of the ninth to pull it out 4–3, thanks to two misplayed fly balls by ne'er-do-well Cubs center fielder Don Young. The next night Tom Seaver came within two outs of a perfect game in his victory. In Chicago .217-hitter Al Weis, the ultimate good-field, no-hit middle infielder, slugged crucial homers to win back-to-back games before disbelieving throngs on July 15 and 16. A hot rivalry was born.

RON SWOBODA: When it became obvious it was going to be us and the Cubs, that thing heated up real good. When you got in Wrigley Field, people would yell things at you that were totally, completely, unbridled obscene. Young girls would yell stuff at you that would singe your ears. They threw pennies. They were always on you. I never took that stuff personally. I had fun with it. It made it all more intense. [Dick] Selma was on that team, a former Met. [Jim] Hickman [another ex-Met] was on that team.

The Cubs fought off the Mets' initial charge and had a five-game lead on July 26 when they hosted the Dodgers at Wrigley Field. Durocher suddenly left the ballpark in the third inning, the official explanation being a recurring stomach problem. But the manager in fact had plotted to hop a chartered plane to attend Parents' Night that same day at Camp Ojibwa, Wisconsin, 400 miles to the north, where his wife's son was enrolled—without asking owner Phil Wrigley for permission, which he likely would have granted. The misdirection play did not work. The Cubs were suspicious when team physician Jacob Suker was dispatched to Durocher's apartment and found nobody home. Then a parent at Camp Ojibwa noticed Durocher's presence while his team was playing a weekend series, and contacted Cubs beat writer James Enright. When Wrigley was informed of Durocher's AWOL affair, he wanted to fire him on the spot and replace him with Herman Franks, who had left as Giants manager after a quartet of second-place seasons from 1965 to 1968. Franks had been a coach under Durocher for the early 1950s Giants and had a long business relationship with him, but dissuaded Wrigley in a behind-the-scenes appeal that never surfaced in the media at the time. In 2004, five years before his death at 95, Franks recalled his conversation with Wrigley.

HERMAN FRANKS (Cubs coach 1970, Cubs manager 1977–79): I told him, "You can't fire him, that would disrupt the team too much. I'm not going to replace him." At the time I was handling Leo's business affairs and making investments for him.

Wrigley opted to keep Durocher. Without this lightning-rod figure, the whole tenor of the 1969 season throughout baseball would have changed. The owner cooled down, apparently remembering Durocher's revival of his sad-sack team. They conferred at Wrigley's Chicago apartment on July 29, with Durocher getting a mere slap on the wrist.

By then the Cubs were a marked team, partially due to Durocher. Teams were reluctant to trade with the Cubs, reluctant to help Durocher. The lovable-losers-becoming-winners were not the Cubs but the Mets in 1969, according to then-Cubs traveling secretary Blake Cullen, who later became a top National League official.

BLAKE CULLEN (Cubs traveling secretary, 1969–75): Everybody hated the Cubs. In Cincinnati or Pittsburgh they'd put a Mets score up, people would cheer. It's the only year it's been that way; otherwise, you'd see Cubs fans everywhere, all over the country. That season we were the enemy, the bad guy.

Cubs players picked up on a little of this, but as August 1969 commenced, they were focused only on the upstarts from Queens. One of Durocher's stalwarts was right-hander Bill Hands, who actually was pitching better than ace Fergie Jenkins in late summer. Hands was the winning pitcher in the only two Cubs victories in the pair of July Mets series on his way to a 20–14 season and 2.49 ERA, which still ranks as the fourth-lowest ERA by a Cubs starting pitcher since World War II.

BILL HANDS (Cubs, Twins, Rangers, 1969–75): [On whether Durocher was the most hated man in the National League.] That's without question. But I don't think, other than the Mets, I felt it from any of the other teams. Maybe I was just not aware of it. We felt the Mets were the team we needed to beat. We knew it early on with their pitching.

Trouble surfaced during an 11-game late-August home stand. The Cubs' pitching started to look shaky in a 4–7 run. Durocher continued to play his regulars day in and day out. Capable switch-hitting utility infielder Paul Popovich, who could have easily spelled Ron Santo, Don Kessinger, and Glenn

Beckert at third, short, and second, respectively, saw only scattered pinch-hitting appearances on the home stand. Meanwhile, Hodges's roster moves had spurred the Mets to rally from a 9½-game deficit to within easy hailing distance of the Cubs by the end of August.

The *Chicago Tribune*'s Richard Dozer sniffed trouble in the air. After an 8–2 Cubs loss to the Astros on August 22, Dozer, breaking out of his timid pack, asked Durocher, while the latter was shaving in his office: "Is anybody tired on the ball club? Do you plan to make any changes, give anybody a rest?"

Easily agitated, Durocher marched the writers into the clubhouse and ordered all players to be present, pulling several out of the shower. "Now ask them what you asked me," Durocher told Dozer. The writer complied, but not one Cub publicly admitted exhaustion. Privately, several later hinted Dozer was on the right track, but no one dared ask out of the lineup. Durocher was more forthcoming for his wife when she asked him why he did not use his bullpen more.

LYNN WALKER GOLDBLATT DUROCHER: He said, "What does the press want me to do, not use my best players? I don't know if these other players can do it. I have to go with my best."

Some 800 miles away, Gil Hodges made up for the Cubs frontline quality with quantity, literally two platoons of role players. While Durocher was behind the curve, stuck in a bygone Gashouse Gang–era mentality, the ol' Dodger was forward-thinking to win without any Hall of Fame–bound everyday players. He used almost all his 25-man roster. Only center fielder Tommie Agee played as many as 140 games. He platooned at first with Donn Clendenon and Ed Kranepool, at third with Wayne Garrett and Ed Charles, and in right with Ron Swoboda and Art Shamsky. Ken Boswell was spelled frequently at second by Al Weis, while catcher Jerry Grote's workload did not remotely approach

Randy Hundley's with J. C. Martin a capable backup. Hodges employed two relievers, Ron Taylor and Tug McGraw, to close out games. He used five starters, even six, long before that was popular.

Such a divergent approach to personnel prompted an interesting historical military analogy.

RON SWOBODA: His [Durocher's] best roster was the guys he played every day, and we felt that worked in our favor. Man-for-man, we may not have been better than them on any given day. We were able to do that because we had the buttons for Hodges to push. And we were way deeper in pitching. Our bench was deeper because those guys played all the time. They didn't repeat till '73 and that was maybe more magical than '69 because they only won 82 games.

When you have more guys, it's the second day of Shiloh in the Civil War. Grant had his ass kicked on the first day, but had more guys coming in the second day—he had more troops coming. We were ready to play, not sitting on the bench watching other people play for a week or two weeks. It's hard to say now. There was a sense of Leo going with his guns and the Mets had more guns. Our guns were a smaller bore but we had more of them. We were Sherman tanks against their Tiger tanks, but we had more of them. It wasn't a better tank, but we had more of them. And we used better fuel.

Meanwhile, the Mets became one-year wonders after their 37–9 season-ending run left the Cubs in the dust—eight games behind. They didn't stop until they had shocked a 109-win Orioles team in five games in the World Series. But no hint of the old magic was seen in back-to-back 83–79 seasons in 1970 and 1971. And the Mets suffered a massive body blow when Gil Hodges died of a heart attack at age 47 while playing golf with

his coaches in West Palm Beach on April 2, 1972. Yogi Berra succeeded Hodges, but the Mets stayed also-rans until a frantic
September 1973 matched the mystical final month of 1969.

In a new era when players did not blindly accept a Captain
Bligh approach to management, Durocher was beyond his time
in his next 2½ stormy seasons as manager, which included an
August 1971 player revolt in the clubhouse. After a one-year
stint as Astros manager in 1972–73, Durocher faded into history.

Luckily, the much-admired DiMaggio and Williams had
a more positive reentry into baseball, their old-school styles
somehow meshing with a new breed of players and their legendary reputations staying intact as a result.

TEDDY BALLGAME HITS D.C.

Ted Williams and Joe DiMaggio, the latter voted baseball's
greatest living player in 1969, graced American League ballparks during baseball's centennial season as manager of the
Washington Senators and coach with the Oakland A's, respectively. It was the first time they had been in uniform at the same
time after their playing days ended. While the impact of their
playing careers far outlasted their mortality, their abbrevi-
ated managing and coaching tenures had staying power in the
majors. The Splendid Splinter and Joltin' Joe then transitioned
into exalted retirement.

Williams, baseball's resident perfectionist whether hitting
a baseball, flying a jet, or fly-fishing, now tried his hand at managing a franchise so steeped in losing that one of its fictional
fans had to make a deal with the devil in the stage and screen
tale *Damn Yankees.* "First in war, first in peace, and last in the
American League" was the unofficial motto of two versions of
the Washington Senators—the first of which had to escape the
capital to win a pennant as the Minnesota Twins in 1965.

But managing—handling pitchers and clubhouse psychology—proved a lot harder than tutoring Carl Yastrzemski, Wil-

liams's other uniformed coaching gig. In what may have been a baseball first, Williams's players counseled him in how to work a pitching staff. One teacher of Pitching 101 was reliever Darold Knowles. Some of the lessons must have stuck as Williams guided the second version of the Senators, a 1961 expansion team, to an 86–76 record in 1969—their only winning mark in 12 seasons of operation in D.C.—earning the Splendid Splinter AL Manager of the Year honors.

DAROLD KNOWLES (Senators, Athletics, Cubs, Rangers, Expos, Cardinals, 1969–79): He was animated and so knowledgeable and had a passion for the game. But it took him about half that season to realize he did not know much about handling pitchers. We used to talk to him every day—and it's kind of crazy when pitchers are talking to the manager, to tell him you can't do this and can't do that. That wasn't his thing with pitchers, knowing their patterns. He had to learn how to handle a staff. He didn't expect it to be that hard. I recall one time I had pitched six days in a row. I went to [pitching coach] Sid Hudson and asked to give me one day off, I'll be fine. He went to Ted and he said [mimicking Williams's twangy voice], "What, holy cow, Casanova throws every day, why can't he throw every day?" I heard about it and said forget it, I'll be OK.

I'll give him credit. He got better. He was such a perfectionist in everything he did—a camera, a fly rod, or hitting. That year he finally started letting the coaches help. He told Wayne Terwilliger, if you want to put the bunt on, put the bunt on. He had a veto. He started believing in his coaches and he started listening. He got so much better. It was a pleasure playing for him even though he didn't know what he was doing when he started.

I do think so [that he became a good manager]. He was not going to be embarrassed. Originally he was embarrassed. He found out what he was doing wrong and tried to fix it. The ball clubs he had were not deep in talent . . . and you're not going to win.

At batting practice everyone would want to be around the cage to listen to Ted talk. He had some ideas, some theories and thought processes and mental paths for these guys to take and it helped them. With Eddie Brinkman, he got him to hit the ball on the ground. Eddie had a great year that year. [Mike] Epstein, he helped. Brant Alyea, he helped. [Paul] Casanova, he helped. They started believing in him because they knew he was Ted Williams, and he knew something about hitting.

Indeed, it was worth the price of admission to hear Williams talk about hitting. He set up shop in some of the most unusual places, in the recall of infielder-outfielder Davey Nelson, now in a dual role as Milwaukee Brewers announcer and director of the Brewers' alumni association. As with all his hitters, Williams took a personal interest in him.

DAVEY NELSON (Indians, Senators, Rangers, Royals, 1969–77): Ted was a manager who was very offensive-minded. They never worked on a lot of fundamentals. We were at a restaurant in Pompano Beach, Florida. When Ted talks about hitting, he commands everyone to listen. All of a sudden, he's moving all the tables out of the way to demonstrate a stance, a swing, how you come down through the ball, how some left-handers have an uplift. He takes over a room.

Ted was a perfectionist. That was part of the problem. He truly believed that everybody could do the things he could do if they worked hard at it. I kept saying, "Ted, I can work hard for eight hours a day, 365 days a year, and I couldn't do the things you do. You're an exception. Your eyesight, your hand-eye coordination." He was very emotional.

I hadn't had a home run in my first two years in the big leagues. During one game I got jammed on a pitch, a 2–0 fastball, and he just screamed at me: "How can you get jammed? You were looking for that fastball. How can you let that ball get in on you? You have to be ready!" Later in the game, I'm batting with a 3–1 count off Sonny Siebert, a former teammate of mine, and Williams yells, "Be ready, be ready" from the dugout. Boom! I hit a three-run homer to win the game. Before I passed first base, he was on the top step of the dugout yelling, "I told you that's the way to go!" He felt he couldn't understand why guys would take a cut at a good fastball and foul it back. He'd yell, "You weren't ready; you weren't ready!"

Second baseman Lenny Randle, the Senators' number one draft pick out of Arizona State in 1970, already had been exposed to Williams, who had been around Tempe before his managing days to give hitting instruction. So he was thrilled that after he was drafted, Williams put him on the fast track to RFK Stadium, arriving in 1971 after a short minor-league apprenticeship.

LENNY RANDLE (Senators, Rangers, Mets, Yankees, 1971–79): Ted said, "I want you to hit like Joe Morgan." I said I'm a switch-hitter—you want me to pump the arm and go deep? That was who he admired at the time. Nellie [Fox, the Senators' first-base and bunting coach] would talk out of the side of his mouth, spit tobacco on my shoe, and say, "Just listen to him, but do as I say." I tried Ted's stuff because his philosophy was pitchers were nothing but outfielders pitching. They're throwing nothing but batting practice. Never give them too much credit. They're only going to last five innings; they're not real athletes. So he pretty much put pitchers down.

His point was he could really handle personnel. He was trying to use reverse psychology to build self-esteem.

Unfortunately, the Senators could not bottle their moderate success of 1969. They reverted to their old form with 92 and 96 losses, respectively, in 1970 and 1971. When Williams moved with the franchise to Texas in 1972, they were even more dreadful, 54–100, in the strike-shortened season. Some quick fixes backfired, made worse by Williams's reaction to less-than-perfect acquisitions such as Denny McLain, who according to Knowles, "had his own rebel style and it wasn't a good fit."

> **DAVEY NELSON:** Losing kind of got to him. We made this five-player trade for Denny McLain. It could have been Ted's downfall. [Owner] Bob Short wanted to draw more fans. He brought Curt Flood from Europe to draw fans. McLain was just horrible by now. One day we're all out by the mound. McLain is getting bombed. Ted sent Sid Hudson out there to take him out of the game. Denny wouldn't come out of the game. He said, "If that fat guy wants to take me out, he better come out and do it himself." So Hudson goes back in and Ted comes back out. About halfway to the mound, Denny flips him the ball. When Ted brought the other pitcher in, I said, "Oh, Lord." Ted shot down back to the dugout and they held him back. He was getting ready to kill McLain.

McLain had not endeared himself to Williams or his new Senators teammates with a grand entrance one day during batting practice. Randle recalled McLain—a renowned private pilot—landing in a helicopter in the ballpark. Despite the matter/antimatter personalities, Williams did not give up on his effort to get through to McLain.

> **LENNY RANDLE:** Ted told Denny, "If you listen to me, I can get you 30 to 40 wins." So Ted actually challenged him

one day in Baltimore. He said he wanted Denny to get out on the field and "I'll humble you. . . . I don't care what you throw, I'll hit you wherever I want. . . . [Elliott] Maddox, go to left-center field, [Toby] Harrah, go to right-center field. [Jim] Mason, go to shortstop." Mike Epstein asked, if he was going to call the shot, where he was going to hit it? Ted says, "Mike, I beat the [Williams] shift. I knew how to hit through a shift so I think I know how to do this."

Denny jumped out on the mound. First ball, line shot left-center field, like a billiard cue he called it. Second ball, line-shot right-center field. He told Denny, "Look, I don't want to embarrass you and humble you to the point where you're going to quit on me. I don't want to take you deep." Then Denny brushed him back, under his chin. "I respect you for that, I'm used to that," Ted said. "I played in the era without helmets and I also dodged bullets in the war. You think your little fastball's going to hurt me?" Unbeliev- able hand-eye coordination. Denny said, "I'm going to get you out with my slider. They didn't have sliders when you played and curveballs and gloves with strings." Ted said, "If a pitcher listens to a good hitter, you'll learn how to get the hitters out." Denny was in his own world.

McLain left the franchise before Williams, exiting after going 10–22 in 1971. Williams departed the transplanted Rang- ers after the '72 season. "The only thing I like about Texas are the [cowboy] boots and the fishing," Randle recalls him saying. The end of his tenure gave Whitey Herzog his first managerial job. Then Billy Martin got the Rangers back over .500. "Billy got the glory from most of the same troops," Randle said. Teddy Ballgame never returned to an active baseball role, but it didn't matter. He had passed into legend. And his Senators/Rangers stint became simply a humor-filled sidelight to an incompara- ble life in baseball.

JOLTIN' JOE PASSES ALONG HIS EXPERTISE TO A'S KIDS

It's probable that Williams compared notes with Joe DiMaggio in 1969, when DiMaggio passed up a return to the Yankees in favor of the Oakland A's, across the bay from his San Francisco hometown. Owner Charlie Finley did DiMaggio a favor: The Yankee Clipper needed two more years in uniform to qualify for the highest level of baseball's pension plan.

But DiMaggio was not just a ceremonial coach or glad-hander, even though he held the title of vice president of community relations when Finley took him aboard after the A's moved to Oakland from Kansas City in 1968. His consummate knowledge of playing the outfield helped the large crop of young A's players. And the lessons absorbed played a role in one of the most famous catches in World Series history, made by Joe Rudi, who has worked in real estate for the past three decades in remote Baker City, Oregon. As a second-year big-leaguer in 1969, he was the beneficiary of one-on-one tutoring from DiMaggio.

JOE RUDI (Athletics, Angels, 1969–79): It was so much different being around him than for people who didn't get a chance to know him. He was very personable, had a great sense of humor, just a super-nice guy. To the guys who were around him on a regular basis, he was so popular. He couldn't go anywhere or do anything. He really enjoyed being around the guys, especially the younger guys. He enjoyed talking, telling stories, and teaching. Those two years he was with us were very enjoyable for him. I learned so much from him. That was right at the period where I was converting to the outfield. I had played shortstop all throughout high school and played infield the first couple of years of minors.

Bob Kennedy, my first manager, and DiMaggio sort of took me under their wing to make me a better outfielder. Joe would come out in the outfield with me every day and

Bob would stay by the third-base coaching box to hit me fly balls. Joe would come out and work with me. It was amazing. One of the early things Joe taught me was having a ball hit over my head, turn with your back to the ball, run to a spot, turn back in, and keeping the proper line. At first the ball would land 50 feet away from me. Literally it paid off because in the 1972 World Series, the catch I made up against the fence [against the Reds' Denis Menke] was where the ball was hit way over my head, and I turned and leaped.

I can't tell how many hundreds of hours I spent in the outfield—learning how to turn and go over my head, line drives hit right at you, the proper footwork. Joe taught me how to turn sideways quickly on a line drive, because you don't know whether the ball's going to take off or sink. The stuff he learned in the outfield was to immediately hop sideways like a baserunner between first and second. In that position I could either cross over [step] toward home plate or toward the fence if the ball took off, and still get a good jump on it. The ball hit between you and the line always is going to go to the line.

We didn't spend a whole lot of time hitting. We talked more about mental preparation. He was of the feeling that by the time you got to the big leagues, most of your technique was pretty much set. Most of your growth would be in approach, things you did at the plate to set up the pitcher and catcher. I learned by far the most from him day-to-day taking instruction in the outfield. It wasn't a fatherly type thing. He was just a person you greatly respected as a coach. Any kind of little tidbits he threw your way, you listened with wide-open ears and went to work on what he had told you.

I think he would have really enjoyed it if not for his notoriety. He loved coaching, he loved being around the guys and road trips and plane rides. He was a different person than when he was trying to get from the bus to the ballpark, or the bus to the hotel, and people were bugging him. They were just fans wanting his autograph, but he was just overwhelmed. That's why he did not stay in the game. The best place for him was back in New York as a coach with the Yankees, but I don't think he could have lived there.

His two years in uniform finished, DiMaggio returned to the role that the public demanded, as Joltin' Joe. Soon he developed a public alter ego—as "Mr. Coffee," the TV endorser of the coffeemaker brand. Baseball missed DiMaggio's knowledge. But as Rudi suggested, his own celebrity and exalted status probably would have gotten in the way of his easily blending into the season-long rhythms of a team.

3

The Greatest Collection
of Talent Ever?

Two ballparks and two leagues in the same city allowed Chicagoans to watch perhaps the finest collection of baseball talent in history as the 20th century rounded into its final third.

Start out at Wrigley Field, where the local nine fielded three future Hall of Famers—the beloved Ernie Banks, Billy Williams, and Fergie Jenkins—and Ron Santo, an all-around third baseman who should by all standards have been enshrined in Cooperstown. Entertainment came in dizzying fashion from the visiting teams. One could expect Willie Mays and Henry Aaron—the latter in particular—to show flashes of their early-career brilliance. Aaron actually lost what would have been career homer number 756 when he launched a fastball toward the left-field bleachers against Cubs lefty Ken Holtzman on August 19, 1969. The ball passed over several rows of bleachers, but then hit a wall of wind and made, if this can be believed, an abrupt left turn. Knowing never to give up on a ball when the wind blew in, Williams backed into the left-field vines and waited for the ball to drop seemingly straight down into his glove. A fortuitous interference by the elements, indeed, as Holtzman would go on to pitch a no-hitter that afternoon without a strikeout, retiring Aaron for the final out.

A spectator could gape at Roberto Clemente, playing with unbridled passion in right field, the occasional foolhardy rookie testing—and succumbing—to the Great One's one-of-a-kind throwing arm. Hitting? Clemente had the distinction of, back in

1959, being the only hitter to belt a baseball out of Wrigley Field to the left of the famed center-field scoreboard.

Whenever the Reds hit town, there was Pete Rose, possessor of baseball's last crew cut (even shorter hairstyles, including chrome domes, would come back into vogue 25 years later). Charlie Hustle would do anything to beat you, and your eyes had to try hard to dart about and keep up with his frenetic pace. He was so confident he probably would have bet on himself. More about that in other books.

Banks, Williams, Mays, Aaron, and Clemente all began their careers in the 1950s. As the 1970s began, they were joined as teammates and opponents by a new crop of future Cooperstown colleagues passing through Clark and Addison. Fans could witness Tom "Terrific" Seaver at his best and worst, such as the September afternoon in 1972 when he served up a grand-slam homer to rookie Cubs hurler Burt Hooton. A few years later a young Phillies third baseman named Mike Schmidt began hitting homers at Wrigley Field as if there were a tee at home plate. He wouldn't stop until he had belted as many homers in Chicago in 18 seasons as Aaron had done in 21.

Eight miles south, at claustrophobic, smoky old Comiskey Park, the talent flow was just as impressive, and they knew it while it was happening.

"It was to me, absolutely," replied Brooks Robinson when asked if he played in the greatest era for talent in history. "I don't like to toot the old guys' horn, but no doubt in my mind that was the greatest time in baseball."

Robinson's first big-league at-bats took place in 1955, but his string of 16 consecutive Gold Gloves for his hot-corner Houdini talents did not end until 1975. You could get two Robinsons for the admission price of one when the mighty Orioles came to the South Side, Brooks having been joined in 1966 by outfielder/leader Frank, whose own career began in tiny Crosley Field in 1956. For 2½ memorable seasons, the White Sox fielded perhaps the era's greatest player, Dick Allen, whose personality quirks perhaps cost him a Cooperstown berth. Allen was a true child of the '60s. But a throwback was good ol' country hardballer Nolan Ryan, who came on strong in 1972 at Anaheim Stadium after four-plus seasons of wandering among roles and efforts to control the lightning firing out of his right arm at Shea Stadium. On Opening Day 1974, with the chill struggling to get above 30 degrees, you knew the White Sox would have a hard time hitting Ryan while the only other heat was generated by a streaker who stumbled out of the stands in the left-field corner. You hoped the poor chap would not get frostbite where such an affliction usually does not strike.

The best example of the confluence of this fantastic array of talent took place at another old, closed-off ballpark, gritty Tiger Stadium in Detroit on the night of July 13, 1971. As each member of the NL and AL squads—managed by Sparky Anderson and Earl Weaver—was introduced, the names rolling past would have comprised the ultimate all-time fantasy team.

"I've been told there are more guys from the 1971 All-Star Game who have gone to the Hall of Fame than any of the All-Star games in history," said AL starter Vida Blue.

The future Cooperstown enshrinees started with Anderson and Weaver. From the NL team: Mays, Aaron, Clemente, Jenkins, Seaver, Willie Stargell, Willie McCovey, Johnny Bench, Lou Brock, Steve Carlton, and Juan Marichal. AL Cooperstown-bound players were Frank and Brooks Robinson, Rod Carew, Carl Yastrzemski, Luis Aparicio, Reggie Jackson, Al Kaline, Harmon Killebrew, and Jim Palmer. The spotlight-lovin' Jackson, of course, put the cherry on the occasion with his titanic homer off a right-field rooftop transformer that will be replayed and talked about for all time.

Not invited to the Motor City that night but bound for Cooperstown induction were '71 active players Banks, Williams, Ryan, Tony Perez, Bob Gibson, Joe Morgan, Orlando Cepeda, Jim Bunning, Don Sutton, Phil Niekro, Catfish Hunter, and Rollie Fingers. Having already made his big-league debut, but not in the Red Sox's lineup for good until season's end, was future Hall member Carlton Fisk. And you could make a good case for Hall membership for Joe Torre, the NL All-Stars' cleanup hitter; Santo, his third-base backup; NL reserve Rose; AL reserve Tony Oliva, and other '71 luminaries like Bert Blyleven, Tommy John, and Thurman Munson.

Within five years of the '71 game, the future Cooperstown ranks were swelled by the debuts of Schmidt, Goose Gossage, George Brett, Dave Winfield, Robin Yount, Dennis Eckersley, and Bruce Sutter. Still another skilled batsman who was later enshrined made his debut in 1978: Paul Molitor.

A star player of the era could not avoid teaming up with fellow greats even when he moved from team to team, as Cepeda did from the Giants to the Cardinals to the Braves to the Red Sox.

"I really, really feel very fortunate to spend some time with Hank [Aaron]," Cepeda said. "Such a great teammate. I was with Yastrzemski. Dusty [Baker] came up in '69. You look back, and how many people can say that you hit behind Aaron? I hit behind Mays and McCovey . . . behind Yaz."

The '71 managerial ranks also were swelled by Cooperstown-bound Durocher (inducted despite the seamy side of his career), Red Schoendienst, Walter Alston, and Bob Lemon. The most prominent Hall of Fame managerial name of them all, despite his team falling into their typical "Damn Yankees" needy routine, was the Washington Senators' Ted Williams.

Perhaps the best analysis of the surplus of talent of the time is offered up by a pitcher who spanned several baseball generations. Tommy John pitched from the administrations of JFK to George H. W. Bush, his extended time fueled by desire, dedication, and a breakthrough in sports medicine that bears his name. The eternal left-hander faced everyone—and is buoyed by that fact.

TOMMY JOHN (White Sox, Dodgers, Yankees, 1969–79):
From the time I broke into baseball in 1963 up until the

'70s, 15 years or so, they had some of the greatest ball-players. I had a chance in 1972 to pitch against Roberto Clemente. I pitched against him only four times. He hit the balls in the same spot—two found the outfield, two found the second baseman. You faced [Willie] Stargell, Billy Williams, [Ron] Santo, Ernie Banks, [Al] Kaline, Frank Robinson, Brooks Robinson. That's just Baltimore.

Usually the good teams had at least two [aces]. Baltimore sometimes had three or even four. That will never happen again. Four guys back then took the mound every four games. I went over to the Dodgers, and our pitching staffs were great. It was a very good time in baseball.

Cooperstown may not be big enough and its electors may not possess enough of a vision to include all the great players from baseball's True Golden Age who deserve enshrinement.

4

Batsmen in Business Again

The "Year of the Pitcher" did not cause mass amnesia among the huge Hall of Fame–bound crop of hitters practicing their trade at the dawn of the True Golden Age. The greats never *forget* how to hit. But Major League Baseball's late-1968 actions to restore some equilibrium to the game perhaps worked better than expected. Many of the great hitters, even those in their 30s, enjoyed their peak years from 1969 on, with a new group of batsmen taking their places and grabbing headlines. And in the most high-profile case, Henry Aaron seemed to realize he had a date with Babe Ruth in a few years, picking up the pace by slugging 40 or more homers three times between 1969 and 1973, including a career-high 47 in 1971. The lone power benchmark that remained elusive was the 50-homer mark, last achieved by Willie Mays with 52 in 1965. Only George Foster of the Reds passed the mark with 52 in 1977. The game may have achieved the balance its lords desired.

Battles between aces and all-time hitters were a daily occurrence as the 1970s wore on, providing some interesting scouting reports. But behind every batter's hitting mechanics was a story of pride and passion to tackle the most difficult skill in all of pro sports.

BEST AGAINST THE BEST: FERGIE JENKINS

Hall of Famers vs. Hall of Famers were daily occurrences in baseball's True Golden Age. Fergie Jenkins (Cubs, Rangers, Red Sox, 1969–79) racked up more than 300 innings each year amid his string of six consecutive 20-win seasons from 1967 to 1972.

Decades later, Jenkins exuded both confidence and trepidation in describing how he pitched against the greatest hitters of his time.

JENKINS ON HANK AARON: Hank was a hitter who was even in the batter's box. He wanted the ball down or down and away. That was my strength, to devise a theory of trying to get around his strength and make it work in my strength. What I tried to do is change speeds. I used to throw him off-speed curveballs, bounce them in front or on top of the plate. Pitch him hard in on his hands. If I needed to throw that slider and paint it away, that was my pitch. Pitching 11 or 12 years against Hank, he hit two home runs against me—one in Wrigley, one in Atlanta. I slowed him down to pitch him hard in. The nice thing about it: I knew he'd swing the bat. I pitched hard in. I knocked people off the plate.

JENKINS ON WILLIE MAYS: I knew on the road at Candlestick Park, I could challenge [Willie with] fastballs over the plate because the ball didn't carry to left or left-center. The ball was hit, you think it was gone, but the wind brought it back in. Here in Wrigley Field or Shea Stadium, it was different. The nice thing about it was he had a bad habit of stepping in the bucket. A lot of times he couldn't hit that slider with full force. He hit a lot of balls to right or right-center. I got him out fairly easy at times. With men on base, he kind of bore down a little more.

JENKINS ON WILLIE MCCOVEY: He hit me pretty good. Of all the left-handed hitters—[Willie] Stargell, Rusty Staub—probably Willie McCovey hit me the hardest. I pitched down and down and in, and this is how he swung at pitches. I couldn't fool him on breaking balls and very seldom threw him sliders or fastballs hard in. I tried to pick the corners away and pitch him up. Sometimes I jammed him up. At one time Randy Hundley and I just told him what was coming—he hit the Cubs so well. He hit balls foul over the roof [at Wrigley]. He and Willie Stargell hit screamers down the line foul.

JENKINS ON WILLIE STARGELL: I used to get him in between swings. He used to whip that bat a lot in the warm-up. I used to change speeds on Willie, bouncing curveballs and sliders down. I used to get him fanning at a lot of pitches down and in. Very seldom did I throw fastballs away to Willie because he hit the ball hard up the middle. To stay on the hill, you couldn't afford to be undressed a couple of different times when he came to the plate. There were a couple of times I pitched around [Roberto] Clemente to try to face Stargell, because I knew I had pretty good success against him.

JENKINS ON ROBERTO CLEMENTE: He didn't have a strike zone. He would swing at a ball up around his nose or at his ankles, or maybe at his shoe tops. He hit me fairly well. Where there were times to face him, I put him on. They [the Pirates] were well known as the Lumber Company. Roberto by far gave me the most problems. I had to start five or six times against Pittsburgh each season. Just jokingly, it seemed he came up every inning. Number 21 was in the on-deck circle all the time. A lot of times there were games he'd break up when I'd have a winning performance going in the eighth or ninth inning. Here it is, Clemente with a double, Clemente with a single. Clemente with a home run. Clemente with a walk would get someone else coming up to the plate.

JENKINS ON PETE ROSE: Pete Rose hit the ball the other way. Pete hit it up the middle with authority. He didn't

strike out much. He looked to hit good, solid strikes. Charlie Hustle, I couldn't pitch around Pete, because then I'd
have [Joe] Morgan, [Johnny] Bench, [Tony] Perez, before
that Lee May, so I had to get Pete Rose. I threw him lots of
strikes, tried to sink the ball, make him hit it on the ground.
The number one thing: I didn't walk Pete Rose because
that just started a dilemma for yourself.

BEST AGAINST THE BEST: BERT BLYLEVEN

Bert Blyleven, with just one 20-win season, may not have been
as dominant as Jenkins, but he certainly was enduring. Starting with the Twins at age 19 in 1970, he finished with 287 wins,
three more than Jenkins, in 1992. Such feats got him excruciat-
ingly close to Hall of Fame induction, having missed by just five
votes in 2010 in his 13th year of eligibility. Certainly that bodes
well for eventual enshrinement in upcoming votes.

Blyleven (Twins, Rangers, Pirates 1970–79), possessor of one
of the game's best curveballs, faced the greats in both leagues.
He recalled his strategies against superb batsmen:

BLYLEVEN ON FRANK ROBINSON: He was a guy who
was right on top of the plate. The consensus was you don't
pitch him inside. You don't wake him up. You pitch him
hard away. You try to change speeds.

BLYLEVEN ON ALEX JOHNSON: He was a great hitter. A
guy who could hit a two-hopper to short and beat it out.
A guy who when he got on first you didn't throw over. You
let him sleep.

BLYLEVEN ON GEORGE BRETT: George was a great hitter. One time I got behind 2-and-0. There was a runner on
second. I didn't want him to beat me in that situation early
in the ball game. I threw two good, hard fastballs up and in

on him to make him kind of move his feet a little bit. That helped me in his next at-bat—he hit a little fly ball to left.

BLYLEVEN ON REGGIE JACKSON: Of course my curveball was my strikeout pitch. I'd try to bust him inside. He hit a two-seam fastball off me and took it the other way over the left-field fence. I was impressed with his power the other way. There are certain guys in each lineup you don't want to beat you, and he beat me going the other way.

BLYLEVEN ON CARL YASTRZEMSKI: He held that bat way up high. Carl had very quick hands. You try to change speeds on him. I tried throwing him a lot of breaking balls. I was a guy who didn't walk a lot of guys. I challenged him. A lot of times you get beat. There aren't that many guys like him—you think of Albert Pujols and Alex Rodriguez—who can hurt you with the long ball *and* getting three or four hits in a game.

ROBERTO CLEMENTE: "THE GREAT ONE" HONORED AT LAST

It was better late than never for Roberto Clemente. Branded for the majority of his career as a hypochondriac because he complained of chronic back and neck pain, Clemente at last enjoyed the acclaim of all of baseball as he entered his mid-30s with the Pittsburgh Pirates. Commissioner Bowie Kuhn called him "baseball royalty."

To ensure the new accolades would not be lost in translation, Clemente put the Buccos on his back with a 1971 World Series for all time. His 12 hits in 29 at-bats (.414), including two homers, held off the powerful Baltimore Orioles, possessors of four 20-game winners, in a riveting seven games. Almost a year later he collected his 3,000th hit, a double off the Mets' Jon

Matlack, in his final regular-season big-league at-bat, his image passing into tragic legend when he was killed in a plane crash off San Juan, Puerto Rico, on a humanitarian mission delivering relief supplies to earthquake-torn Nicaragua.

The best views of Clemente are from those he touched, whom he helped mold, and who tried to carry on after a life cut short at 38. If Clemente had a protégé, it was Pirates first baseman/outfielder Al Oliver, who came under his wing for Clemente's final four seasons starting in 1969. Clemente was driven to draw the respect that was due to him—and was denied for so long because he was honest about his aches and pains.

AL OLIVER (Pirates, Rangers, 1969–79): [Clemente] was motivated by the false accusations against him. I wonder to this day how they could have misread an individual so badly. When I came up, I had no problem understanding him at all. If he was approached by someone open-minded and was willing to listen to what he had to say, they really shouldn't have had a problem with him.

He and I had a special relationship. When I first came up, I was misunderstood because of my confidence level, [because of my] honesty. He could relate. I wasn't going to change my personality. If you're honest with people, you're not going to change your personality. I was brought up properly. I had great parents who raised me. Words like *cocky* and *arrogant*—I never heard those words before. They didn't raise a son who was cocky and arrogant. They raised a son who was self-assured. They made me feel good about myself growing up. Sometimes people take things the wrong way.

[Roberto] sat down and told me. He said, "I know what you're going through." I was being platooned. The only thing I knew about platooning was Fort Knox in 1967 in basic training. As far as not hitting left-handers, it was something I couldn't relate to. He told me, what you need to do is stay calm, stay ready, because one day you'll be one of the best players to ever play the game. That meant a lot to me coming from him. He understood my personality. Our personalities were very similar. Even at the time, our wives had said the same things. We were kind of laid-back, but if you approached us, very cordial. The right word would have been very "engaging." It's too bad he didn't live to see my career. I lost my dad the same day I found out I was coming to the major leagues.

Just what he said to me that one time helped. We were both very body-conscious. We both had the body. We took care of ourselves. So, therefore, without any serious injuries, we were destined to play a long time.

To my knowledge [he was baseball's greatest humanitarian]. In the fashion and the way he left here, it brought to light the kind of human being he was all along. He wasn't doing it for notoriety. He was doing it from his heart. There's no telling [how many he helped behind the scenes]. To know the guy, this guy really cared about people. He recognized my personality was similar to his, and that's the reason why we hit it off from day one.

He was my manager when I was sent to the Puerto Rico winter league in 1970 to make the adjustment from first base to center field [to make room for Bob Robertson at first]. He'd have been a great manager. He had the right temperament. A lot of great players do not become great managers. First of all, you've got to know individuals. Once you get to know an individual, you know how to handle him. Some managers never get to know their own players. They might have this one rule or two rules for everybody. Bottom line, you've got to treat all players differently, but all have to play by the same rules. They have to play within the confines of team rules and rules of the game. You know what to say and not to say at the right time—that's the key to being a successful manager.

Roberto knew how to read people. He had great people skills.

Roberto gave the Pirates the OK I was ready to play center field. Once they got the OK, they traded Matty Alou. That opened up the gate for both me and Bob Robertson to play. He emphasized the cutoff man.

He almost had a built-in clock and a built-in notebook about how they were going to pitch him. He knew they weren't going to throw him inside in the strike zone because he had great power.

Those in the know about baseball realized Clemente's sublime talents. An 18-year-old outfielder named Fred Lynn, about to enter Southern Cal, decided to get an up-close view of Clemente's legendary throwing arm while on vacation at his grandfather's house near Wrigley Field in June 1969. Lynn and his family were veterans of the ivy-covered bandbox. His uncle Bob had once obtained a ball hit into the ivy from Mel Ott, with Fred donating it decades later to a friend's sports museum in Newport Beach, California. But Clemente made the greatest impression of any player Lynn watched at Clark and Addison. He and a buddy staked out seats right behind Clemente before one game. He'd take what he saw into his own big-league career, which included American League and All-Star MVP awards.

FRED LYNN (Red Sox, 1975–79): It was a packed house that day. I wanted to get by Clemente in the right-field bleachers and see him play. I wanted to make sure we got there for infield practice to see him throw. He was built like me, not a real tall guy, not bulky. It was fun to watch him throw. He was proud of his arm and would show it off. The ball would take off—*shweeeeewh*—I said, "Whoa, that guy can throw." It was the best arm I had seen to that point. Dwight Evans had a great arm and so did Ichiro. But Clemente got his whole body behind it. When he threw, his feet came off the ground. He was having a ball. He was having fun playing. You could see it.

Clemente had only a supporting role, with nine hits and three RBIs, in the 1960 Pirates' World Series victory over the Yankees. He wasn't the senior or mainstay Pirate then. But by 1971 he was team elder. He would be the centerpiece on a national stage, finally, including the first-ever night Fall Classic game on October 13, 1971. Oddly enough, that was one of his quieter games despite a 3-for-4 performance in a 4–3 Buccos win in which rookie reliever Bruce Kison was the star. Otherwise, Clemente took over clutch-hitting duties while his arm took on errant Orioles runners on defense.

AL OLIVER: It was his presence. You could feel it. He was not going to let us lose. He didn't have to say anything. It was just the way he played. He was our leader. All he wanted us to do was a little bit and he would do the rest. If we showed up, we were going to do something. He went to work in '71.

He did it all the time. We saw it all the time. That's what made the difference [a national stage]. You can be right or you can be off. He was just on. When he got his pitches, he didn't miss them. Defensively, great. Great baserunner. The Man Upstairs said, "Roberto, it's your time to show the world what kind of player you are." He was hungry [for another championship ring]. Plus, in 1960 it was different than '71. The '71 team was his team, and he was well aware of that. He wasn't going to let us lose—it was his team. It was the greatest one-man performance I've ever seen. I can't see anything that can come close to that, all-around, defensively and offensively. I just took off the ring just before you called. I wear it all the time. Who'd have thought that would be the last world championship I'd be on?

Those who knew Clemente best still haven't gotten over his death in the crash of a chartered old DC-7, a plane that probably was not air-worthy, on his mission of mercy. Life is indeed unfair. But Clemente left enough of a great legacy to keep them going through their grief.

AL OLIVER: Maybe two or three months into the season [it took me to recover]. Opening Day 1973 was terrible for me. I can only speak for myself. When I got that call from [Willie] Stargell early that morning and he said a plane had gone down off San Juan and Roberto was supposed to be on board—that was terrible news. I had just left his New Year's Eve party; quite a few of the players were there. I jumped out of bed and got in the shower, feeling this is unreal. I turned on the TV, and they had not confirmed it.

What really bothered me more than anything else is he just didn't get what he deserved as a person. When you leave here like he did, for anyone to question him and say anything negative, they got a serious problem. All the news then was good, how great a humanitarian he was. Some of the people who knocked him now came to light and said how great he was. They called him a hypochondriac? So many people were hypocritical.

Even to this day, I still think about him. I know the influence he had on me. I would say from a personal standpoint, it came to light to me as I inherited the number three spot in the lineup. That usually goes to your best all-around hitter on the team. I really felt a great sense of responsibility to not be like Roberto, although we were good hitters who used the whole field. If I could just be Al Oliver. When I look back at it, it was an honor and a privilege to be the third hitter.

Grief overcame Clemente's native Puerto Rico when his death was confirmed. One of the mourners was outfielder Jose Cruz, who, of course, looked up to Clemente growing up in Puerto Rico. He recalled how as a young Cardinals player in 1971–72, he was hesitant to approach Clemente because he was busy.

JOSE CRUZ (Cardinals, Astros, 1970–79): He was my manager in Puerto Rico in the All-Star Game in 1970–71. To me, I was too excited, I was afraid to talk to him. We had a lot of respect for guys in the big leagues. I talked more to Orlando Cepeda in St. Louis. He was there for us, the young guys, [to] help us out.

I was in my house. We were watching the news and we couldn't believe it. That was a bad day. We stayed together with the family. Everybody was crying. I had just gotten married. It was a long time to get over it. Clemente was the number one star. Then [Juan] Pizarro. Vic Power, Cepeda. Then me, Willie Montanez, Ed Figueroa, Jerry Morales.

In a late-April 1973 series at Wrigley Field, an overly excited Latin fan held up a black-bordered photo of Clemente in the back aisle of the right-field bleachers. He practically was in apoplexy as he exhorted the Pirates team that Clemente had left behind to rally. *"Panamanio!"* he yelled at Panamanian Manny Sanguillen, who often took Clemente's place in right field in that downer '73 campaign. "Rich-eee, come to me!" the rooter implored to left-handed-hitting third baseman Richie Hebner, who loved hitting in Wrigley Field. After a one-year dip, the Pirates returned to either winning the National League East or contending well into September the rest of the '70s. Clemente had taught his teammates well. But the better lesson was for the rest of the world: Don't rush to judgment. His legacy is as secure as anyone's in baseball history.

DICK ALLEN: THE BEST OF HIS TIME?

Excursions for a carless teenager from West Rogers Park on Chicago's far North Side to 15-miles-distant Comiskey Park had to be planned for weekend day games or the few weekday matinee contests. Taking the L train at night in 1972, particularly down to Chicago's South Side, was perceived as less-than-safe. So a Wednesday, August 23, afternoon game against the New York Yankees was perfect, given it was also an off-day from stock boy duties at the downtown Goldblatt's department store.

The timing was perfect to watch the game from the third-base grandstands. The only pennant race in town was here: The Cubs were far off the Pirates' pace in the NL East. The White Sox kept creeping up on the Oakland A's in the AL West, no small thanks to an MVP-season-in-the-making by first baseman Dick Allen. GM Roland Hemond's gamble to acquire the controversial Allen for lefty Tommy John the previous winter was paying off handsomely. Despite Allen's continued eccentricities, viewed by many as rebelliousness, he was like a one-man gang for the Sox.

In the seventh, old war-horse reliever Lindy McDaniel faced Allen. With the voluble Harry Caray broadcasting and armed with a big fishnet in the center-field bleachers, more than 445 feet from home plate, Allen teed off with his 40-ounce club. It was not a majestic parabola of a shot. Allen's brute strength and bat speed shot the baseball almost on a straight line 15 feet off the ground, straight in Caray's direction. Shocked, the announcer began waving the fishnet as the ball landed with a thud just out of reach on some empty benches. Allen had been known for his outer-limits bombs. But this beat 'em all as an entire ballpark of players and fans gaped in amazement. "Nobody has ever hit a ball any farther," bellowed Caray.

If only Allen's entire career had been as focused. . . .

After a 1964 Rookie-of-the-Year season with the Phillies, Allen's tenure in the City of Brotherly Love steadily deteriorated amid a series of controversies. By 1969 a disgruntled Allen was drawing messages in the dirt with his foot at first base: MOM, for the number one person in his life. COKE, after the sign atop the Connie Mack Stadium roof, for the expectation that he'd hit it with a baseball. NO when told to stop drawing in the dirt. WEYER for ump Lee Weyer. OCT. 3 for the last day of the '69 season. And the most famous: BOO, denoting the tough Phillies fans' reactions to him.

Allen wondered how good he could have been without the attendant controversies, many of them his own doing, but he also acknowledged the baseball "outlaw" label. He didn't mind the rebel image, posing for a *Sports Illustrated* cover in 1972 juggling baseballs while smoking a cigarette in the White Sox dugout.

Allen was traded to the Cardinals for the 1970 season. He then moved on to the Dodgers in 1971. Then came the deal with the White Sox for John. Soon after the trade he tried to explain his vagabond nature in the game in a radio interview with Caray.

DICK ALLEN (Phillies, Cardinals, Dodgers, White Sox, Athletics, 1969-79): I really don't know, Harry [why he played with four clubs in four years]. I think it's part of baseball's business. The only thing that really keeps me going is I don't think a club would trade for a fellow that couldn't play. I'm in the horse business. I wouldn't want a horse that couldn't run no longer. I kind of accepted it with a grain of salt. The other two clubs, St. Louis and the Dodgers, I didn't feel I was part of the organization by not coming up in their farm system. But here, with [Chuck] Tanner and [Joe] Lonnett and a few of the coaches, it's kind of like being at home. I really feel like I did come through their system even though I haven't. I think this is it and I'm sure this is my last move.

There's been a lot of talk about me not being able to get along with managers, and two sets of rules, one for Allen and one for the club. When I was in St. Louis, they got rid of a lot of the large salaries, and carried like 10 rookies and three sophomores. They brought me down there to try to change my image and keep people coming through the gate. They lose none of that money coming through the gate and pay the small salaries to the younger players. I was kind of glad to go. With the Dodgers, I didn't want to go back there, either.

Without Allen's presence, the White Sox might have moved out of Chicago. Between 1968 and 1988 the franchise had dalliances with potential owners in Milwaukee, Seattle, Denver, and St. Petersburg. He was the right man at the right time.

Allen's image to his teammates was different than portrayed to the public, according to third baseman Bill Melton, the defending AL home-run champion when Allen was acquired. It was the Sox's bad luck that Melton hurt his back two months into Allen's great '72 season. A team with the one-two punch of Allen and Melton at full health could have matched, and perhaps passed, the A's in the standings.

BILL MELTON (White Sox, Angels, Indians, 1969–77): He was very well received in the clubhouse. When he left the clubhouse, there were times he rubbed the press the wrong way. He didn't like talking to the press. He didn't mind talking to the traveling scribes—he was pretty friendly. His annoyance came on the road with outside press that always wanted to know things that he concealed. He thought it was unfair that he got all the attention; he wanted us to get the attention.

Overall, an outstanding teammate, a good guy, a very funny guy, a very bright guy. We had a lot of fun in the clubhouse. The attacks that took place were usually from the media on the road. They didn't know him and he didn't want them to know him. He had a lot of energy.

It was his M.O. [skipping batting practice]. If the game started at seven thirty, he got there a quarter to seven, seven o'clock. He never took batting practice. When he did get there an hour early, he always liked to take ground balls at second base, shortstop, anyplace but first base. He actually had terrific hands. This guy was a terrific first baseman. So many things came natural to him. He liked to come into the clubhouse [within an hour of the first pitch], jump around the middle of the floor, and do a little shadow boxing with Pat Kelly. He'd take that big cape of his off like Superman, hang it in his locker, put on his uniform, and grabbed his bat. We were like, hey the game's not that easy. He made it easy. That was his ritual. Some guys get to the ballpark at one o'clock and lift weights. For Dick Allen, it was all about when the game started till when it was ended. That's what mattered to him the most.

He was the best player I played with and against. He had exceptional speed and was an outstanding baserunner. I actually saw him hit left-handed, hitting home runs, in the only time he took batting practice. He walked out onto the field one day and started hitting left-handed. We almost fell over that he was hitting the ball as hard left-handed as right-handed. A lot of the times you could see him rounding third, I'd get behind home plate signaling him to slide. He'd turn around to look at the outfielder. As soon as the ball was let go, he put on the after-burners. Everything was natural. He was like Henry Aaron. Nobody knew Henry stole 20 out of 20 bases. You rarely threw him out.

I didn't see him in a lot of slumps. Usually you see guys struggle a lot. He was so consistent. When we faced the Oakland staff, he often excelled as if they took him up another level. He looked at you and said, "If I played a lot, I might have been in the Hall of Fame." He kind of giggled, and you had to giggle with him. He did what he wanted to do. He had fun in the game. He got down when he broke his leg. You could read the fact he [Allen] had enough playing baseball. If you were 10, 15, 20 games back, a lot of passion left.

You rarely if ever saw him in the training room. A guy that's good to you and a good teammate, you kind of never second-guess him. It's hard for outsiders to look into that and not understand what a player feels after 140 games, and walks away. To us, he was done with baseball [in late 1974].

The only manager who came close to properly focusing Allen was Chuck Tanner, practically a neighbor back in their western Pennsylvania hometowns. Tanner was from New Castle, near Allen's Wampum hometown. So he had a better vantage point into Allen's psyche than most. Tanner was accused of coddling Allen and allowing him to play by his own set of rules apart from the White Sox. But that isn't the whole story, according to the outspoken ex-manager.

CHUCK TANNER (manager White Sox, Athletics, Pirates, 1970–79): By far, he was the best player [in the American League]. He's a Hall of Famer. He carried us on his back. We almost beat the great Oakland A's that year. He was like being a manager on the field. He took care of the young kids, not only on the field, but in the clubhouse. We had a lot of kids, like Bucky Dent, Brian Downing, Jorge Orta, Terry Forster, and Goose Gossage.

I don't know why [Allen is not in the Hall of Fame]. He's the best player I ever managed, that carried the team by himself. Oh, definitely [he'd match Allen with Hank Aaron, an old Braves teammate of Tanner's, in talent]. They both were great. He said one time he wished I had been his first manager, when Aaron broke the all-time home-run record.

Nobody had to take batting practice if they could hit like him. Shit, he used to sit in the dugout with a bat and not take it. Before nine o'clock at night, he hit more home runs than anyone in baseball. I talked to him all the time. He said, "Y'know, this batting practice, you got guys throwing 40 mph, it throws my timing off." I said I don't care if you do. I witnessed him hitting left-handed in BP.

I just treated him like anyone else, like an individual. My rules were this: I have one for every one on the team, whatever I wanted it to be. I didn't allow Terry Forster to go to a bar when he was 19. I kicked his ass and sent him to his room. If you were 30 like Wilbur Wood or Joel Horlen, you could [go to] a bar and I'll have one with you.

When it came to hitting and pitching, there was nobody any smarter [than Allen]. He used to set up the pitchers. He'd take a pitch the first inning and look for it with the game on the line in the seventh, and pound it.

I knew him from when he was a little kid and I knew his mother well. I used to go visit her, even before he played for me. His mother was the motivator. He'd talk to her and she'd tell him, don't worry about what other people say or do. You just listen to Chuck, he's from our neighborhood and he's one of us. I'd take care of him.

Three weeks before the laser shot against the Yankees, on July 31, 1972, Allen almost outdid himself with his bat and legs. Taking advantage of old Metropolitan Stadium's spacious center field, he slugged a three-run inside-the-park homer off Bert Blyleven in the first. Then in the fifth, with one man on base, Allen connected to nearly the same spot against Blyleven and dashed around the bases for another inside-the-park job.

BERT BLYLEVEN: He was a tough out. You could see the bat he swung was a 40-ounce bat. It was like a telephone pole. He was so strong and so quick that the barrel of the bat went out so quickly. The two inside-the-park home runs he hit off me—Bobby Darwin, a former pitcher, filled in for Cesar Tovar, our regular guy [in center]. The first one short-hopped Bobby. He came in and tried to make a shoestring catch, and the ball got by him and went all the way to the wall, which was 410, 420 at the old Met. It was a three-run homer. Next at-bat it was like a knuckleball. Darwin came in like he was going to catch it. The ball went past him again. A two-run inside-the-park homer.

Allen completed his dream '72 season with the AL-leading 37 homers and 113 RBIs along with a .308 average and 19 stolen bases. That made for an AL MVP award and cemented his image as the game's best all-around player. But Allen would never repeat that kind of performance the rest of his career. Bothered by the aftereffects of a broken leg suffered in 1973 and distraught that the Sox were out of the pennant race, Allen showed up at Comiskey Park before a September 16, 1974, game, waited until after batting practice, and then announced to the entire Sox team that he was walking away from baseball, despite leading the AL in homers with 32. "This is hard for me to say," he tearfully told his teammates, who relayed the remarks to Chicago newspapers, including the *Tribune*. "I've never been happier anywhere but here. You're still gonna be a good ball club without me. You got a good manager [in Tanner]." Allen gave up a baseball-best $250,000 annual salary with his abdication. Refreshed after a winter's break, though, he returned to the Phillies in 1975–76 and finished up in obscurity on the 1977 Oakland A's. He had 351 homers, 133 stolen bases, and a .292 average. Prorated, those are Hall of Fame numbers. Dick Allen had everything but longevity and enough inner discipline to not jump the track so often.

THE MANY DIMENSIONS OF "MR. OCTOBER"

The most colorful player of the 1970s was Reggie Jackson, hands down. "Mr. October" and the "Straw That Stirs the Drink" were two apropos tags for the man who could back up his strut with clutch performances for the Oakland A's, New York Yankees, and California Angels. He could talk as well as he could hit. Not all of his material was family-friendly, but Jackson was unabashed. A day after he tussled with manager Billy Martin in the dugout at Fenway Park in 1977, Jackson was defiant to a reporter who projected that a Red Sox lead would balloon proportionally to 24 games: "Nobody's going to run away with it in this division, not even the Red Sox. It's a long season. . . . If they win by 24 games, I'll suck your dick," he told Fenway Park media, the remark preserved through the decades by then–AP reporter Tom Shaer.

Jackson grabbed headlines in just his third season, eight years before he outdid himself with three home runs for the Yankees in a World Series game. He took a run at Babe Ruth's home-run record in the first half of 1969. He had 37 homers before the All-Star break, on pace to reach Ruth, before slowing down in the season's dog days.

Jackson confirmed he had a flair for center-stage drama when he launched his homer toward the right-field rooftop transformer at Tiger Stadium in the '71 All-Star Game. The distance classic amazed his AL teammates, who gestured toward the transformer after Jackson circled the bases. One of his A's teammates, who had seen Jackson's heroics all the time, was equally impressed.

VIDA BLUE (Athletics, Giants, 1969–79): Reggie was pinch-hitting for me. I had worked my three innings. You really had to be there to see where that ball landed. It was one of those shots where if it had not hit the transformer, it was still going up when you lost sight of it. Reggie has a knack of doing some tremendous feats when there's national publicity to be attained. He was always a good showman.

The outspoken Jackson could sometimes rub teammates the wrong way. The worst incident took place June 5, 1974, at Tiger Stadium. Jackson and A's center fielder Bill North brawled in the clubhouse. Jackson hurt his shoulder, while A's catcher Ray

Fosse, who had been smoked at home plate by Pete Rose to end the 1970 All-Star Game, broke a bone in his neck trying to break up the fight. But that did not damage Jackson's relationships with North and others long-term.

BILL NORTH (Cubs, Athletics, Dodgers, Giants, 1971–79): It was a fuckin' mental disagreement, things that happen when you're teammates. It happened and it was over. We ended up having a conversation about what we wanted to accomplish. It's something I'm not comfortable talking about. When that happened between Reggie and me, some of the white guys on the team liked what happened. They didn't like Reggie as much.

Reggie was like most ballplayers—they're insecure. I was 5-for-55 one time, and I can run. That will give you some insecurity. In time you find individuals that like the big stage. He didn't shrink from the pressure. There are 70 percent of ballplayers that don't want to hit in the ninth inning with two outs.

He was a superstar. If you get in a situation, you perform enough, it becomes natural. Whenever everyone was watching with all the cameras, he was the best player I ever saw. [Away from the game] he was like anyone else. I consider him a friend. Only problem about hanging with Reggie off the field was people. He was glib and fun to be around. But when people would come around, they would get in our relationship because they wanted to hang around. People were so obtrusive, I said I'll catch you next time. It wasn't mean. I like to enjoy him. He was a good dude and we ran together. Reggie was cool.

Despite his controversies with Billy Martin and Yankees owner George Steinbrenner, Jackson was the final touch on back-to-back Yankees world champions in 1977–78. He was respected by the top competitors among his teammates.

LOU PINIELLA (Royals, Yankees, 1969–79): Reggie liked the limelight, period. Reggie had ability. Reggie liked to play. Reggie wanted to be up there at the moment the ball game was decided. He wanted to be the guy. Most of the time he was the guy. He liked being up there. Mr. Steinbrenner named him Mr. October. This guy performed here well at the bigger moments.

Reggie was another guy [who had] toughness about him. He took his share of criticism. I'll tell you this, the guy performed. The bigger the moment, the more he gave. Does anybody do it all the time? No. But he did it his share of the time and other people's, too.

Jackson also got the respect of opponents, including those playing for the archrival Red Sox.

LUIS TIANT (Indians, Twins, Red Sox, Yankees, 1969–79): I had pretty good luck with Reggie. I used to throw the hesitation pitch to him. He'd swing and he couldn't hit it. He looked at me and laughed. But he hit two home runs against me, in Oakland. He swung late and hit the ball into the left-field bleachers. I used to challenge him. I had good control. Then I changed speeds, fastball in, fastball rising. I played with him twice on two different teams. He was dangerous. He didn't hit cheap home runs.

RICK BURLESON (Red Sox, 1974–79): He was definitely a winning ballplayer and I had seen him while I was a high school senior watching a game at Anaheim Stadium. He hit a home run in each game of a doubleheader. We're playing him in the playoffs in '75, here they come again. The Red Sox were underdogs and we swept them. I remember he came over to our locker room after the game and congratulated us. It was the first time we had really seen him with that kind of professional move. I didn't get to know him as a Yankee. I followed his problems with Billy. I think he liked the limelight. I think whether it was a negative or positive, he wanted to be front and center all the time. That's the one thing—most players don't want the negative part. He seemed to treasure it.

Then I got to know him when he came to the Angels in 1982. We became friends. He came to my home and met my children. As a Yankee, he didn't really like us. He may have respected our players. But Reggie was into himself more than any other player. If you didn't like him, it's probably because of that. He wanted to hit in the last group in batting practice so when the opposing team came out to warm up, they'd watch him hit. With most players, you hit [in batting practice] where you hit in the lineup. If he was the number four hitter, he'd [normally] hit early. He wanted to hit in the last group as the gates opened at Yankee Stadium and the visiting team was coming on the field getting ready for their BP, he'd be hitting and putting on his show. He wanted that limelight.

Jackson actually counseled young opposing ballplayers, contrary to his self-centered image. Confirmation came from a shortstop who also knew about the pressure of coming through with the spotlight on.

ALAN TRAMMELL (Tigers, 1977–79): I enjoyed watching Reggie play. Because I thought, watching him play, that he hustled his butt off. He ran out ground balls. People remember home runs and strikeouts. But I remember the hustling part. He ran the bases hard. Those are the kinds of things that caught my attention. He was a star, doing all those things in the World Series. He was cocky to a point—but he backed it up. Jack Morris was cocky and he backed it up. I had a nice relationship with him. For whatever reason, he took the time to seek me out when I was a young player to chat for a couple of minutes. I appreciated it very much and never forgot it. He was trying to help and pass the torch to younger players on how to do it and how to conduct yourself.

Reggie can live off his image as he goes about the game as a senior statesman. Few had come through under pressure as well as he did. His 563 home runs were solid Hall of Fame caliber, but being the right man at the right place at the right time is his all-time legacy.

MIKE SCHMIDT: A PHILLIE WHO WAS MASTER OF WRIGLEY FIELD

Sometime in the late 1980s, I walked through the visitors' clubhouse at Wrigley Field with Mike Schmidt directly in my sights. He spotted me at 20 paces and rolled his eyes. Like Greg Maddux, Schmidt seemingly could read minds. He figured that I intended to ask him why he treated Wrigley as his personal playground. Often reticent with his public demands, Schmidt had been asked that question too many times. When his career finally ended in 1989, he had belted 50 homers in 18 seasons in his own special on-the-road Friendly Confines.

I had witnessed Schmidt's two most memorable Wrigley performances. He hit four homers in four consecutive at-bats on April 17, 1976. Then, on May 17, 1979, he powered a 3–2 hanging split-fingered fastball from Bruce Sutter onto Waveland Avenue for the 10th-inning, game-winning homer in the outlandish 23–22 runfest, the second-highest-scoring game in big-league history. Both games had a common link—Schmidt took advantage of unusually warm spring days that produced vigorous outblowing winds. Of course, the man who might be the greatest all-around third baseman in history hit almost everywhere, drawing the respect of all his contemporaries. Strangely enough, at times his own fans—the toughest in baseball—at

Veterans Stadium booed him. Perhaps they didn't know what they had in Schmidt, the mold of which comes along once in a lifetime in a franchise's history.

DAVE PARKER (Pirates, 1973-79): Mike was the best offensive third baseman. He was a disciplined hitter. He would get in there and wouldn't swing at a lot of pitches out of the zone. He did a lot of cripple-shooting. He'd get ahead in the count and look in the zone for a pitch and take advantage of it. That's when he got a lot of his home runs. He'd work the count in his favor and he capitalized on pitchers behind in the count against him.

Mike was a strong fly-ball hitter. If you get it up in the jet-stream, it goes. Mike could hit it out anywhere. The ballpark [Wrigley Field] was ideal for a strong fly-ball hitter. He always hit with the pitcher behind in the count.

FERGIE JENKINS: You couldn't pitch him away. He liked to get his arms extended. And he had enough power inside to get around on a pitch. I tried to pitch him hard in and then go away, or vice versa, and then stay down. He seemed to be able to counteract a lot of different pitchers. He made his mind up that he was looking for a pitch down, and a lot of guys made their living down. Not that many made their living up.

Future Cubs clutch hitter Keith Moreland, who came up with the Phillies as a catcher, had a good inside-out insight into the complicated man always referred to as "Michael . . . Jack . . . Schmidt" by Phillies announcer Harry Kalas.

KEITH MORELAND (Phillies, 1978-79): You got to start with the man himself. He was a highly intelligent monster of a man, 6-foot-2, 215, 220 pounds. He had a great mind. He was very smart. Sometimes he was too smart for himself; he would outthink himself. There's very few that can just see it and hit it. But Mike was one of those guys. Sometimes he would think "a pitcher was going to do *this* to me," and he would outthink himself. I saw it as a young player hitting behind him, watching this guy have the only struggling year of his career. He was a great athlete, he could have been a good major-league shortstop. They would pitch around him and he would steal a bag. He had great speed.

Mike sort of made you speechless. He could do things that very few players in that group can do. He had a great work ethic. He broke in, he was a home-run guy who struck out a lot. You could see that transition into becoming a complete player.

[Phillies fans] booed him a lot. They thought he should hit a home run every time. I was in total amazement. I think they probably knew that [Mike being the best third baseman in history] late, but by the time they recognized it, it was too late. Part of Mike not wanting to talk to people was the way he was treated at home. He was not treated very well by the Phillies fan, no question. If he was in Chicago, like when Andre [Dawson] was in Chicago, it would have been so much better for him.

Cubs fans certainly would have treated Schmidt like a baseball god had he worn the blue pinstripes. Instead, they faced his godlike wrath every time he took a swing at Wrigley Field. His 50 Wrigley homers, to go along with a .307 average, were amassed in 524 career at-bats over 16-plus seasons on the North Side. In comparison, Hank Aaron required 719 at-bats over 21 seasons to get his 50 homers at Wrigley. The all-time visiting long-ball man was Willie Mays with 54 homers in 691 at-bats over 21-plus seasons.

All the while, Cubs pitchers were working Schmidt wrong by pitching him the right way—logically. They'd have done better hanging off-speed pitches to Schmidt, according to one Chicago starter who dueled Mike for five seasons in his Clark and Addison prime, then became his Phillies teammate.

MIKE KRUKOW (Cubs, 1976–79): I really learned a lot about Mike Schmidt when I played with him in 1982. Mike was a good low-ball hitter, away. You want to get Mike Schmidt out? Hang a slider. He couldn't hit a hanging slider. We were trying to put the ball down around the knees to keep the ball in the ballpark, and we were feeding his strength. You want it down and away. But that was his zone. He'd wear you out. We'd talk about it when we became teammates. He was lucky. It seemed every time the wind was blowing out and the Phillies were coming to town. Mike told me, "I could go 0-for-St. Louis and 0-for-Pittsburgh and the third city in the trip was Chicago, and I knew I'd get hits there." He always got good weather and good wind to hit in. That was his ballpark.

In the four-homer game in 1976, none of the 28,287 fans nearly filling the ballpark on the uncommonly balmy Saturday afternoon would have predicted a football score with Steve Carlton, who usually dominated the Cubs, going up against sinkerballer Rick Reuschel. But the Cubs amazingly took a 13–2 lead in the bottom of the fourth.

Schmidt used teammate Tony Taylor's lighter bat in an attempt to change the bad luck of nine strikeouts in his first four games of the season. The NL's two-time defending home-run champ, he was dropped to sixth, behind Dick Allen, in the batting order. Schmidt slugged his first homer with two outs in the fifth off Reuschel to make it 13–4.

Then, in the top of the seventh, Reuschel gave up two more Phillies runs before serving up a solo shot to Schmidt with two outs to make it 13–7. That brought in a shaky Cubs bullpen for the eighth. Mike Garman gave up two more runs before Schmidt connected for number three with two on and two out, to cut the deficit to 13–12. Astoundingly, the Phillies took a 15–13 lead in the top of the ninth, without Schmidt's help, off lefty Darold Knowles before Cubs catcher Steve Swisher slashed a two-out, two-run single in the bottom of the inning for a 15–15 tie.

Right-hander Paul Reuschel, Rick's brother, came in after Knowles had walked Dick Allen to lead off the 10th. What happened next probably crosses Reuschel's mind as he tends the fairways as the groundskeeper at Western Illinois University's golf course in Macomb, Illinois.

PAUL REUSCHEL (Cubs, Indians, 1975–79): The wind was blowing out about 30 mph. When [Schmidt] hit one off me, I actually thought the shortstop would catch it or the left fielder would come in and run him off. When he hit it, I said, "All right, there's another out." But it just kept carrying and carrying till it landed in the basket.

When he was hot, you couldn't get him out. When he wasn't, anybody could get him out. He was real streaky. You don't think about those things [dominating Wrigley Field] when you're pitching—you're just trying to get him out. I was a sinker-slider pitcher and I tried to get ahead inside and make him chase it if I could.

Schmidt's feats inspired young Phillies fans, including one who had the honor of playing center field at Veterans Stadium a generation later. To imitate Schmidt's stance and style as a grade-school kid in Teaneck, New Jersey, was the highest calling.

DOUG GLANVILLE: Michael Jack Schmidt was a big part of what my childhood meant to me. My older brother, Ken, had me involved in baseball as soon as I could read, and part of his grand plan to make me a major-league ballplayer was to learn the art of Wiffle ball. In no time we had plastic helmets from all of our favorite teams and would switch out one for another when the whim hit us. I was a loyal Phillies fan so most of my time, I would find the red Phillies helmet and walk through their lineup, replicating each player with every idiosyncrasy in consideration. But Mike Schmidt would stand tall. That tap on the plate, the wiggle of the hips, the wrist flick that would send the ball flying. It is no wonder I tapped the plate in his honor for my entire major league career.

He was the complete package, and I knew this when I was 7 years old. He could run, he could field with precision, hit for average, he knew the strike zone, he could drive the ball out of the park, and most of all, he was out there every day on bad knees on Astroturf. I even remembered his anti-drug commercial to help kids avoid the pitfalls of drug use. He was everywhere and I loved every minute of it.

Once I wore the Phillies uniform, I was part of what made my childhood a time of magic. I wore the same fabric that Mike Schmidt wore and that meant a lot. I spent some time with him as he helped coach the next generation of Phillies from time to time. Talking hitting, talking shop. A tremendous honor for me.

Schmidt's 548 homers, three NL MVP awards and 12 All-Star berths is a typical résumé for a player who populated baseball's True Golden Age, an all-around third baseman who succeeded Brooks Robinson and Ron Santo in that role, then far exceeded their accomplishments. There are no boos for Schmidt in his golf-filled retirement.

THURMAN MUNSON: THE PRIDE OF THE YANKEES

Some of the greats are taken from us much too soon. Thurman Munson was one of them, killed while practicing takeoffs and landings in his private jet in Canton, Ohio, on August 2, 1979.

The tragedy took the true heart and soul of the Yankees. Catcher Munson, the captain of the Bombers, was the toughest and smartest of the bunch as the Yanks returned to dominance after a 12-year absence from the postseason.

As valuable as his numbers was Munson's old-school attitude, worthy of the Yankees' all-time greats. His best friend on the team summed up his career best.

LOU PINIELLA: Thurman basically was a tough kid. He enjoyed playing, he enjoyed talking baseball. And he loved playing every day. He played a very demanding position. A year or two after I was there, he was named captain of the Yankees, which in itself was a huge honor. Thurman basically was very tough-minded.

Thurman was well liked in the clubhouse and respected. The guy was really a good catcher and a clutch hitter. He had the respect of everybody in that clubhouse. He played hard. I remember many times a guy would slide into home plate and he'd cut him up pretty good. They'd stitch him up between innings and he'd stay in the ball game—basically like a hockey player. He had this gruff exterior about him, but if you really got to know him, he was a good guy.

Better yet, Munson had a way of getting inside opponents' heads, starting with the ace pitcher of the Yanks' top opponent.

LUIS TIANT: One day I pitched against him in Boston. He hit the left-field screen against me. As he's running around the bases, he's hollering, "I got you, I finally got you." We had a good respect between us. In New York he was my catcher. A good catcher, a good person. He put the uniform on, he wanted to beat you. He played hard nine innings every day.

From his vantage point in his catcher's crouch, Munson played mind games.

RICK BURLESON: It was around 1977. The Yankees came into Winter Haven. I had gone to Don Zimmer in spring training and told him I want to run on my own, steal bags on my own. He said, "I'll tell you what. I'll let you do it in spring training and at the end of spring training, we'll decide what we want to do." The Red Sox weren't big on running. In this particular game I happen to get two bags at second and even stole third. I didn't think much of it, I'm just working on stealing bags. Then the season starts, and Thurman goes out of his way to take me out at second, gets a piece of me, and knocks me on my keester. Next time I come up to bat, he gets into his crouch and he looks up at me and says, "Rooster, now we're even." I step out. I look back and said, "What are you talking about?" He said, "Remember in spring training, you stole those bags on me." I said, "Yeah." He said "My arm was killing me. I didn't appreciate you running on me at that time."

My favorite player, without a doubt. I was totally crushed when we lost Thurman Munson. You had to respect the way he played the game, the way he went about his business on a daily basis as Yankees captain. He was always under a lot of scrutiny from the press.

FRED LYNN: I liked Thurman. Gawd, he'd talk your ear off as an opposing hitter. He'd try to distract you, especially when I was a rookie. He'd be talking about how far he hit that last ball. I'm a rookie, I can't say shut up. I just tried to block all that stuff out and focus on the pitcher. It was gamesmanship.

As long as the Yankees dominate baseball, their history is highlighted in the books. That means Thurman Munson's persona will always be front and center.

THE SWEET SWINGER'S BIGGEST DAY

Billy Williams always possessed a perfect swing worthy of a batting champion. But Williams, nicknamed the "Sweet Swinger" and "Whistler" for his hometown near Mobile, Alabama, never attained the top of the stats his first 11 Cubs seasons through 1971. Perhaps his own endurance did him in. He played 1,117 consecutive games, setting an NL record, from 1963 to 1970. All those day games at Wrigley Field couldn't have done much for his late-season bat speed on a lithe 170-pound frame.

In 1972 it was different. A combination of maturity, at 34, and a little more rest kept Williams fresh for his run at the batting title. Putting him into position to win the crown was a memorable 8-for-8 performance in a July 11 doubleheader against the Astros at Wrigley Field. The hits spree, which included two homers and a double, boosted his average from .310 to .328 in one afternoon. Williams was used to coming through big-time in twin bills. On June 29, 1969, at Wrigley Field, when he was honored between games for breaking Stan Musial's old NL consecutive-games-played mark, he was 5-for-9 in the doubleheader with two doubles and two triples, running counter to the trend that a player being honored ends up a flop on the field that day.

BILLY WILLIAMS: When you're playing in the major leagues, you want to stay in the top 10. You had [Roberto] Clemente, [Pete] Rose, [Willie] Mays, Henry Aaron. If you could stay up there, you'd be compared with the great hitters. On this one day, playing Houston in July, I'm swinging the bat well. Nothing was special. I swung the bat so-so in batting practice. But during the game I started swinging the bat well. I hit every ball on the nose. I hit eight balls on the nose, which is unusual for a player to do. All of them found the hole. It kind of spurred me to go on to win the batting title.

That particular day I was [unconscious]. I was swinging the bat good. The ball looked like a basketball coming up there. It seemed like it came up 60 feet, 6 inches, stopped, and sat on a tee. I hit the ball every time I went up to the plate. You're seeing the ball well, and if I was told you're sitting out the second game, you would have heard me all over Chicago.

The last couple of weeks, I felt confident, I was swinging the bat really well. I was aware of what they were doing [batting-title challengers Dusty Baker and Ralph Garr of the Braves]. I could pick up the Atlanta games at night [on the radio]. I put pressure on them during the day [at Wrigley Field]. I'd get two or three hits, and they had to work a little bit that evening. Ralph Garr could put the ball into play and run like a deer. Aaron used to tell [Baker] a lot of things to do up at the plate. I felt I was secure I'd win the batting title.

Williams won the crown with a .333 mark. But he missed out on the triple crown by three homers and three RBIs, finishing with 37 and 122, with Johnny Bench of the Reds capturing both categories. That also was the second season Bench's modest statistical edge in homers and RBIs, plus the Reds' finishing first compared to the Cubs' second-place standing, enabled the Cincy catcher to cop the NL MVP award over Williams.

A NEW PROFESSION: DESIGNATED HITTER

Ron Blomberg has made a second career out of his status as baseball's first designated hitter with the Yankees in 1973. But the introduction of the DH had more far-ranging effects than on

Blomberg's résumé. The ability to get three or four at-bats a game without playing defense extended the careers of all-time greats like Hank Aaron and Frank Robinson in the mid-1970s. Other older or less-fielding-adept players soon gravitated to the role.

The DH was the most radical change in the way baseball was played in the 1970s. But it only was adopted by the attendance-hungry American League. The National League resisted then and has never bent. Even more radical changes were proposed by commissioner Bowie Kuhn. Advocating limited interleague play with some AL clubs' backing at baseball's summer owners' meetings in 1973, Kuhn was resoundingly shot down by the NL clubs. Although the seed was planted, interleague play would not become a reality for 24 more years.

But the DH was enough change for the likes of Hal McRae. He had been a part-time outfielder on some good Cincinnati Reds teams from 1970 to 1972. But in moving to the Kansas City Royals at the dawn of the DH era, he found a new role to ensure he'd be a 500 at-bat regular. It did not take that long for McRae to bury his leather-wielding ego.

HAL McRAE (Reds, Royals, 1969–79): It was tough in the beginning because no one wanted to do it. They used to call you half of a ballplayer because you didn't play in the field. Nobody wanted to do it initially. I was given that role. I had to learn to adapt to that role. It was a lot of fun for me because we were a better club with me as a DH. I wanted to win most of all. We had Amos [Otis] in center, [Al] Cowens in right, and [Tom] Poquette in left. A lot of good arms out there. We were a better club if I was DH.

I had to learn to stay in the game, number one. Follow the rhythm of the game, watch the pitchers. Stay loose [mentally] to where you had four at-bats rather than four pinch-hit [appearances]. That's what everyone had to overcome. That had to be learned. Nobody knew how to do it. Guys sort of accepted the role.

I ran in the tunnel. I'd walk around in the clubhouse listening to the radio or watch TV. We had a laundry basket in Kansas City and I'd push at the basket to stretch my legs. I would move around the clubhouse with that basket in order to keep the hammies stretched out. If I broke a sweat, I tried to maintain a sweat. The condition of your body had to be at the same level as if you're playing. I had to feel like my body is playing and mentally I'm playing, not just DHing and playing only half the time. Initially there were no indoor cages. I'd just swing to stay loose.

I think it's good for the game. It used to allow a veteran player whose legs were gone [to play] in those AL cities where they never saw this guy play. Now it's a position where the guy's not an old guy, he's going to bat third or fourth in the order. He's going to be a real productive player. The role has evolved into just a good hitter regardless of his age. As a rule, that guy is not one of your better defensive players. It allows him to help the club win more than hurting the club.

McRae indeed found the perfect role. He was the Royals' primary DH during the franchise's greatest period of success from 1976 to 1985, when Kansas City finally captured its lone World Series victory. McRae led the AL in RBIs with 133 in 1982. Son Brian McRae never followed in his old man's footsteps, though. He was a pretty good center fielder for the Royals and Cubs in the 1990s. Meanwhile, the DH transformed the AL into an offense-oriented league, where a 4.00 ERA was considered good by Brian McRae's time. And the onslaught of hitters up and down the lineups eventually meant more pitchers would be needed. Change came to baseball in the True Golden Age, and it was never rolled back.

5

Duels to a Standstill, Complete Games, and Rubber Arms

Tuesday, April 6, 1971, was Election Day in Chicago. Mayor Richard J. Daley, Hizzoner and eventual mayor for life, stood for his fifth term and wasn't going to be denied by a reformer. The bars were closed.

But the continuation of the Daley Machine was of little consequence at 6310 North Artesian Street on the Far North Side, compared to the first of 40 consecutive Wrigley Field Opening Days I would attend, stretching well into another century. This was a dream come true. I finally summoned the gumption to cut classes as a sophomore at Mather High School. I studied my mother's handwriting carefully for weeks to craft the note excusing my absence. In these more innocent times, schools did not call home to make sure you were indeed ill and confined to your bed. I guess the assistant principals weren't baseball fans and couldn't put two plus two together.

As clever as I branded myself in playing hooky, I also made a rookie mistake. The deceptive, bright sunshine masked the early-spring chill's bite. I neglected to take gloves and a hat when I hopped the number 155 Devon bus for the 2-mile ride to the Loyola L station, transferring to the B train for the 3-mile scoot to the Addison Street stop for Wrigley Field.

You could never arrive too early for a Cubs opener in this era. The majority of seats were sold day-of-game, and much of the expected 40,000 crowd cramming into the then-36,000-seat bandbox arrived by daybreak, or even earlier. When I arrived at 9:30 a.m., the $1 sun-drenched bleachers, the only place where the chill was not overwhelming, were already full. I settled for a $1.75 shaded seat in the right-field grandstand. I immediately started cooling down as the four-hour wait for the first pitch commenced.

Curious, I bounded down the steps to the first row of the boxes, where the Cardinals started loosening up. Nearby, a wise guy spotted newly acquired outfielder Matty Alou. "Hey, Mateo," he bellowed. "How's your brother *Gee-sus*?" When I returned to my seat in the shade, I simply got more chilled. My fingers grew stiff. I tried to write the lineup in the 15-cent cardboard scorecard. I could barely scrawl the name "Brock" in the visitors section before I gave up.

Too bad. A fully filled-out scorecard would have been a proper memento of one of baseball's most talent-laden eras. Both the Cubs and Cardinals were full of Hall of Famers and should-be-enshrinees. Such as Cards' stolen-base king Lou Brock, signed and developed by the Cubs—but that's another book. The managers—Leo Durocher of the Cubs and Red Schoendienst of the Redbirds—eventually landed in Cooperstown. Billy Williams in the Cubs lineup and Ernie Banks on the bench would get the summons. The competing third basemen, Ron Santo of the Cubs and Joe Torre of the Cardinals, should be enshrined, but mysteriously haven't been.

But the best examples of Hall of Fame–caliber talent on hand were the opposing pitchers, taking their by-now famous duels to an Opening Day for the first time. Fergie Jenkins, fresh off four consecutive 20-win seasons for the Cubs, squared off against Bob Gibson, with three straight 20-win campaigns under his belt, just three years removed from a record-low 1.12 ERA. If four or five runs would be scored today between these all-time aces and the cold weather, it would be an accomplishment. Instead, runs were scarce, and my only consolation for frozen hands was that Jenkins and Gibson were on their games and moved the game into the express lane. Nine scattered hits—including a Torre homer—yielded by both pitchers and four walks off Gibson, and here we were tied 1–1 going into the 10th inning. Not even an hour and 50 minutes had transpired.

It was a different era than today. Aces were allowed to go nine and beyond, even in their first start of the year, and in adverse weather. Jenkins and Gibson had gone into the 10th locked up in 95-degree heat in St. Louis on July 4, 1969, so they'd go just as far in Arctic conditions. Jenkins retired the Cardinals easily in the top of the 10th. Then, with one out in the bottom of the inning, Billy Williams took the measure of Gibson as he often did. He slammed a fastball into the right-field bleachers to end it, Cubs 2, Cards 1, in one hour, 58 minutes. Gibson walked off the mound with his head held high. Two decades later the man who only begrudgingly conceded defeat remembered losing this game, but not the Williams homer, one Hall of Famer beating another. Gibson just would not admit a weakness even after such a passage of time.

Scrambling amid the mobs surging toward the L station and trying to defrost, I was warmed with the thought of the classic I had just witnessed, while sad I had no written record of the Jenkins-Gibson battle. I would soon have other chances, though, to see similar matchups. This was an age of aces. Baseball was dotted with rubber-armed pitchers who started every four days, amassing 40 starts, 20 or more complete games, and 300-plus innings every year. Such classics were a regular feature of baseball's landscape, pitchers going the distance against each other with the game riding on every pitch. The era would not last much longer, but it was riveting to watch while it carried on. The memory cannot be supplanted by anything in the "five-and-fly" era of fragile starters and eight-man bullpens.

The duelists of April 6, 1971, were the front-liners in an unforgettable era of pitching in baseball's True Golden Age.

FERGIE AND GIBBY DUEL TO THE DEATH

Jenkins and Gibson had personalities at polar opposites of the spectrum. Fergie was the "Fly" who merrily buzzed around his teammates, while "Gibby" could be an acerbic, hard man who would not tolerate fools.

But both were lean and limber, lending themselves to all-around athleticism in which they could play basketball for the Harlem Globetrotters in the off-season. They had rubber arms and a devotion to going nine or more innings. Jenkins established a streak that won't likely be matched soon: six consecutive 20-win seasons from 1967 to 1972. After an off-year in 1973 and a trade to the Texas Rangers, he won a career-high 25 games in 1974. Gibson had 56 complete games in 1968–69; Jenkins finished 30 of his 39 starts in 1971. Both had six complete-game losses in their peak seasons. Each worked quickly and was a good hitter. They'd prefer to get three groundball outs on three pitches, but their stuff was so good that 250 or more strikeouts a season was the norm.

They were inexorably linked during baseball's True Golden Age, Gibson the older, established pitcher on a frequent contender, Jenkins the up-and-coming control artist on a Cubs team emerging from generation-long doldrums. They were the aces-on old-time geographic arch-rivals and their duels thus counted even more. Jenkins squeaked out a 5–3 record in the nine head-to-head matchups between 1967 and 1972. He had a 1.78 ERA in those starts; Gibson 2.43. Gibson won the pair of 1–0 games. Jenkins was victor in two 10-inning contests. There were two 2–1 affairs and two 3–1 games.

Jenkins was so affable he could have been the Cubs' director of community relations after his career. Gibson was more distant, stating he never wanted his opponents to know much about him. He mellowed a bit when the two met for their first radio interview together for the syndicated *Diamond Gems* show when both were pitching coaches in 1996.

BOB GIBSON (Cardinals, 1969–75): I was aware [of Jenkins], of course. He was the enemy pitcher. The problem was, everyone thought I loved to pitch against Fergie and I liked the competition. Not really. You'd rather pitch against somebody you know you're going to get four or five runs off of. We weren't going to get but one or two runs off of him, and that made it tough.

FERGIE JENKINS: I knew if I was pitching against Gibson, runs would be at a minimum. Same with [Juan] Marichal, [Gaylord] Perry. Bobby was one of the top five in the National League in the time before I got established. If I gave up two or three runs, I was a loser.

Gibson felt there was a logical reason to keep his distance, mentally and physically, from opponents. Thus he never reached out to his worthy opponent in Cubbie blue to talk shop.

BOB GIBSON: I felt that hitters just love to get comfortable with you. The more you consorted with them, the more you talked with them, the more comfortable they get with you. I felt that if I just stayed away from them and they didn't have any idea of what I was about, it would work in my favor. I still believe in that.

I didn't care what he [Jenkins] was thinking. I knew I was going to have to be on my best game in order to beat him. I wasn't concerned about how he did it. He did it differently than me. I was a high fastball pitcher; he was a sinker-baller. We both had a pretty good slider. He was in and out more than me; I tried to overpower the guy most of the time.

No offense taken for his foe's standoffishness.

FERGIE JENKINS: Bobby was always fielding ground balls at short or third. That's how he got his exercise in. He was the kind of guy who concentrated on what he had to do. We might exchange glances and say hi. But when the game started, we're all business. Both of us knew if we let up, we'd be in trouble.

When Bob was on the mound, he was all business, he didn't mess around. That's very important. When you're out there, your concentration is 100 percent pitching, no foolishness. That's how you win ball games.

Both pitchers were so good they were regarded as their own best relievers. Actually, once they got into a rhythm in midgame, they rarely faltered late. The best time to get Jenkins and Gibson was early on, before they got their momentum in high gear. The end result was astounding. Gibson's 56 complete jobs in 1968–69 came in a total of 69 starts. Jenkins had at least 20 complete games in each of his 20-win Cubs seasons.

BOB GIBSON: I doubt that we'll ever see that happen again. It's really sad that everybody blames the pitchers for not completing ball games. It really has nothing to do with the pitchers. It has to do with the way the game is played today. They have the setup men and the closers, and that's who they look to in the sixth, seventh, and eighth innings. [Back in my time] the press would criticize you if you didn't finish ball games.

No one questioned when Gibson threw inside to hitters. He was simply an ornery competitor who believed the plate was his. But one hitter he largely left alone was Billy Williams, Jenkins's fishing buddy. Williams's game-winning Opening Day homer in 1971 against Gibson was 1 of 10 lifetime he belted against Gibson.

BILLY WILLIAMS: Gibson threw me a slider down and in. For about 10 or 12 years, he threw me that same pitch. He didn't think I could hit it. When Gibson's pitching, because he was an aggressive pitcher and I was an aggressive hitter, something had to happen. Several times I connected, the ball went out of the ballpark. Many years you hit 30 homers, you get a $2,500 raise. When I knew that Fergie and Gibson were pitching, I always planned something after the game. I knew it was a game that would be played around two hours. When Gibson was pitching, Leo [Durocher] tried to get us to disrupt his tempo. When he got into a good-tempo game, you didn't want him to get in that groove. Everybody was reluctant to step out because if you stepped out and broke his rhythm, the next pitch would be at your head.

Also escaping the worst of Gibson's wrath was Pirates outfielder Al Oliver, who could only watch one day as a prominent teammate stood in as a big target for the Cardinals pitcher.

AL OLIVER: He brushed you back, but he never drilled me like he drilled my teammates. I was on deck one night in St. Louis. He hit Will [Willie Stargell], and Will was peppering him that night. He threw the ball at his ribs and it was like the ball stuck there for a while. Two or three seconds and it dropped to the ground. One thing about a pitcher, if he wants to hit you, he's going to hit you. That's why we didn't have any problems in Pittsburgh—our pitchers would protect us. With the great hitting we had, we would do damage to a lot of teams.

He was probably the most intimidating pitcher I've faced, and I'm thankful he was right-handed. I've had chances to carry on conversations with him since we've both been out of the game, and he's enjoyable to talk to. But one time I went down to the Hilton Hotel [in Pittsburgh] to pick up [Cardinals pitcher] Scipio Spinks to go to the ballpark, and he got on the elevator with me at the same time, going up. He never said a word. That was intimidation.

The one-hour, 58-minute Opening Day game was not the quickest Gibson–Jenkins contest. On May 31, 1972, at Wrigley Field, Gibson bested Jenkins 1–0 in just one hour, 47 minutes.

FERGIE JENKINS: Both of us were equally fast. Once we got the tempo of the game the way we wanted, we didn't want to slow it up. Guys were hitting first or second pitches. The thing that's different now compared to then is you don't see so many [long] commercial breaks. We didn't beat around the bush, nibbling here, nibbling there. Both of us had the positive attitude [that] if the hitter beat you, he'd have to beat you with your best stuff.

Gibson was what could be termed a maximum-effort pitcher. He fell off toward the first-base mound in his delivery, so a shot through the middle could be hazardous. He sweated a waterfall. In contrast, Jenkins must have had the same kind of ice water in his veins that he'd see in winter fishing holes in his native Ontario. In the Amazon-like climate of July 4, 1969, at Busch Stadium, he hardly sweated through his heavy gray flannel road jersey, while Gibson was soaked. Plate umpire Shag Crawford had to leave due to heat exhaustion after six innings. But Jenkins was the coolest dude, pitching the full 10 innings for the win as Gibson faltered in the top of the 10th. The lack of sweat and his runs to and from the mound were a psychological ploy.

FERGIE JENKINS: That's exactly what it was. You put those hot sweaters on and that flannel uniform on and you run out, back and forth on that turf, not [showing] it's hot out. Telling the hitters in the opposing dugout, I'm fresh, I'm ready to go. That's the way I performed. I ran on and off the field. If I got a base hit, I ran out the ground ball. I think the nice thing about it you had to let the other team know they were not going to beat you that day.

Jenkins used the Opening Day '71 triumph over Gibson as his springboard to his only Cy Young Award season. Jenkins went 24–13 and walked just 37 in 325 innings. For good measure, he slugged six homers—including two in one game against Montreal—and drove in 20 runs, batting .243.

FERGIE JENKINS: I knew I'd have to face the number one pitcher on their ball club. You're only going to win half your games. In that season I won two-thirds of my games. When I look back at it, the competition of being able to face the number one pitcher on the other ball club was satisfying. I'd have to do it every fourth day.

I was coming off a pretty good spring training. I was healthy. I'm not sure you could predict [a Cy Young season]. You knew you'd get on an average . . . I'd get six or seven starts a month. I'd have to win three or four of those starts.

I knew my control was good enough to do that [only 37 walks]. I could always hear in the back of my mind there's no defense for a walk. Let the hitter to do the work. You have the ball, you could throw strikes.

I always knew I could make contact [at the plate]. I knew I would go to the plate a lot, 90 to 100 times. If the pitcher threw strikes to me, I could hit the ball. You're always happy you hit the ball hard a couple of times. I could see [the two-homer game] like it was yesterday.

Jenkins was with Texas by the time Gibson appeared in his final game on September 3, 1975, at Busch Stadium. Appropriately, it was against the Cubs. Fading fast at 40, Gibby was consigned to middle relief. In the seventh inning he issued three walks (one intentional) and gave up a hit and a run-scoring wild pitch before serving up a pinch-hit grand slam to little-known Pete LaCock, son of *Hollywood Squares* host Peter Marshall. Such a humiliation caused Gibson to hang it up for good with 251 victories and a 2.91 ERA.

Jenkins lasted till spring training 1984, finishing with 284 wins. His last career shutout? A four-hitter against the Cardinals on June 10, 1983, at age 40 at Wrigley Field.

LEFTY: MUM'S THE WORD, BUT A VERY LOUD SLIDER

By 1969 a 6-foot-5 southpaw with outstanding stuff had worked himself up to the number two Cardinals starter's job behind Gibson. Steve Carlton was nearly a finished product with his repertoire, but his one-of-a-kind persona would require a couple more years and a change of teams to become recognized as baseball's strong, silent type for the balance of the 1970s.

Early on, though, Carlton's claim to fame was losing one of the toughest-luck games in history on September 15, 1969, at Busch Stadium. He struck out a record 19 New York Mets, but lost 4–3 to the World Series–bound team on a pair of two-run homers by right-fielder Ron Swoboda, one in the fourth and the other in the eighth.

Swoboda certainly had not made a history of hitting Carlton.

RON SWOBODA: I don't know what happened. I had one game with him. The only thing that was different is I struggled a bit [going into the game]. St. Louis had one of the few [indoor] hitting cages that existed then, behind the left-field wall. They had the old pitching machines that spun between the tires—it could throw a little slider. Someone could feed the balls to you and it would pitch to you. I asked [broadcaster] Ralph Kiner [to help] because I was fucked up. Come down there and look at me, see if you see anything. He looked at some stances and he said they looked good. I got into a good groove. Hitting for me was so much of a feel thing and I got comfortable, I got the bat out front. I took that into the game against Carlton. He had interstellar stuff, man, you knew it.

He struck me out the first time, and they take a 1-0 lead. Next time up he gets two strikes on me with Tommie Agee onboard. I bang him. I hit a high fastball upstairs in left field. He strikes me out the third time up and they take a 3-2 lead. The fourth time up he throws me a slider with two strikes that was on me, but I got the head of the bat on it and hit a line drive that just makes it over the left-field wall, and we beat him 4-3. I don't know how it happened. I think I had three base hits off him my whole life.

Right after him Harry Caray had his postgame [radio] show. I walk in the room and here's Steve Carlton looking like he just heard somebody ran over his dog. You look at big strikeout games, more times than you think they end up as losses.

Carlton had an interesting habit, then and postcareer, of saying the wrong thing at the wrong time. When Caray asked Carlton where one of the Swoboda gopher balls had been located, he responded, "It was cock high," by Caray's remembrance. He would later learn his lesson and deprive a national baseball audience of the secret of his success to come.

Carlton racked up his first 20-win season in 1971, but was traded to the Phillies for pitcher Rick Wise during the following spring training when Cards owner Gussie Busch couldn't compromise over a relative pittance in difference between the team's and Carlton's contract demands. Despite Wise's competence, the trade ended up as the worst in Cardinals history. Carlton made Busch pay with an astounding 27–10 season, the most wins in one season of any National League pitcher in the 1970s. He added 30 complete games, 346⅓ innings, and 310 strikeouts. The Phils won just 59 games all season, but played like champions when Carlton took the mound. Shortstop Larry Bowa had one of the best views of Carlton's otherworldly season in which his nickname "Lefty" stuck for good.

LARRY BOWA (Phillies, 1970–79): I just think when he took the mound, it elevated the team to another level. It didn't matter what our record was when he was on the mound—we felt we could win the ball game. The record could be 30 games under .500. When he was on the mound, everyone on the team knew if we could score two or three runs, we would have a good chance to win the game. He elevated everybody's play.

Poor Wise. Nobody could measure up to Carlton's sheer excellence. Wise had back-to-back 16-win seasons in St. Louis and a creditable career that lasted until 1982, but he was not in Carlton's ballpark. No one really was.

RICK WISE (Phillies, Cardinals, Red Sox, Indians, 1969–79): Sure, it [27 wins] was a surprise. You kidding me? I was doing the same thing, trying to win some games in Philly. He was fantastic. He had overpowering stuff. They wouldn't even put the ball in play. You have to bury the bottom of the order. Stay away from those three-run homers. He certainly did.

Carlton perfected a devastating slider to complement a blazing fastball. That's all he needed. Five years after his dream Phillies season, a young Braves hitter who would go on to back-to-back MVP awards had to figure out how to hit Carlton.

DALE MURPHY (Braves, 1976–79): You didn't do much with it [slider]. To a right-hander it would be low and inside and then he'd throw his fastball away, then come with a fastball in. Then right when you thought he'd throw another fastball inside, he'd throw that slider. That slider would come out of his hand looking like a fastball and the last 5, 6 feet would dive straight down. You didn't hit that. What you'd try to hit was one of those fastballs. Willie

Stargell told me, "You want to be a good curveball hitter?" I said, "Yeah." He said, "Then don't miss the fastball." If Lefty threw it where he wanted to throw it in the count he wanted to throw it, you'd have to fight to foul it off. I said to myself every time up, I'm going to get something to hit in the strike zone. He couldn't throw three sliders in the dirt. Lefty's got to throw me a strike sometime. I have to be ready to hit it.

If it was a challenge for right-handers to figure out Carlton, imagine the dilemma for left-handed swingers. The Pirates' Al Oliver took pride in being able to hit almost all kinds of pitching. Carlton, however, was in a different class.

AL OLIVER: The one good and great pitcher that I didn't hit that I thought I did a lot better [against] was Steve Carlton. My batting average was under .200 against him. I thought it was a misprint. He was a great pitcher, no question about it. What he did was he didn't make me look bad. Sometimes you wish you would look bad. He never allowed me to really get comfortable. He kept me honest. He made me hit his pitches. That is the key to great pitching. The slider was definitely the equalizer. He wasn't going to allow me to dive into the ball, because I went into the ball. He would throw his fastball inside to get me off the plate and then come with the slider. If I did hit the slider, I'd hit a hard ground ball to shortstop. I remember one home run I hit off him. The count was in my favor, 3–1 or 3–2, and it was in Pittsburgh. Great pitchers make you [try to] hit their pitches. Steve did that to me consistently, to his credit.

He got the ball and threw the ball. Personally I loved that part about a pitcher. I never stepped out of the batter's box. [Carlton's '72 performance was the] best I saw for a whole season. I missed [Sandy] Koufax, and I can only relate to Steve.

Already left-handed in personality with his devotion to martial arts and cutting-edge training method of immersing his left arm in a bowl of rice, Carlton clammed up permanently after taking knocks over a rare pratfall, a 20-loss season in Philly in 1973. He became the most prominent "zipped-lipped personality," in baseball, avoiding the media like the plague.

His energy conserved by not talking, Carlton went on to four more 20-win seasons with the Phillies and won 329 games, second-best all-time for a left-hander, before finally hanging it up in 1988.

RYAN EXPRESS AND HIS FASTBALL DETOURED OUT OF NEW YORK

Speed always fascinates. But in the 1970s, with the moon conquered and a 55-mph national limit put in place to conserve gas in the wake of the first oil shock, one of the top points of interest was measuring the pace of Nolan Ryan's fastball.

So that's why the *Chicago Tribune* city room stirred to life on a normally quiet Saturday midnight on September 7, 1974. Gazing over from my copy clerk's station at the switchboard, I noticed a telecopier whirring to life, beginning its transmission of Richard Dozer's final Sunday-edition deadline story from Anaheim Stadium. The measuring device at the ballpark and the gizmo delivering Dozer's copy were a lot more low-tech than their more portable, efficient successors. The cylinder began spinning ever faster, although not rivaling Ryan's speed, as a pungent, inky smell wafted from its immediate vicinity. After a few minutes of spins, the telecopier spewed forth Dozer's story, reporting how the Rockwell International radar device installed in the press box timed Ryan as fast as 100.8 mph against the White Sox's Bee Bee Richard in the ninth inning.

More than 6,000 entries from 38 states were received guessing Ryan's speed in a contest conducted by the Angels in 1974. Guesses ranged from 48 to 200 mph, but the median estimate was 99 to 100 mph. The winner got an all-expenses-paid trip to the first two games of the American League Championship Series.

To be sure, others threw almost as hard, if not faster, than Ryan over the decades, when clocking velocity was less frequent. But officially, he beat Bob Feller's 98.6 mph, clocked in Washington, D.C., in 1946 via even more primitive means. Anyone following baseball figured Ryan was a century-mark guy in speed. The big question was whether Ryan, in 1974 in his third season with the Angels, always knew where his heater was going.

Harnessing control was a sometimes frustrating process—somewhat mimicking the path taken 15 years earlier by Sandy Koufax—for Ryan in a career that began in 1966 as part of the New York Mets' bumper crop of young hard throwers. Ryan never had a chance to develop a season-long rhythm as a starter. His control troubles kept Mets manager Gil Hodges from installing him in his core rotation. The Alvin, Texas, native shuttled in and out of spot starts and came in from the bullpen, making no discernible progress in taking his place with Tom Seaver and Jerry Koosman. Finally, on December 10, 1971, Ryan was traded with three other youngish Mets to the Angels for veteran shortstop Jim Fregosi.

Like the Steve Carlton deal for the Phillies, dispatching Ryan would turn out to be the Mets' worst-ever transaction. But for Ryan, it was liberating. He would start on his own express path to the Hall of Fame, even though his postseason experiences would be few and far between. He'd work in a big ballpark with people who began figuring out how to properly harness his enormous pitching power. Never again would he be consigned to a bullpen.

The most accomplished of his old Mets pitching mates figured that a regular rotation slot was all Ryan needed to get going.

TOM SEAVER (Mets, Reds, 1969–79): That's one of the reasons why Nolan Ryan went to California and blossomed into the great pitcher he was. Unfortunately, the Mets were in a situation with myself, Koosman, [Gary] Gentry, etc., and Nolan being a little bit wild and young at the time, they didn't give him the ball. He didn't have the luxury of "here's the ball, you're going to pitch every fifth day, come hell or high water." They [the Angels] said, you're pitching every fourth or fifth day, we don't care what happens, you're pitching and you're going to make 36 or 38 starts and we'll evaluate it at the end of the year.

Ryan also needed to get out of the National League at the time, reasoned yet another old Mets teammate who had watched Ryan when he broke in back in '66.

RON SWOBODA: It was hard to get in that rotation. His biggest problem was he was a high fastball pitcher in a lowball league. Back in the 1960s the National League umpires had their internal gear and were much closer to the strike zone. Augie Donatelli would get down next to the catcher's face. They saw the low ball better and it was not a high-ball league. In the American League, when I went over there in '71, they were still using the inner tube—the external gear—and they saw the high pitch better.

Also, Nolan's wife [Ruth] did not like New York. Nolan did ask them to trade him. They were small-town people. She was not comfortable living in New York and Nolan was sensitive to that. Nolan precipitated that trade, I am fairly certain. When we had the '69 guys back at Citi Field on the 40th anniversary, he more or less said that.

Whatever Ryan's fate, the Mets certainly did not get their end of the bargain from Fregosi, who batted just .232 and .234 playing out of position at Shea Stadium in 1972–73.

JIM FREGOSI (Angels, Mets, Rangers, Pirates, 1969–78):
Even when a new general manager comes into a ball club
[Harry Dalton with the Angels], I still was surprised I was
traded. It was a big adjustment [in New York] because I
wasn't going to play shortstop. I had some trouble adjust-
ing to third base. I was either going to the Yankees or the
Mets—two clubs I found out later were interested in making a deal for me. I had been around for a relatively long
time and the change of leagues was difficult for me.

But you know how things turn out in this game? Nolan
Ryan pitched for me when I managed the Angels and we
won the first division title ever there [1979]. He became a
great pitcher in Anaheim. Nolan became a Hall of Fame
pitcher. You can always tell your grandkids you got traded
for a Hall of Fame player. He was a power pitcher who had
to be out there. The Angels at that time were in position
where they could pitch him every fourth day. Consistently,
Nolan threw the hardest of anyone in the game.

Jeff Torborg channeled the best of Sandy Koufax in time to
help put Ryan on a two-decade-long path of excellence. Once
a young catcher with the Dodgers who was tutored in the fine
points of pitching by Koufax and buddy Don Drysdale, including catching Koufax's perfect game against the Cubs on September 9, 1965, Torborg was by 1972 a wizened Angels veteran who
was prepping for his coaching and managing days. He immediately set out to smooth over Ryan's delivery in the most informal of workouts during the strike that delayed the start of the
'72 season.

JEFF TORBORG (Dodgers, Angels, 1969–73): I was a
player rep with the Angels. When we had that short strike,
we worked out at La Palma Park on State College Bou-
levard, just a little north of Anaheim Stadium. When the
workout was over, I'd catch Nolan. My wife, Susie, and his

wife, Ruth, would sit with the kids on the blanket away from us. There was a home plate and a mound—it was a little chewed up. We'd start working on his delivery. He was wild. God, he could throw bullets. He threw as hard as any human being could throw the ball. He had a tendency to overthrow where it would run in and up on a right-handed hitter because he would spin open a little bit. I came aboard with Sandy when he had it all together. They taught me.

I stressed [to] him [not to take] his front leg back past the rubber, but to raise it parallel to the rubber. The coaches couldn't be with us due to the strike. I was trying to use all the stuff that [John] Roseboro and Koufax and Drysdale and Carroll Beringer had used with me, with Nolan.

Besides the mechanical side, I kept pounding into him, "Get strike one, low and away, no matter who the hitter." We cut the plate in halves and got the outer half of the plate for strike one. Sandy said to set up in the middle of the plate and then we can start moving.

We carried this forward to Anaheim Stadium [after the strike]. Tom Morgan was the pitching coach—an exceptional coach. He had great confidence in Tom, who would stand out in front of him, close to him, to make Nolan stride out in front in him so he couldn't spin off and not bump into him when he threw the ball, which is what I was trying to get Nolan to do. He was taking his left [front] leg back past the rubber. He would fly open, his shoulder would come up, and that's why that fastball would almost crown right-handed hitters when he overthrew. We got him to lift his leg straight up parallel to the rubber, enabling him to come straight to the plate.

I don't know if he threw harder [than Koufax] up in the strike zone. But down in the strike zone, Nolan threw a pitch we called the "dry spitter," not intentionally. He had a tendency to choke the fastball, hold it so tightly that the bottom would drop out. The action of the ball was like a spitball. It had the same rotation as Sutter's split-finger. Get ahead in the count, 100-mph fastball low and away. Nolan threw so hard and down he would handcuff you. If the ball was kneecap level, you as a catcher couldn't get your hand turned quickly enough to really catch it smoothly. He could really beat your hand up. Sandy could do the same thing, only up in the zone, the ball exploded and pounded into your glove up.

Torborg caught one of Koufax's four no-hitters and one of Ryan's record-breaking seven no-no's. He had the honor of back-stopping Ryan's first hitless gem, against the Royals in Kansas City on May 15, 1973.

JEFF TORBORG: Jack McKeon [who replaced Torborg as Marlins manager 29 years later] was manager of K.C. Nolan had a way of tapping the top of the rubber with his right foot as he's going to make the right turn. McKeon protested the game [claiming] he was breaking contact with the rubber. . . .

I walked up to Nolan and said we got a no-hitter going. You look at the fifth inning, see zeroes, and see you've got something special going. I was trying to take [pressure] away from them. These guys aren't stupid. They know what's going on. We talked the latter part of the game, what we were trying to do.

Amos Otis hit a long fly ball to right field as the final hitter, Ken Berry, a really good outfielder, came in for defense. When the ball goes, I think, "Oh, no, it's off the wall." But Berry got it right at the wall.

Exactly two months later, on July 15, 1973, in Detroit, Ryan recorded his second no-hitter against the Tigers. But Torborg insists he could have had still another no-no, on August 29, 1973, at Anaheim Stadium.

JEFF TORBORG: Nolan almost had three in one year. He really has another no-hitter. Thurman Munson hits a pop-up behind second base in this game. Shortstop Rudy Meoli and second baseman Sandy Alomar Sr. go for it and it bounces on the dirt behind second. Scorer Dick Miller calls it a base hit. Nolan goes on to pitch a one-hitter. You give the error to the one closest. If a pop-up goes up and the catcher lets it fall with the first baseman or third baseman near him, they give him the error. Dick Miller did not change it. His comment about not changing it—"you took the pressure off Nolan." That's baloney. If Nolan had problems, it was in the early innings. When he got rolling near the end of the game, it was lights-out.

On a Friday night in Detroit, I break a finger. Two days later Art Kusnyer catches his [second] no-hitter. In Nolan's next start [July 19 in Anaheim], he has a no-hitter in the eighth against Baltimore with Kusnyer catching. He walks someone [actually hits Brooks Robinson] and then Mark Belanger is up. Weaver puts on the bunt. He changes the sign to let him hit. Nolan throws a get-me-over pitch in a bunt situation and he gets a base hit in a bunt situation— the only hit till extra innings. That would have been back-to-back no-hitters like [Johnny] Vander Meer.

Torborg completed a special trifecta of catching historic games on September 27 at Anaheim Stadium. Ryan needed 16 strikeouts to break Koufax's season-whiff record of 382. The Express got the mark—but barely.

JEFF TORBORG: It was his last start against the Twins. He almost didn't make it through the second. They scored four runs early. He needed 16 punch-outs and he had 15 by the ninth. Fortunately, as a team we tied the game and it went extra innings. In the 10th the last Twins batter, Rich Reese, swung in one area and the ball was 2 feet above his bat. He missed it by a larger distance than I've ever seen a pitch missed. He broke Sandy [Koufax]'s record by one in extra innings. We knew exactly what the record was. He struggled to get there. Nolan had cramps in his legs and they were giving him salt. They were rubbing his calves.

A GUY NAMED BLUE EARNED SOME GREEN

Once-in-a-lifetime seasons are cherished, such as the Koufaxian 1971 campaign for then–Oakland A Vida Blue.

Baseball's absolute sensation, start to finish, Blue in his first full big-league season racked up staggering numbers. He was 24–8. His 1.82 ERA and eight shutouts led the AL. He struck out 301 and gave up just 209 hits in 312 innings. All of which earned him both the AL MVP and Cy Young Awards.

Surely he couldn't repeat it, and Blue didn't. But a pair of 20-win seasons for the A's, then an 18-win effort for the Giants in 1978 when he jumped the bay in the huge exodus of championship Oakland players, proved he was made to last in a career that finally ended in 1986 in a second stint in San Francisco.

VIDA BLUE: You gotta think you're going to be successful. It probably took me half a season till I'd feel comfortable with myself. Oakland had a great team. I was just another piece of the puzzle. I can't say I mastered anyone. Luckily I did have movement on my fastball. I think that was a key factor why I attained a little success. I don't think I succeeded that much. I thought I could have done a whole lot better.

My first full year it probably was a combination of the hitters not seeing me as well as me not knowing them. Basically, the stupidity of me just going out there pitching was probably a big part of it. You have no fear. When you're that young and green, you don't think in terms of "it's the bases loaded and I'm facing the 3-4-5 hitters in the Minnesota Twins lineup," which would have included Harmon Killebrew. That's a very scary situation to be in. When you're a young pitcher, you don't think about it. You don't have time to get nervous.

I can't even recall the emotions I had at the time. You do expect good things out of yourself. A lot of people thought I was worthy of winning the Cy Young and MVP, and I'm very grateful that I did win them. If I had to do it all over again, I wouldn't change a thing.

THE TRICKSTERS

There's the macho-man fireballer. Then there's the sinker-baller who wants worm-killing ground balls. And finally there's a master of deception, who will use strange deliveries or pitches that seemingly defy gravity or who works at a frenetic pace to distract hitters. After all, the game of power and speed is also one for mind games.

Luis Tiant seemingly pitched from everywhere but between his legs and twitched his head (baseball's closest thing to Linda Blair's 360-degree spin in *The Exorcist,* the scariest movie of the True Golden Age) as he mesmerized hitters with the Indians and then, especially, as a beloved New England hero branded "El Tiante" with the Red Sox.

LUIS TIANT: Look into center field, look in the sky, release the ball sidearm—my control was better. In Cleveland I challenged guys fastball, fastball, fastball with a slider. I started [the gyrations] in Boston in '72.

I threw sliders, curves, changeups, fastballs, moving, rising, going in, going out. I used to throw a knuckleball to some left-handers. [Daisuke] Matsuzaka said he commanded six different pitches in one game. Nobody can command six different pitches. If he's telling you that, he's lying. You got three pitches in one game, that's good. That's when Pedro [Martinez] was good. You hit the spot consistently, you have a chance. Pedro had pitches—changeup, fastball, and slider.

The problem is the hitter is looking where the ball is coming from. They're looking at your hand. I used to throw the slider same way as the fastball. Three pitches sidearm, three pitches from the top. That's why I was effective.

A son of Massachusetts himself and an original Red Sox product, lefty knuckleballer Wilbur Wood wouldn't distract hitters like El Tiante while first closing, then starting, for the White Sox. He simply dared them to follow the midair bouncing ball, which screwed up timing. The flutterball was so easy on its practitioner's shoulder that Wood was tapped for some amazing pitching-endurance feats, especially in 1973.

Wood started regularly on just two days' rest in 1973. And several times even more frequently than that. When a suspended game with the Indians was resumed in the top of the 17th inning on Memorial Day, May 28, 1973, at old Comiskey Park, Wood took the ball and pitched five more innings, giving up one run for the victory. Then he started the regularly scheduled game, recording a complete-game four-hit shutout. Tempting fate, the Sox were much less successful with Wood on July 20 at Yankee Stadium. He started Game 1 of the twi-night doubleheader, but lasted just six batters in the first, charged with six runs in a 12–2 loss. Figuring he hadn't used up many pitches, Wood came back to start Game 2. He pitched 4⅓ innings, giving up seven runs as the Sox were thrashed 7–2.

WILBUR WOOD (White Sox, 1969–78): When that knuckleball doesn't move, they can hit it a long way. I came over to the Sox after I'd kicked around quite a bit with the Red Sox and Pirates. That fastball was all right in the minor leagues. You could only throw so many curves. For me to have a successful career, I had to come up with something else—that's when I started throwing the knuckleball.

Three-hundred fifty innings? Start both ends of a doubleheader. The one I liked to remember was against Cleveland. The night game was suspended due to curfew. I was scheduled to pitch on Monday night. I picked up where that game left off. It ended up going five innings, Dick Allen hit a two-run homer to win that game. I started the second game and we won that one also. The only time a pitcher has any fun in the game is when he's on the mound. I felt a four-man rotation would be ideal for a starting pitcher.

Jim Kaat, Wood's fellow lefty and White Sox rotation mate, did not throw a knuckler. But the batter had to pay attention and stay loose with Kaat on the mound. He developed a no-windup, quick-pitch style. The only nonfast pace of "Kitty Kaat's" baseball life was the length of his career. In the True Golden Age, he and catcher Tim McCarver were the last of the four-decade players. Kaat began with the old Washington Senators in 1959 and lasted until 1983 with the Cardinals.

JIM KAAT (Twins, White Sox, Phillies, Yankees, 1969–79): [Sox pitching coach] Johnny Sain suggested I make a little change in my pitching motion in mid-1974. It was new. We didn't have the two-minute commercial breaks for TV. There was an article about how much time I actually spent on the mound each inning. One inning was like 36 seconds. Several innings were less than a minute. We'd have some five-, six-pitch innings and we'd be out of there. Of course I'd also have seven- or eight-pitch innings where I'd give up five runs and I'd be out of there, too. Win or lose, I'd be out of there in a hurry.

I doubt that we will [have any more four-decade players]. A combination of the travel and the money, primarily the money. If guys are successful, that sets them up for life. I don't think you ever feel secure enough at the major-league level to say you're going to pitch another five years or 10 years. Every year when I went to spring training, I felt like I was a rookie that had to make the club and prove myself. That was a good motivating factor. As the years rolled on, every spring I said I'm good, I'm competing, and I hope I get to play another year. Before long I was 44 years old and I had played 25 of them.

MARATHON MEN

The hitter-friendly rules enacted at the end of 1968 did not change the workload of the game's busiest pitchers. At least for the time being, the credo of starting what one finished held firm.

Inclusion in four-man rotations and 37 to 40-plus starts were the norm for starting pitchers. Some thrifty teams such as the A's did not even carry 10 pitchers—they depended on four starters and a closer, and the rest filled in where necessary. Endurance usually meant victory. In 1969 the NL had eight pitchers log at least 300 innings; all won 20 or more. Only two AL pitchers, both 20-game winners, reached the 300-inning plateau.

This marathon-man routine was carried to several extremes. Mickey Lolich of the Tigers and Wilbur Wood of the White Sox topped the 376-inning mark in 1971 and 1972, respectively. The number of 300-inning pitchers in the NL declined, but the inclusion of the designated hitter in the AL in 1973 permitted that league's pitchers to stay in longer without being pulled for pinch hitters. Seven AL hurlers topped 300 innings in both 1973 and 1974. But as the decade waned, the 300-inning crowd thinned dramatically. Knuckleballer Phil Niekro of the Braves was the only consistent 300-inning pitcher as the 1970s closed.

Steve Carlton of the Phillies recorded the last 300-inning year with 304 in 1980, resulting in a 24–9 record. A year earlier a typical ace's workload had dropped to around 260 innings.

Subtly, team by team, the concept of the five-man rotation, augmented by a bullpen with relievers designated in specific roles, began to creep through baseball. The addition of another starter could be traced back to 1969 with the Mets, when ace Tom Seaver suggested he'd be more effective with another day's rest. But even as workloads became lighter, the concept of throwing more often instead of less frequently, of rationing pitch counts, was foreign through much of the game. The physical training of arms to pitch more frequently has been cited as explanation for the breakdowns of latter-day pitchers in spite of light years of advances in sports medicine.

FERGIE JENKINS: I'd throw at least 10 minutes a day. Warming up in the bullpen prior to the game, I'd throw at least 100 pitches to make sure my arm was good and loose, and extended. . . . if I had to throw 100 pitches, 97 or 130 to win the game, I'd do it. I had a nice, relaxed windup. I didn't try to overthrow. I had four basic pitches: fastball, curve, slider, and changeup. I just went out there and had some fun.

In a four-man rotation, you prepare yourself to make that start worthwhile. Your preparation is your own individual liking. I never lifted weights. It's something I've never, ever touched. Now, they don't throw enough. To make this work, right from high school, you have to work your arm to strengthen it. I used to do a lot of swimming. A lot of isometrics.

PHIL NIEKRO (Braves, 1969–79): We'd throw batting practice between starts and we threw a little bit more on the side. Our arms probably were a little stronger. We weren't the best-conditioned pitchers in those days. We didn't have the bulging out of our forearms and back. We looked at your heart and your guts to get ready to pitch every four days.

I remember many times talking with my trainer. I didn't feel well, but [I wanted to] get the knots out of my arm so I can pitch. There wasn't any security in the game and there weren't as many teams, [which meant] more pitchers trying to get your job. In spring training there'd be 250 guys trying to find jobs in the minor-league system. If you weren't doing real good, there was a good chance you'd get sent down and somebody would take your job. You signed one-year contracts and pretty much signed for pretty much what they gave you.

GAYLORD PERRY (Giants, Indians, Rangers, Padres, 1969-79): When I was tired after pitching every fourth day, my ball would move a little more. I wouldn't register high on the radar gun, but I might easily win the game, 5–1, 3–2. I don't think these pitchers throw enough in the game. If you pitch 200 innings, it seems like a great deal. I can remember two or three pitchers on a good club would pitch 300 innings.

Next day after I pitched, I'd take off. The managers would let me play the infield and I'd played long toss from shortstop to first base, to stretch my arm out. A long throw would loosen my arm out. I did not throw off the bullpen mound.

BERT BLYLEVEN: Complete games and pitching shutouts and no-pitch counts were prevalent. That's just the way it was. We pitched every fourth day and you were expected to keep your club in the game. Your whole concept at that time was to be out on the field shaking hands with your teammates because you just had a victory instead of being the clubhouse waiting for you to come in.

I've always been a firm believer the more you throw the better off you are. In the '70s guys were expected to go out there eight or nine innings, win or lose. They didn't have 12 pitchers then. I love the DH as a pitcher. I liked the AL, because you had a chance for more victories—and more losses—but [you would] also pitch more innings. In 1973 I pitched 325 innings in 40 starts. It helped me as a young kid, if I lost 1-0 or 2-1, it made me more of a competitor or a pitcher. I always took it as my fault that we lost 1-0. That's why I had so many shutouts. You go out there with the intentions of shutting out your opponents.

Marv Grissom was my first pitching coach [with the Twins]. I had a bad habit of throwing across my body. He put a folding chair where he wanted me to land, to the right. [You] got on that pitching rubber and used the lower part of your body, your ass and your legs, and take less pressure on [your] arm. That enabled me to pitch as long as I did.

NO-HITTERS AND WOULD-BE PERFECTOS

What are the odds of pitching a no-hitter on any given day? One hundred thousand to one? And if you do, how 'bout adding a pair of homers in the no-no?

On June 23, 1971, at Riverfront Stadium in Cincinnati, just three weeks after the Cubs' Ken Holtzman threw his second no-hitter in the same ballpark, Phillies ace Rick Wise held the Reds hitless while belting homers in the fifth off Ross Grimsley and the eighth off Clay Carroll. Wise's recollection is crystal clear after decades as a pitching coach led him to retirement in his native Oregon.

RICK WISE: I had six home runs that year and hit two home runs twice that year to tie an NL record. The other was a grand slam and a solo shot to beat the Giants. Theoretically, every starting pitcher had the ability to pitch a no-hitter. I always did that as a Little Leaguer, Babe Ruth, high school, I always hit third or fourth. I worked at it—I was good at it. It didn't surprise me. When you're throwing a no-hitter, it is exceptional. The second home run was in the eighth inning against Clay Carroll on a 2–0 pitch. That's why you're a professional, you concentrate. That's what you train to do. There were a lot of good-hitting pitchers in both leagues, before the DH. That was big, to stay in the game—at least you can bunt.

I got the [dugout] greetings for the home runs. [Manager] Frank Lucchesi was going nuts. He was the nervous one. The big scoreboard in center field, of course you know what's going on. It isn't hard to do. It wouldn't matter if I had a no-no or an eight-hitter, I still had to go out there to get the outs. And with Cincinnati's lineup, they were capable of scoring runs in bunches. It was only 4–0 at the time. Stuff can happen in a hurry. I threw that game in an hour and 53 minutes with 94 pitches.

But Wise ran into a buzz saw trying for his second no-no four years later, as a member of the Red Sox, on July 2, 1975, at County Stadium in Milwaukee. Wise had two giant hurdles—George "Boomer" Scott and me. Scott could break up any no-hitter—and did on this night. Your friendly neighborhood author is a Flying Dutchman, a jinx when it comes to would-be no-hit pitchers. I've seen a number of no-no's busted up in the ninth inning. In addition, I'd often attend the game before or after a no-hitter. So on this nice evening, driving with a friend up to Milwaukee for a twi-night doubleheader in my battered '65 Buick Special, I witnessed Wise work in the ninth inning in Game 1 against the Brewers with a 6–0 lead, a no-hitter, two outs and .241-hitting outfielder Bill Sharp up, followed by Scott.

RICK WISE: I was going after him with my number one pitch, a fastball. Especially when the count got even, 2–2, I challenged him. In all fairness Don Money could have been awarded a base hit in the third or fourth. They gave Burley [shortstop Rick Burleson] a tough error on a ball in the hole. I wouldn't have been upset one bit if it was a hit.

Both pitches were right at the knees. Sharp never offered at them. Just took them and he walked. You get another opportunity with Boomer's talent. He was a tremendous player. I was at the end of my strength there. Throwing complete games is a tough business. I still challenged Boomer with a fastball. I got the win—that's all that counts.

Scott broke up the no-hitter with a booming 430-foot homer. No doubt about ending the no-no this way, no disputes or second-guesses. Bobby Darwin, the next Brewers hitter, also homered. Wise truly was at the end of his rope. He then gave up a single to Darrell Porter to put the tying run in the on-deck circle. But he fanned Mike Hegan for the final out and a 6–3 complete-game win. Wise should blame the college kid with the beat-up Buick for simply showing up. Maybe Scott gets under the ball and hits a warning-track fly ball instead.

But Milt Pappas could not have faulted me nearly three years earlier, on September 2, 1972, at Wrigley Field. I was 6 miles south, working my final day as a summer stock boy at the downtown Goldblatt's department store. Pappas reported to the ballpark with a cold, but still took his start against the woeful San Diego Padres.

I was going between floors when I noticed a crowd in the TV department just after 3 p.m. Approaching the console color TV they were watching, I saw the image of Cubs shortstop Don Kessinger throw out the Padres' Nate Colbert for the first out in the eighth inning. Someone said Pappas had a no-hitter going. A perfect game, too. I decided to shirk my duties and join the crowd. Pappas mowed down the Padres, the Cubs went out in the bottom of the eighth, and the drama heightened.

Pappas got the first batter of the ninth, John Jeter, to fly to left-center. But center fielder Bill North, tracking the ball, slipped and fell on his face. Out of the corner of the screen came left fielder Billy Williams, backing up the play. He caught the ball at full speed. *"Aww, brotherrr!"* overly excited announcer Jack Brickhouse bellowed. Fred Kendall grounded to short for out number two. Then pinch-hitter Larry Stahl, a .232 hitter, was the last Padres hope to spoil perfect. Pappas got ahead of Stahl 1-and-2. Then something strange happened. He threw a couple of close pitches, but Stahl would not offer at either and second-year plate ump Bruce Froemming did not slightly expand his zone. With the full count, Pappas delivered near the corner. Stahl again did not offer and Froemming's arm did not move. Stahl took his base.

The TV viewers groaned. Pappas, enraged at Froemming, somehow collected enough composure to get Garry Jestadt to pop up to second to complete the no-hitter. For the next 38 years, Pappas bitched at Froemming every chance he got for not giving him the break that, say, a Hall of Famer might have received. He even cited the apparent smirk on Froemming's face, shown on TV, as another example of the ump going the other way against him.

MILT PAPPAS (Braves, Cubs, 1969–73): Unfortunately, at that time, Bruce Froemming was a [second-year] umpire. He didn't see it as he called it. All three final pitches were close enough to be a strike. When you look at the perfect game of Don Larsen, that umpire knew exactly what was going on. He knew Larsen was pitching a perfect game. That last pitch he threw to Dale Mitchell was two feet inside and three feet high. But the umpire was no dummy. He knew history was in the making and he knew he was going to be a part of history. And nobody argued with him.

Same thing with Bruce Froemming. You're winning 8–0 in Wrigley Field and you have a perfect game. It's going to go into the history book and he's going to be part of history. But obviously he's not as bright as I thought he was.

Randy [catcher Hundley] and Ron Santo both came to the mound, said the perfect game is gone, nothing you can do but you still have a no-hitter. That put a lot of things into perspective. I took a deep breath and told Randy let's go get the no-hitter. The one he [Jestadt] popped up was a fastball inside.

After Pappas completed the no-hitter, the Goldblatt's men's department assistant manager, Rick Osney, spotted me leaving the TV department. Although Osney called himself a Cubs fan, duty called first. He was livid. "If this wasn't your last day on the job, I would have kicked your ass," Osney said, reaming me out good.

The next day, true to form, I went to Wrigley Field and witnessed lefty Fred Norman shut out the Cubs 3–0. Pappas was luckier than he could have imagined.

6

Immortalized by a Ligament

If a pitcher's arm went bad in the middle of the 20th century, he had three choices. He could conceal the pain, keep chucking, and hope for the best in squeezing a few more years out of it. He could submit to invasive surgery that often did as much damage as it was designed to correct. Or he could simply quit.

For Dodgers southpaw starter Tommy John, 31 in midseason 1974, the choice was even more black-and-white after he broke down with an NL-leading 13–3 record to his credit: Either become orthopedic surgeon Frank Jobe's guinea pig or walk away from the game.

John went along with Jobe's gamble. The result radically altered baseball history and saved scores of pitchers' arms. The tendon transplant in John's aching left elbow was termed "Tommy John surgery" and represented the greatest-ever leap forward in sports medicine.

For Jobe, there was a sense of regret. His willingness to improvise the transplant procedure did not come quickly enough to save the most golden arm of them all. Sports medicine wasn't as bad as witch doctoring when Sandy Koufax was in his prime and John was starting out in the 1960s—but it was a lot of macho posturing disguising the fact that the sawbones often were groping in the dark.

TOMMY JOHN: He [Jobe] told me a year or so ago [in 2008]—he's a great surgeon because he's very, very, very humble—had he been a better doctor and known more about the physiology of the body, I can almost guarantee you that Sandy Koufax needed Tommy John surgery.

He just said he didn't know enough about the physiology of the body. All of what Sandy had, all of his complaints [pointed to] Tommy John surgery. It was one of those things that he couldn't figure out. He said, "Stevie Wonder could have seen yours, yours was so blatant."

With the White Sox, Frank Robinson slid into [second baseman] Al Weis. In the trainer's room they moved his knee side to side. You tore a ligament in your knee. That's the only way they could have diagnosed it, there were no MRIs. This is what Dr. Jobe said, that had I known more . . . Yours was so obvious.

John was the classic number two starter in his career, starting with the Indians, then moving to full-time rotation duty with the White Sox in 1965 and finally with the Dodgers via a trade for Dick Allen in late 1971. Now in business in Fort Worth, Texas, he has a vivid memory of how he came to be in Jobe's operating room and thus gave pitchers hope where none previously existed.

TOMMY JOHN: My arm started hurting me in 1962–63 in the minor leagues. In 1963 I was in Puerto Rico. I pitched a nine-inning shutout. The next day I could not move my arm. I went to the ball club. They sent me to a physical therapist for a week. It wasn't any better. I tried to throw and it hurt. The Indians sent me home. They sent me to St. Louis to work with Cards trainer Bob Bowman. I went in and had my first [cortisone] injection.

There are dates that stand out. Where were you on 9/11? And where were you on November 22, 1963? I can tell you where I was. I was in Dr. I. C. Middleman's office waiting to get my first injection. Between '63 and '74, I probably had 40 injections in my elbow. Back then if your elbow was sore, you got an injection. They didn't know you could only take a few of those injections. Dr. Jobe was amazed I lasted as long as I did.

He said it was like putting . . . pebbles in a pot of water. They will make the water overflow. What pitch would do it? I threw one pitch in July 1974, and that was the one that shredded the ligament.

He just said we're going to rest it and it will heal on its own. I did for three weeks, threw, and it wasn't any better. Our trainer, the late Bill Buhler, taped it up like a sprained ankle. I could pitch like that, but not good enough to get big-league hitters out. Dr. Jobe said [he] was afraid of it. He said you do not have to have the surgery. But if you don't have it, you won't pitch major-league baseball again. You can play catch with your kids, you can throw batting practice to your kids, stuff like that, but never be able to throw major-league ball again. My whole thing was I wanted to keep playing. I asked what's our choices? He said we could do a ligament transplant. I asked him if it's been done before. He said no, but it's been done in the hand and wrist all the time. Never on a player who was going to abuse his elbow like a pitcher.

There was no doubt. People thought I laid awake at night anguishing over it. I told you why I knew he was the right doctor. I asked him to do it right now. He said he had to schedule it, that [he wanted] as many brilliant minds in the operating room with [him as possible]. He said, "I really don't know what I'm doing on this. I want other people in there I trust to guide me." One surgeon who had experience was a hand surgeon named Herb Stark. He examined me. He had done transplants in the hand and wrist, and he knew the techniques. He wanted Dr. [Robert] Kerlan in there, he wanted Dr. [Lewis] Yocum in there. The minute a doctor tells you he is humble, that's the doctor I want operating on me. I knew, number one, Dr. Jobe was a friend first. He was a doctor second. He would not tell me something that was not in my best interest.

The operation was on September 25, 1974, the day he could assemble all those doctors in Centinela Hospital [Inglewood, California]. He told me all the various scenarios that would happen. If we have to go in and do the transplant, we'll take it [the tendon] out of the right forearm. First thing I did when I woke up is feel around my right forearm. I felt a bandage on my right forearm. I said, "Damn, they had to do a transplant." He came in and said we opened you up, the ligament was like a bowl of spaghetti. There wasn't enough left to maybe tack it on [to something else]. What are we going to do? Let the incision heal, then start range of motion. Do nothing for 16 weeks post-op. I just went along at my pace.

About halfway through the next baseball season [1975], I started to get a little something on my fastball, after I started throwing in spring training. That's what I told [former Twins GM] Terry Ryan after [Nelson] Liriano had the surgery. He's having it at the best time. You have it in the fall. You'll miss all of the next baseball season, so you're not going to try to pitch in that season. You'll have all the season and then the following off-season, then spring training to get yourself ready for the next season. You have 16 months to get ready. This was not something that was done before.

When I first started throwing in 1975, the catcher in the bullpen said the ball is starting to have a little life it never had. I asked Dr. Jobe two, three months ago, all this stuff, what is your timeframe? He said the best result he ever had was 12 months. I tell them 12 months. I pitched in the [Arizona] Instructional League one year, one day after my surgery. I then had seven starts in the next 28 days—I was pitching once every four days.

I felt normal. From that time on till I retired in 1989, I never had a bit of elbow problems. I threw the ball every day off the mound to a catcher. I threw on three days' rest, I threw on four days' rest. In Game 2 of the '81 World Series, I beat the Dodgers, then came out of the bullpen to pitch two innings in Game 4, then I started Game 6.

In the big leagues now, there's probably over 100 who have had the surgery. The [revolution in the] way the medical game was played. If you want to do something bad enough, you'll go to whatever means to get through it and get out and play. I wanted to play major-league baseball again.

In 1977, in his second full season back from the surgery, Tommy John won 20 games for the Dodgers. His spectacular comeback earned him a lucrative free-agent deal with the Yankees. He twice won 20 or more games in New York. Lefties often have nine lives, but John had far more by baseball's measurement. After Jobe completed his handiwork, John pitched 13-plus additional seasons, finally retiring at age 46 in 1989 as a Yankee with 288 career victories.

He has not received a commission from the multimillion-dollar contracts earned by many subsequent recipients of Tommy John surgery. But that doesn't matter to the operation's namesake. He helped change baseball forever, and that's satisfaction enough.

7

Everyday Men,
Splitters, and Setting It Up

Macho starters pushed the innings-pitched envelope past the 350-inning mark at times in the True Golden Age. Meanwhile, two revolutions occurred in relief pitching, which finally were legitimized in the record book in 1969 when the save was made an official statistic a decade after Chicago sportswriter Jerome Holtzman concocted the numerical measurement of a reliever's effectiveness.

Closers per se had existed since earlier in the 20th century, but they sometimes had to do double-duty as fill-in starters. They might go more than three innings or even pitch extra innings, as long as necessary, until the game was decided. Managers did not mind abusing them, either, just as they did not mind starters moonlighting as relievers on their supposed off days.

When Dizzy Dean was baseball's next-to-last 30-game winner (30–7) as a Cardinal in 1934, he completed 24 of 33 starts. But Dean also made 17 relief appearances, picking up four wins and seven unofficial saves. He finished 14 games coming out of the bullpen. Apparently, Dean's fellow country boys like Glen Hobbie, from central Illinois, had the same rubber-armed mindset in more "modern" times. In 1959 Hobbie was 16–13, making 33 starts and 13 relief appearances. He was just as busy in 1960, finishing 16–20 overall on 36 starts and 10 bullpen outings, (2–3 in relief).

In a Saturday night game on August 10, 1968, at Crosley Field in Cincinnati, Cubs manager Leo Durocher gave a sneak preview of his barbaric handling of pitchers for the ill-fated pennant run of 1969. The Lip summoned closer Phil "the Vulture"

Regan during a 3–3 tie game with two out in the sixth. Regan pitched 3⅓ innings for the win as the Cubs rallied. The next afternoon Durocher brought Regan back to protect a 5–3 lead with one out in the seventh. Regan allowed the Reds to tie the game on a two-run homer by Johnny Bench in the eighth, then continued pitching a total of 7⅔ innings all the way through the 14th in the deadlocked contest. Finally, Durocher pinch-hit for Regan in the top of the 15th, and the spitballer's achin' arm was rewarded with another win via Billy Williams's three-run, inside-the-park homer.

Wins seemed just as important to relievers as saves. Roy Face was renowned for crafting baseball's best winning percentage ever with an 18–1 mark exclusively as a reliever for the Pirates in 1959. Regan picked up his "Vulture" nickname swooping in on starters' potential victories with a 14–1 record for the 1966 Dodgers. He had a seemingly modest 21 saves. Regan led the NL with 25 saves with the Cubs in 1968.

But by this time, the craft of closing became a specialty. Practitioners of a trick pitch or sinker were just as common as the hard thrower. Hoyt Wilhelm had the game's best knuckleball working for the Orioles and White Sox. Dave Giusti and his palmball staked out the late innings for the Pirates. Mike Marshall and Jim Brewers established their screwballs for the Expos and Dodgers, respectively. The trickiest pitch, though, was Bruce Sutter's straight-dropping split-fingered fastball, most effective with the Cubs before he moved on to the Cardinals and Braves.

From this crop came the first closers who would eventually make the Hall of Fame. Rollie Fingers, busy in the last third of the game for the Athletics, Padres, and Brewers, would be first to enter Cooperstown. He was followed in eventual enshrinement by Sutter and the intimidating Goose Gossage. Their emergence finally persuaded managers, pitching coaches, and starting pitchers that the starters did not have to be pushed to go nine innings in every outing.

GAYLORD PERRY: The first three-fourths of my career, I had to let the manager know I was in good shape and I wanted to pitch. Then the big year, 1978, at San Diego, I won 21 and the Cy Young, when Roger Craig would come out and say I got Rollie Fingers ready, I said, "What are you waiting for?" It was a different story. I never had such a great relief pitcher. I was 40 and I would have not argued. I would have if I was 25.

The Hall of Fame electors certainly did not reward the busiest of the closers. Long before the save totals pushed into the 40s and 50s each season, the super-closer who would pitch at least every other day, breaking stamina records every time he swooped in during the late innings, was the vogue by the mid-1970s. There was a price for employing too much of a good thing. Regan, who toiled 134⅔ innings over 73 games as NL "Fireman of the Year" in 1968, was pitched out two years later, possibly costing the Cubs a craved-for NL East title, and out of the game by 1972. Wayne Granger, who appeared in a record 90 games along with 144⅔ innings and 27 saves for the Reds in 1969, would have just two seasons of double-digit saves after 1970 and was finished after 1976.

THE KINESIOLOGIST-TURNED-EVERYDAY-RELIEVER

Meanwhile, Mike Marshall tried to buck the trend by becoming a nearly everyday closer. He broke Granger's record with 92 games and 179 innings in Montreal in 1973, then outdid himself 3,000 miles away with the Dodgers in 1974 via three all-time records: 106 games, 208⅓ innings, and 13 consecutive games pitched.

The screwball-throwing Marshall defied the laws of human endurance with his academic devotion to kinesiology, the relationship of muscles and tendons in body movements.

Yet the ability to pitch at least every other day, often for two innings, was not a happenstance or old-school tough-it-out act for Marshall, who now counsels pitchers as a Florida-based consultant with philosophies on mechanics usually considered too radical for organized baseball.

The genesis for Marshall's daily availability in relief started while he was a graduate teaching assistant in kinesiology at Michigan State University in the winter of 1967–68, after a decent rookie season with the Tigers. Marshall found he couldn't fully bend his right arm while shaving. X-rays and two high-speed cameras recording his pitching motion found he had lost 12 degrees' worth of range of motion and helped him make an adjustment in his pitching delivery. But he was not able to apply the adjustment, which he claimed put no strain on his arm and enabled it to handle a constant workload, until 1972 in Montreal, after Marshall had passed through the Tigers, Seattle Pilots, and Houston Astros organizations. Marshall found the one big-league manager—Gene Mauch—who was cerebral enough to understand him.

MIKE MARSHALL (Pilots, Astros, Expos, Dodgers, Braves, Rangers, Twins, 1969–79): Nineteen seventy-two was when I got to do what I wanted to do the way I wanted to do it. Mauch said, "Marshall, if you worked to *stay* out of trouble as you do to *get* out of trouble, you'd never be in trouble." He wouldn't mess with me one bit. He gave me full room to do whatever I wanted to do. He was a little concerned about overusing me. After '72 I told him you can use me *more.*

We found out in 1967 that the motion that protects your pitching elbow is *pronation*—turning your thumb downward. After high-speed filming I took in 1971, I found it's the side-to-side movement of the baseball that injures pitchers. If you apply force straight forward, then you're not going to injure your pitching arm. The key to it all was the broad muscle, a huge muscle, that attaches to the lower half of your back. It attaches to your hip bone and the head of the humerus bone [near the biceps]. It attaches to the bone of the pitching arm. It's the most powerful muscle that attaches to your arm, by far. Nothing else is even close. I figured out how to use that muscle. It allows you to inwardly rotate the forearm and drive in a straight line. It's not the least bit fatiguing. I trained in the off-season with a 30-pound wrist weight and threw a 16-pound iron ball off my fingertips.

I told Gene, don't wait till the game is lost. If the game is lost in the sixth or seventh, I can't save it in the ninth. If you got a game to win, let me finish that sixth inning. The key to the game is the third time through the lineup. You got to shut them down then. You can't trust your starter to do it so you better find somebody else to do it. It's special if you can get batters out three different ways. There are very few human beings like that. They're the guys [Hall of Fame–caliber pitchers] who are genetically superior to the rest of us, we just have to be smarter.

I'd go out and throw batting practice to the extra guys every day. I'd throw 15 to 20 minutes of as-hard-as-I-could. No stress at all, it didn't bother me. I was getting stronger and stronger. He [Mauch] said, "Will you stop throwing batting practice if I put you in more games?" I said, "It sounds like a deal." I said, if you don't pitch me tonight, I'm throwing batting practice the next day.

I also watched the other team take batting practice. I did it at home, too, when you're supposed to be back in your locker room playing cards or grab-ass. I told Mauch that I hope to pitch to them, I don't know them and I want to see what they're doing. I'd tell Gene what I intended to do and what defense would be needed against the hitter. Gene would give me that defense.

But when Marshall was traded to the Dodgers for center fielder Willie Davis after the 1973 season, he figured he'd have to sell his modus operandi to a new manager, Walter Alston, all over again. Fortunately, Alston had taken a kinesiology class himself in college, so Marshall was not starting out from square one with the venerable Alston.

MIKE MARSHALL: Walter was one of the smartest gentlemen in baseball. Gene Mauch was very smart, but he also had quirks that were really not too good. He could really get furious and drive some of his players out of the game. When I got to spring training [in Vero Beach, Florida], Alston asked to talk. He asked me to explain what I was doing. It was fabulous. I started talking about it, how to train the body so you could be very effective with the force you apply. It was absolutely no problem for me to throw 150 pitches every single day with no stress, and do it the next day and not be stiff or sore.

Alston said, as far as I'm concerned, you're able to pitch every day unless you tell me you're not. I said you got it. I never told him I was never ready to pitch. I kept track of every pitch I threw in the major leagues in the '73 and '74 seasons. I analyzed the sequence of pitches. I figured out that right-handed spray hitters gave me a lot of trouble. The little bastards stay far away from the plate and they'd flop that slider of mine down the right-field line, and they could turn on the sinker inside and the fastball inside, fight the ball in the hole.

Marshall concluded he had to counteract the slap-hitters by developing a curveball. But in snapping off a hook against the Giants early in the 1975 season, Marshall broke a rib on his left side. That mishap and a knee injury hampered him much of the next three years until he signed with the Twins as a free agent and was reunited with Mauch, who in 1979 restored Marshall to his everyday status. He pitched in 90 games and finished a record 84, one more than his previous mark in Los Angeles, and worked 142⅔ innings. Two years later Marshall's run was finally over, but he believes he's proved a point, even if others in the game won't listen.

"ONLY THE LORD SAVES MORE THAN SUTTER"

Almost losing his career actually saved Bruce Sutter's career, with perhaps the most tricky pitch ever invented.

Never a big-time prospect in the Cubs farm system, Sutter adopted a "split-fingered" fastball under the tutelage of crafty minor-league pitching coach Fred Martin after arm surgery in 1973 robbed him of what was an average fastball anyway. Similar to the forkball thrown by the likes of Lindy McDaniel and others in past decades, Sutter's splitter was an improvement on the old model. The pitch came in like a straight fastball, then broke straight down, often under the batter's swing, as it crossed the plate.

Sutter made his big-league debut on May 9, 1976, called up to help a Cubs pitching staff in complete shambles, which had included blowing a 13–2 fourth-inning lead and allowing Mike Schmidt to club four consecutive homers in an 18–16, 10-inning Phillies win on April 17. The splitter was an immediate success. He was phenomenally better in 1977, his splitter totally unhittable. Only a little slap-hitter named Julio Gonzalez of the Astros solved Sutter with a ground-ball single through the right side to beat him. Otherwise, he'd whiff two or three hitters at a time, his ERA a microscopic 0.77 by July 3. Sutter had 24 saves by July 16. An orange bumper sticker proclaiming ONLY THE LORD SAVES MORE THAN SUTTER was slapped on numerous cars, including my '65 Buick Special.

BRUCE SUTTER (Cubs, 1976–79): It was definitely new at the time. Without the splitter I wouldn't have pitched in the majors. Mike Scott, Jack Morris, and Dave Stewart really had good ones. Sooner or later someone would have figured it out if it wouldn't have been me.

In the decade to come, the splitter would become the rage of the game. Roger Craig, a pitching coach who became the Giants' mid-1980s manager, became its biggest devotee. But many in the game, including a Sutter 1976 Cubs teammate, insist his original version still remains the best.

DAROLD KNOWLES: Without a doubt, no one has ever come close to as good a splitter as he had. It dropped more than any splitter I've ever seen, even though there are some good ones out there. He was unbelievable when he came up. Never saw a guy who didn't throw hard—upper 80s—and threw such a devastating pitch. It was probably the only splitter I ever saw that would start off belt-high and wind up in the dirt. We used to think if guys would take it, he'd walk everybody. But they didn't. He was the best. He would make a mistake every now or then, hang one. That's the only time you ever got Bruce, when he got behind and made a mistake by hanging one.

Future two-time NL MVP Dale Murphy had another rude welcome to the majors not long after Sutter—trying to hit the splitter.

DALE MURPHY: When I did break in, and playing against Bruce with the Cubs, everybody said go up there and make it be at least waist-high before you swing. Otherwise, take it, because it's going to drop. I go up there, OK, it's fine. When you go up there and he releases it, it's waist-high. It's waist-high. But when you start to swing, it's not. The forkball or split-finger is one of the greatest pitches. There was controversy because it puts extra pressure on the elbow. Some guys have had sore arms. The key to that pitch is it works like a changeup because you have great arm speed and you don't cock your wrist. You don't give anything away.

I hated facing Bruce Sutter, no question about it. You could almost go up there and take four pitches, they'd be balls because they'd be out of the strike zone. He threw just enough fastballs to put a little doubt in your mind. It's hard to go up there and just take. Anytime he came into the game, the game was on the line. And if you took, you figured it was going to be a ball, and it was a strike, you were done. Because then you gave up a pitch you could hit. It was a real tough thing that you were going to sit there and think, I'm going to take the first two pitches because they were going to be balls. It was tough to go up there and take because if he threw you a strike, that was your one chance to hit.

When Sutter came in the game, he helped begin the trend of the entire crowd standing and roaring for the last out. The fans took their act on the road, too. On August 12, 1979, the Cardinals fans were seemingly outnumbered with two out in the ninth as some 20,000 Cubs fans at Busch Stadium rose to cheer on Sutter as he struck out George Hendrick for the final out. When healthy, Sutter gave similar confidence to his teammates in the field as he worked for another save.

BILL BUCKNER (Dodgers, Cubs, 1969–79): Bruce was the most dominating pitcher I've ever seen. It didn't matter if you were right-handed or left-handed, you just couldn't hit him, especially that first half of '77. The ball broke straight down. He'd either get a strikeout or ground ball. I hit against him some when he went to the Cardinals and he was still tough. But it was something in '77. It was a six-inning game when he was on. When he was in there, you felt you had a great chance to win.

Unfortunately, Cubs manager Herman Franks wanted too much of a good thing, like Walter Alston with Marshall and Don Zimmer with Bill Campbell. Franks often used Sutter for two or even three innings. His July 16, 1977, save against the Phillies was three innings. He struck out just one. There was good reason. His shoulder was sore, the official description being a "knot" in the shoulder. Sutter missed most of the rest of the next six weeks, and the Cubs season started going down the drain as a result.

Another evolution thus began in baseball. Managers began shortening closers' workloads and employing specialists who'd set up the closers in the seventh and eighth innings.

SETTING UP A NEW BULLPEN SYSTEM

As the 1970s progressed, more relievers found additional work late in the game, but without statistical reward. Baseball began to evolve into the bullpen system presently used. Managers just could not keep using their closers in multiple innings and trips through the lineup.

High-kicking, sidearming Dick "Dirt" Tidrow began to fill a setup role in 1976–77 with the Yankees to bring the game to closer Sparky Lyle. Then Tidrow cemented the setup man in 1979, relieving Bruce Sutter of the extra eighth-inning duty that had caused the shoulder injury two years prior.

BRUCE SUTTER: You can't pitch three innings every day. There's just no way. A guy like Willie Hernandez, the days that I couldn't pitch, Willie saved games. Willie went on to have a nice career as a closer himself. Lee Smith came up and he got me traded. Dick Tidrow was kind of funny—he never did want to pitch the ninth inning. [Before Tidrow] you'd get up in the seventh inning and you didn't worry about tomorrow. You worried about tomorrow tomorrow. It was different. You only had 10 pitchers; you didn't have 12.

DAROLD KNOWLES: I think managers finally figured out that the starter would tire out after a while. Starters would go five or six great innings, and then, *boom,* he'd give up three or four and starts losing it. Someone started figuring it out and got fresh arms in there. The closer thing was big. But you had to get to the closer. Gene Mauch kind of got into that. He used to like to use all his pitchers. It just kind of evolved that way. It proved to be successful and that's probably the way to go now.

There was a period there where we had nine guys [in Oakland] and they often went deep in the ball game. It made the decision easy. But a lot of clubs did not have that luxury. They would take 11 and 12 now.

The Cubs also produced a pioneer setup man—and traded him to the Yankees as a player to be named later for aging starter Ken Holtzman. Ron Davis was used to bring the game to Gossage, whom he thought would have been even more effective had he been used for shorter stints. In his first year as a setup man in 1979, Davis was 14–2.

RON DAVIS (Yankees, 1978–79): I don't know if I was the one who pioneered [setup roles]. There hardly was anybody out there who did the job that I was doing. I did bring up the hold situation. I got beat in arbitration in 1981. The arbitrator said hey, Ron, I understand you were 9–2 and a 1.86 ERA and you pitched in 60-odd games, but you didn't have any saves. The only thing we can do a reliever on is how many saves he has, not by how many appearances or what his ERA is. If you win games, you're not supposed to be winning games, you might be blowing games and not winning these games. There is no stat for you to make any money. I told the reporters they ought to come up with a hold every time a reliever pitches an inning, two or three, and gives us less than one run in three innings, regardless of a winning or losing cause. As long as he doesn't give up a run, he should get a hold. ERA for a reliever is not a just cause to look at.

Holds or not, the evolution continued to the point where the complete game became uncommon. And with starters no longer controlling their own destiny, they had fewer opportunities overall for big-victory seasons. The 20-game winner now sticks out by its infrequency. Those who benefited from the change in the game took note.

BRUCE SUTTER: The starting pitching records will never be broken. Whatever records are in place after Randy Johnson and those guys [like Greg Maddux] retire, they never will be touched again.

8

Centerpieces

On May 17, 1979, the two teams playing before me from my Wrigley right-field bleachers vantage point provided the ultimate distraction from my allergies and lack of sleep. The wind blowing out at 18 mph blew all sorts of stuff toward my nostrils while pushing baseballs to the furthest reaches of the ballpark and beyond. By the end of the first inning, the score was Phillies 7, Cubs 6, with Phillies starter Randy Lerch slicing a home run to left before he ever threw a pitch, and Cubs reliever Donnie Moore, working in place of early-exit starter Dennis Lamp, booming a triple to right-center in the bottom of the first.

The contest would become one of the signature games of the decade, replayed for years to come and often confused with another football-size Wrigley Field score between the Cubs and Phillies. That was Mike Schmidt's four-homers-in-four-at-bats outburst on April 17, 1976. Final: Phillies 18, Cubs 16.

But by the fifth inning on this day, the score was Phillies 21 (after an eight-run third inning), Cubs 9. Something made me think that the game was not over yet. I turned to the cigar-chomping, Runyonesque bookie type with the multiple aliases who always sat with us. "I bet the Cubs get back into this game before it's over," I said to him.

They got back in quickly. The Cubs scored seven in the bottom of the fifth as Dave Kingman powered his way to a memorable afternoon. By the time the Cubs tied it 22–22 in the bottom of the eighth, Kong had three homers. He and Bill Buckner (grand slam) had 13 RBIs between them. All the day's starters had at least one hit. Lost amid the whirlwinds of homers were slap-hitter Larry Bowa's five hits.

But by the top of the 10th, all the hitters except one had spent themselves. And in Cubs-Phillies lore, his identity was obvious. Mike Schmidt slugged a 3-and-2 hanging splitter from Cubs closer Bruce Sutter, powering the ball far out onto Waveland Avenue for the game winner in the 23–22 final. The two teams had combined for 50 hits, including 11 homers, in amassing the second-highest scoring game in history after . . . you guessed it, Cubs 26, Phillies 22, at Wrigley Field in 1922.

The game took its place among the centerpiece events of the True Golden Age: baseball's all-time contests that are replayed well into another century and looked upon with fondness by those who are glad to have witnessed history unfolding.

HANK RESPECTFULLY PASSES THE BABE

Hank Aaron was on everybody's mind in 1974. He broke a record that was considered baseball's most sacred.

Even months after his 715th homer, the Hammer was close to everyone's consciousness. Early Sunday morning on July 7, one of the small cadre of insomniacs and lonely hearts who called the *Chicago Tribune*'s city room switchboard in the wee hours lit up one of the many buttons on the console. As copy clerk on duty, I answered. The caller was a woman who always called up to preach and claim she had the power of God at her fingertips.

I figured I'd get one up on her this time.

"If you have the power of God, then when Hank Aaron comes to bat 12 hours from now in Wrigley Field, the wind will be blowing out. I want you to turn the wind around to blow in against him when Aaron comes up."

Click.

The preacher lady obviously could not deliver and was certainly off-duty when Aaron faced Cubs starter Rick Reuschel in the fourth, a scene I witnessed from the left-field upper deck. Aaron connected for his 50th and final Wrigley Field homer in 21 seasons.

By then, the home-run champ was at ease. The tortuous path to the record, which should have been a joyous road, had long been completed. Aaron had survived the trial by fire in which he attained a nation's acclaim that unfortunately had a dark side. Twenty-seven years after Jackie Robinson endured racist taunts and threats in breaking the major leagues' color line, Aaron discovered that progress in racial understanding had been made—but not enough.

By early in the 1973 season, the math was obvious: Aaron would break Ruth's record within the next two seasons, given good health. A noncontroversial type who usually let his bat and glove do the talking since he began in Milwaukee in 1954, Aaron suddenly ran the gauntlet of verbal abuse and hate mail. "A certain few fans," according to Aaron, in the Fulton County Stadium right-field stands had been insulting him with cries of "nigger" and "son of a bitch," among other epithets, from the season's start. The Braves vowed to protect Aaron, and soon the federal government intervened. Aaron's family was watched over by the FBI.

But the vast majority of Southern fans were supportive of Aaron, who acknowledged their backing while the Braves offered 700 silver dollars for the fan who retrieved homer number 700.

To this day, Aaron's Braves teammates credited him with not letting the hoopla—or the negatives—spill over to them. He literally took it all for the team.

DUSTY BAKER (Braves, Dodgers, 1969–79): It didn't affect me. I felt honored and thrilled to be in the situation, with no clue of the magnitude of what it was going to have on the history of the game. When you're living history, it doesn't have the same magnitude as history itself.

Hank would try to sort of shelter us from some things. I had to pry a lot out of him. I had to ask him questions. I could tell from the look on his face that I had to ask him stuff in order to get an honest answer. Jackie Robinson was his hero—as a kid he saw Jackie play a game in his hometown. That motivated Hank, especially since he was so active in the civil rights movement in Atlanta, with the NAACP and Urban League. I was fortunate to be with him at some of the meetings, some of the happenings. I was with him almost every day. Ralph Garr and Paul Casanova and myself. It was very lonely for him. He had an assigned bodyguard, Calvin Wardlow, who was cool with us. Hank had two rooms on the road—one he slept in, the other he was registered under. It should have been a very happy time, but it really wasn't for him. He remained extremely focused. The more hate mail he got, the more driven, the more motivated that he became.

Hank and Ralph Garr helped me as a young man from California, where my brother and I were the only two African Americans in our high school. It wasn't tough on us because Hank held a lot from us. He was the ultimate teammate, teacher, mentor, father-uncle figure. We could go to Hank for anything. A lot of the hate mail and resentment, from what I saw, more was from the North than the South. I know the people of Atlanta as a whole, at least the baseball fans, were proud to witness it and proud to be there. It was a tough time on Hank and tough on his family.

Knuckleballer Phil Niekro knew Aaron better than any of the '74 Braves. Other than third baseman Eddie Matthews, Niekro had been an Aaron teammate the longest, having broken in during the 1964 season.

PHIL NIEKRO: Anytime, you noticed that [hype over the home-run chase] was in the clubhouse before the game, with all the reporters. Henry was so professional about keeping that end of it away from the game and clubhouse talk. With how many reporters, he had the ability to take that off to the side, take that into another room. He was super-terrific at that.

Henry was always sort of a quiet guy. He led by exam-ple. That was his leadership. He didn't voice a lot of talk in the clubhouse. His leadership was "here's how you play the game," when he took batting practice. You work hard. All that stuff with the hate mail, personally I didn't know that was going on. There was a lot of stuff that maybe Henry kept to himself. He was so good at keeping that away from the players. We'd go on road trips, you wouldn't see him in the lobbies because he couldn't get through. Very seldom he rode our buses. He's feeling for us, too, because he's keeping this stuff away from us. I've always appreciated so much the way he handled that.

I never saw him get out of line, throw a bat, throw a helmet, fly off the handle. He always had the mental-ity [of] "You got me, but I'll get you back and I'll keep coming." I learned a lot from him. Took his infield, took his batting practice, and he kept that going through the home-run chase.

On April 4, 1974, in the season opener at Cincinnati, Aaron tied Ruth with his 714th home run, a three-run first-inning homer off Jack Billingham. The Nixon administration, other-wise embattled in Watergate, gave its blessing to the chase by dispatching Vice President Gerald Ford to the game. Along with commissioner Bowie Kuhn, Ford posed with Aaron immediately after the Ruth-tying blast. But by now, Aaron and the Braves wanted to get the chase over with.

Aaron finally provided himself relief by connecting for the record-breaker against the Dodgers' Al Downing in the fourth inning at Fulton County Stadium on April 8, 1974. He couldn't have timed it better, as the Monday night game was telecast nationally by NBC. Curt Gowdy's network call is rarely heard, while Milo Hamilton's Atlanta radio play-by-play is the one most replayed. However, the most poetic description—fittingly—was Vin Scully's Los Angeles radio version. Scully let the crowd roar for two minutes after the ball cleared the left-field fence—retrieved by Braves reliever Tom House—before he put it all into perspective on KFI Radio in Los Angeles and the Dodgers network.

VIN SCULLY (1974): What a marvelous moment for baseball. What a marvelous moment for Atlanta and the state of Georgia; what a marvelous moment for the country and the world. A black man is getting a standing ovation in the Deep South for breaking a record of an all-time baseball idol. It is a great moment for all of us and particularly for Henry Aaron.

Dusty Baker had the next-best view to Aaron's. He was in the on-deck circle.

DUSTY BAKER: It was one of the greatest moments of my career and it wasn't me doing it. Hank told me that he was going to get it over with. It was a very cold night in Atlanta, the coldest night I remember in Atlanta. Hank said I'm tired of this, I'm going to get it over with now. They stopped the game and his mom and dad and children and wife, Billye, came out and we went home after the game.

Phil Niekro also was grateful for his up-close-and-personal view of history.

PHIL NIEKRO: I was in the dugout when he hit it. When he tied it off Billingham, we wondered if it was going to be the next day. Let's get this over for Henry, so all these thousands of reporters are out of here, and get it behind him and allow him to play baseball in a relaxed manner. I got to see something a lot of people never saw. I played with this guy as long as anybody. I've never seen the guy change his demeanor from the first time I saw him till he hit that homer.

There was little afterglow from Aaron's record-breaker. The Braves were broken up after 1974 as ownership stripped down in preparation for a sale. In a heartfelt homecoming Aaron went on to his final two years in the majors as DH for the Milwaukee Brewers.

Even if Barry Bonds hadn't been stained by steroids when he finally broke Aaron's record 33 years later, Hammering Hank's chase and the dignity he displayed in the face of pressure and threats remains one of baseball's all-time greatest stories. No wonder Aaron is still considered the real home-run champion.

PUDGE'S BODY-ENGLISH HOME RUN

Splitting the decade almost cleanly in half was perhaps the most famous game-ending homer in World Series history. The blast that decided one of the Fall Classic's best games ever was the Boston Red Sox Carlton Fisk's 12th-inning homer off the Reds' Pat Darcy in Game 6 on October 21, 1975. The homer is an important demarcation point in baseball history. Although the tinkering with the mound and introduction of the DH to juice up hitting starting in 1969 revived attendance, the Fisk homer and the wildly fluctuating, drama-by-the-minute theatrics of Game 6 truly gave baseball a massive shot in the arm in a telecast that lasted late into the night in the Eastern and Central time zones.

Famed baseball documentarian Ken Burns claimed he was an out-of-it hippie until Game 6 brought him back to baseball for good. The famed contest also was a talking point about the start of a romance in a conversation Robin Williams had with Matt Damon in the movie *Good Will Hunting*.

The NBC-TV slow-motion replay of Fisk trying to body-English his shot down the left-field line to stay fair has become the most iconic image of triumph in baseball, captured almost by accident when the network camera operator, stationed inside the Green Monster's scoreboard, was spooked by a rat and shifted his position.

CARLTON FISK (Red Sox, 1969–79): People recognize me, but just more in appreciation than individual moments. I haven't forgotten that moment. I keep kidding [Bill] Maze-roski that mine was better than his. Of course his [homer] won the World Series, mine just got us to the next game.

I don't sit and watch myself. When I watch the World Series and [that highlight] comes on, I go, "Who's that young guy?" Jeez. He even has a vertical [leap] I don't have anymore.

Those who helped set up Fisk's heroics believe they participated in one of baseball's greatest games ever. For Red Sox center-fielder Fred Lynn, the game was almost the ultimate capper to his dream Rookie of the Year season.

FRED LYNN: On a personal level, it's too bad it happened to me as a rookie and not, quote, unquote, a veteran player. Afterward, I was listening to Pete Rose and others say it was the greatest game they had played in. I hit a three-run homer in the first, and I was happy about that. It was a roller coaster. I was on second when Bernie Carbo hit that pinch-hit homer [in the bottom of the ninth]. He looked god-awful on the pitch before the homer.

The only thing I could draw upon was my collegiate experience. I won three College World Series and a Triple-A World Series. I never lost a key game so I fully expected to win Game 6. When it wasn't going our way, I never really got down. I knew we had the capacity to come back, but I didn't expect Bernie to hit that three-run homer. [George] Foster makes the play when I hit the ball down the line, Dwight Evans makes the play in right field. Crunch time, you want the ball. I played three other sports. That's what's fun.

I was on-deck for Fisk. We were watching Pat Darcy warm up. That was the first and only time he got in the game. We knew he threw sinkers and Pudge was a low-ball hitter. He said I'm going to get on and you knock me in. Our on-deck circle was pretty close to home plate. I tried to cheat and get as close to home plate as possible to see the movement of the ball, which you're not supposed to do.

When he hit it, I had a great angle, almost like the umpire's. I could see it was going to be fair—just whether it would get up high enough. Pudge was jumping around, but I had a much higher vertical leap than Pudge. You'll catch me as they pan for Pudge—he's pointing and I'm jumping, partly because I knew I didn't have to hit again.

People remember Game 6 and Pudge's home run and think that was Game 7. I wish it was Game 7. Unfortunately, we had to go out there one more time. They got the breaks in that game. Joe Morgan hit a tough pitch from Jim Burton. It was a slider and he just kind of dunked it into center field for the game-winning hit. They were a great team, no question about it. But we were a great team, too. We just came up on the short end. We rallied, forced a Game 7, and lost that one 4–3. We played that series without Jimmy Rice, who had broken his hand in late September when he got hit by a pitch from Vern Ruhle. We played them head-to-head without one of our biggest guns. It would have been like them playing us without Johnny Bench or Tony Perez. I like our chances if they don't have them in the lineup. If we would have Jimmy in there, I'm sure we would have won.

I never experienced losing. I remember sitting at my locker, watching the guys. I don't think anyone was taking any solace in the fact we pushed them to the brink without Jimmy. It was the first time I ever experienced defeat in a championship game.

Reds announcer Marty Brennaman, whose first big-league game had been for Aaron's 714th the previous year, now had back-to-back seasons of all-time highlights he covered. Brennaman announced the first half of the game on the NBC Radio network broadcast.

MARTY BRENNAMAN (Reds announcer, 1974–79): As soon as you saw something you felt like you never saw before, all of a sudden you saw something else. I've told people, if I didn't know better, I thought the Red Sox won that World Series. Everything focused on Game 6. Nobody talked about Game 7.

When it was going on, I was only in my second year as a [Reds] broadcaster, so I had no means of comparison. In retrospect, comparing that game with others I've seen, I've never seen a baseball game any better than that, World Series or regular season. The game incorporated every facet of the game at his highest level. That game had it all. I've often told people I feel privileged to be a part of that game. The '75 World Series Game 6 was about as good as it gets.

Dayton Daily News Reds writer Hal McCoy had to do the deadline dash as the game went into extra innings. Just as Fisk came through under pressure, so did the man who did not leave his newspaper rounds until 2009 as the senior beat writer in all sports before switching to Fox Sports Ohio.

HAL MCCOY (*Dayton Daily News* Reds writer, 1973–79): The pitching staff wasn't that great. You had Don Gullett, who was very good, and Jack Billingham. The rest were suspect. The Reds usually outhit you and outmauled you.

The only chance you had was to stay close and get into that bullpen, which the Red Sox did.

I was still a kid. I started covering the Reds in 1973. A&E did a baseball writers' special. They asked me the biggest game I've ever covered. I mentioned this game. They got a copy of my story and had me read it on the air, and show Fisk hitting the home run. I thought, "Oh my God, I'm just a kid, I shudder to think what I wrote." When they dug it out, I read it and they showed Fisk, I nailed it. It was unbelievable. I was proud of it after that. I was afraid of what I had written that day. I was past deadline and they were holding the paper for me. I had to get it right now as soon as it happened. I was pretty proud of it.

I think it definitely did [boost baseball]. The fact that not just Game 6 but every game was a great game. You had the Red Sox mystique. You had the Big Red Machine. Every game went down almost to the final out. It was so exciting. I remember being drained as if I had played the games myself after the World Series was over. People still talk about that World Series. So I think history has shown it was one of the greatest World Series ever.

But in the eyes of some, maybe Game 6 had some rivals within the '75 World Series for drama. One contrarian view was offered by a Red Sox first baseman who went on to stardom with the Brewers and managed the Astros.

CECIL COOPER (Red Sox, Brewers, 1971–79): I can't say Game 6 was the greatest. No, [it was] Game 4 in Cincinnati [tying the series 2–2] where Luis Tiant threw 200 pitches. To me, that might be the greatest, just because of what he had to do in that game. He threw almost 200 pitches [actually 155, including 87 strikes] in that game. He went the distance and won the game. That might have been the greatest I've ever been part of.

LUIS TIANT: I threw 153. Just do it. I wanted to finish my game. It's in the World Series, you're not there all the time. When you get there, you want to be part of it. You have to do what you have to do. I had 187 complete games. That's the way we grew up, that's the way we learned it. There's no room for thinking about you're tired. When you come into that situation, there's no tomorrow. They were the best-hitting team in baseball. Maybe they didn't see me in the season. With my delivery, they never see anybody throw like that before. It was hard for them to see the ball from me when I release the ball when I turn around, throw three-quarter, sidearm, and overhand. But they could hit the ball off anybody.

Indeed, Game 6 is unusual in being rated an all-time classic. All it did statistically is make the Red Sox fit to be tied. Sometimes you can derive a moral victory in baseball. In this case Boston was a big winner.

"BUCKY DENT GAME" REALLY LOU PINIELLA'S GAME?

They couldn't have handled best-of-three. In the good ol' days, pennant races ending in ties were decided by best-of-three playoffs. That's how Bobby Thomson hit his "Shot Heard Round the World" in 1951—in the deciding Game 3 of the Giants–Dodgers playoff.

But with two rounds in the postseason scheduled instead of just a direct entrée to the World Series in the pre-1969 age, deadlocks at game number 162 were now going to be a one-and-done proposition. That's all the Yankees and Red Sox could take in 1978, anyway, after the Bombers had stormed back from a 14-game deficit behind the Red Sox on July 19 to take a 3½-game lead on September 16, only to have Boston claw its way back into a tie at season's end. The winner-take-all game was scheduled October 2 at Fenway Park.

Bucky Dent's shocking three-run homer off Mike Torrez in the eighth gets all the glory and brands this game with the slap-hitting Dent's name. However, a hitter playing out of position, doing guesswork as he was blinded by the sun, is the unsung hero, according to those who played in the game.

RICK BURLESON: I think every athlete figures out we're going to figure out a way to get it done. They came in there, the Boston Massacre occurred. It got so bad they built a 3½-game lead on us. They were writing us off then. You come to the ballpark, you got to play the games. It's a matter of trying to turn it around. It's a positive, when the offense gets going, everyone hits. When several stop hitting, nobody hits. It was just a matter of winning a couple of tight games and turning it around. We won the last 12 of 15, they lost, we ended up tied. We won the toss and got the game at home.

Over a 24-hour period you had to deal with dishing out playoff tickets to people, you're in this game, you go to the ballpark with your suitcase packed. If you win, you're going to Kansas City and they're there, they're ready to go. Both teams go to the ballpark with suitcases packed. One team's going on to bigger and better things, the other team is ready to go home. So much happened so fast. Suddenly it's game time, we're playing this thing. You have [Ron] Guidry, 25–3 in one of the best one-year performances ever by a pitcher, going against us. We had some success against him. He had a couple of no-decisions in that 25–3 record where they came back and tied the game. We got a standup guy in Mike Torrez. It's not like he's a slouch and we're just pitching a nobody. He's a proven guy who's won a lot of games.

We have a 2–0 lead in the seventh inning. The place was excited and we were pumped. This was our opportunity to get the monkey off our back. To get that choke thing and spit it right back in somebody's face. As fast as that, the 2–0 lead disappeared. With two outs, [Roy] White and [Chris] Chambliss singled. Here comes Bucky Dent, breaks his bat on the 0–2 pitch, Mickey Rivers hands him his bat and says use this. Torrez waited and waited and waited and didn't throw anymore warm-up tosses. Fisk calls for something off the plate, Mike missed, and Bucky hit the three-run homer into the net.

We still weren't done. Reggie [Jackson] hits a two-run homer off Bob Stanley. We end up scoring two runs off Sparky Lyle in the eighth to make it a 5–4 game. They had to bring in the Goose. Goose struck out a pinch hitter, I walk on four pitches, Jerry Remy hits that line drive to right where the sun's coming down behind the third-base dugout. I'm taking off, I'm thinking, it's too high, I just can't go to third, I have to wait to see if it drops. Piniella just throws his glove up and it goes in it. I start to round second and I realize there's no way I can make it, I would have been out a mile. He froze and just stuck his glove out the other way. Now it's first and second, Rice hits a long fly.

Here comes Yaz. Of all people, if you had to have one guy at the plate, Goose gets him to pop up to third and history was made.

Lou Piniella was best known as the Yankees' finest clutch hitter, but just an acceptable left fielder. Strangely enough, Piniella was shifted to right field that day in place of Jackson, who was the DH. Now he had trouble with the sun in the ninth inning, hoping the Red Sox would hit the ball to center fielder Paul Blair. Piniella recalled what happened when Remy came up in his 1986 autobiography *Sweet Lou.*

LOU PINIELLA: Goose threw a low, inside fastball and Remy pulled it hard on a line to right. I saw the ball leave the bat and that was the last time I saw it. I knew if the ball got by me the runner would go to third and maybe score the tying run. I couldn't allow Burleson to see that I had lost it in the sun. I kept my composure and as I searched for the ball, I kept backtracking as hard as I could. I wanted to give myself some more room to find it. Out of the corner of my eye, I saw the damn ball landing a few feet to my left on the grass. . . . I lunged and it slapped into my glove. I whirled to my right and fired a throw to third. It was the best throw I had ever made in my career. I would never make one like that again.

The Red Sox could hardly be consoled postgame.

LUIS TIANT: To me, that was the worst game in my major-league career. Everybody was crying in the clubhouse. The worst feeling we ever had. We played bad in 2004, lost three, and then came back four in a row [against the Yankees in the ALCS]. Baseball, they can talk all they want. People don't know nothing. Baseball is a funny game. You never know what can happen in the game.

I pitched the day before against Toronto to get to that game. What's going to happen is going to happen. Piniella catching the ball after losing the ball in the sun. If the ball gets by, we win the game.

"What if" were the main words in the Red Sox's lexicon for another 26 years until they collected the overwhelmingly due bill from the Yankees in the ALCS, as the only team to ever come back from a 3–0 deficit in the postseason. Some things are indeed worth waiting for, but any Red Sox fan will tell you it was hell counting off the years in the meantime.

BROOKS ROBINSON'S WORLD SERIES

If any single performance ensured a player's entrée into the Hall of Fame, it was Brooks Robinson's 1970 World Series. Robinson didn't just put the Orioles on his back to carry them, he tucked the nascent Big Red Machine neatly into the webbing of his eternally gold glove.

The Robinson play of diving across the foul line, throwing across his body, and nipping Lee May at first could be the all-time textbook Web gem of the World Series—long before there ever was an ESPN. This time, the whole world's baseball watching was concentrated on NBC's telecast, so the images were indelible. Robinson made several other beautiful plays, including spearing a liner by Johnny Bench. At the plate Robinson had two homers, two doubles, and six RBIs in a 9-for-21 performance. He had clutch hits in all four Orioles victories in the five-game series. But the glove work made him a Michelangelo of the hot corner.

BROOKS ROBINSON (Orioles, 1969–77): It was a little unusual, believe me. I tell people I played 23 years professionally and I don't think I had five games in a row where it happened just like the World Series. You can play a whole week and never get a chance to do anything spectacular.

Going into the World Series, the big question for the infielders was we had never played on Astroturf before— should we wear regular cleats or go to Astroturf shoes? We ended up wearing regular spikes. We remembered losing to the Mets in '69. And in the first inning of the first game in '70, Woody Woodward hit me a little 24-hopper in the first inning and I made a high throw to Boog Powell for an error. I'm thinking, can you believe this? I make a high throw to Boog, it has to be pretty high for an error. You just can't handle the pressure here, what's the story?

Going into the series, [shortstop Mark] Belanger and I knew we were going to get a lot of work. We had [Mike] Cuellar and [Dave] McNally, left-handers, going and they had Lee May, Johnny Bench, Tony Perez, and Pete Rose. I just had a chance to make some outstanding plays. After the third or fourth game, I'm saying I hope this gets over in a hurry, I can't keep this up.

You're talking about 6 inches or a foot, you wouldn't be making these plays. You started to believe that something special was happening in that series. I knew they were going to hit the ball my way. The play I made over the bag in foul territory—normally you stop, plant your feet, and try to make the long throw. In this instance, I just caught the ball, turned, whirled, and threw one-hop to Boog Powell for a strike. We got Lee May. Lee May runs like me, which was the good thing about it.

Then Johnny Bench on a diving play, he hit the ball so hard it was curling back to me. I was diving. It was like pulling a one-iron. It was hooking. It was just a reflex action. Many times I dived for balls I never get. It's just a reaction play. Cuellar threw a big, slow hook to Bench. I always like to know when that's coming. Belanger would always say, "Be alive." John started that bat to get it out in front. He kind of hooked it over the bag. I was playing him to pull anyway and I ended up catching that ball a couple of feet in foul territory.

Absolutely. Being in four World Series and being the MVP [in 1970] helped get me in the Hall of Fame.

Orioles manager Earl Weaver wasn't the least bit surprised at Robinson's artistry. He saw it year-round in Baltimore.

EARL WEAVER (Orioles manager, 1969–79): Brooks made those plays throughout the course of the season. But they didn't come in the course of a five-game [World] series. A third baseman only averages three chances a ball game. That's putouts and assists. The fact Cincinnati had a lot of right-handed hitters, the fact we had two left-handed pitchers, there were a lot of balls hit his way in five games. He came up with every one of them that possibly anyone can come up with. You could go the whole series and possibly only have six chances in five games. That was his series.

What did he do that made him so good? Quickness, great hands, the fact that once he got to it, he was going to make the play and that was it.

And in the case of Robinson, nice guys do finish first.

9

Would-Be Dynasties

The entire sporting public knows the soap opera of George Steinbrenner, Billy Martin, and Reggie Jackson by heart.

We recall how it was two against one, then it shifted, and through all the tension between the strong-willed men, the Yankees were finally restored to glory after more than a decade of drift, going to three consecutive World Series, winning two, between 1976 and 1978. Then, like now, the Bronx Bombers were envied, feared, resented, and admired.

But despite what some historians may have you believe, the game did not begin and end with the Yankees, whether it was the 1920s, 1950s, 1970s, or 1990s. Baseball had achievers just as good, maybe even better, than the Yanks in the True Golden Age. The Yanks were a disappointing runner-up for the first half of the 1970s and closed the decade with a down season.

There were the Oakland Athletics, who could surpass the New Yorkers in creative tension and total number of Fall Classics captured—three in a row from 1972 to 1974. Then there were the Cincinnati Reds, more popularly known as the "Big Red Machine," whom some regarded as the greatest team of all time, going to four World Series, winning two, while finishing first in the NL West six times in the decade. Proud but under-credited was a team perhaps more consistent than any—the Baltimore Orioles, presided over by crusty Earl Weaver—whose record was tarnished by winning just one of the four World Series in which they played from 1969 to 1979, a period marked by a half dozen first-place finishes in the beastly AL East. Finally, challenging the Yankees were the upstart Kansas City Royals, a forward-thinking franchise that nevertheless built its success the old-fashioned way, from within.

GREEN AND GOLD AS GOOD AS GOLD

Handling the national broadcast for NBC TV on October 5, 1971, Curt Gowdy aptly described the experienced Baltimore Orioles and the just-swept Oakland Athletics in the American League Championship Series. The A's October play was their first foray into the postseason in 40 years.

CURT GOWDY: A young A's team just reaching maturity . . . The A's are going to be a factor for some years now unless they get hit by hard-luck injuries. . . . They [Orioles] have just been too good for their opposition in the American League [winning nine League Championship Series games in a row]. The best term to describe this [Orioles] team, it's a beautifully balanced baseball machine: age, youth, defense, hitting, speed, bench, good leadership, marvelous esprit de corps on the club. . . . You never hear a note of discord out of this club.

Gowdy was prescient about the A's. They were ready for prime time in 1972, the deft talent-gathering process by maverick owner Charles O. Finley having paid off. Based in Chicago, the self-made medical insurance man Finley had been mostly known for the sizzle, not the steak, when he had acquired the sad-sack A's a decade earlier in Kansas City. But while he gained almost all his fame employing a mascot mule and dressing his players in green-and-gold sleeveless uniforms, among other promotions, Finley was squirreling away talent he and a small cadre of good scouts had signed and developed. He plucked Reggie Jackson, Sal Bando, and Rick Monday out of Arizona State University. Finley would be the classic triumphant/tragic baseball story, building up his champions from scratch, then tearing them down when the new system of free agency thwarted his style of paying his players 75 cents for every dollar that players of comparable talent were earning.

But what a run it was, the A's outsmarting and outexecuting their opponents in the regular season in swashbuckling fashion, their mustaches and long hair encouraged by Finley and changing the look of major leaguers for the rest of the 1970s. While generating headlines off the field with several clubhouse fights, the battling "Mustache Gang" A's were stretched to seven games in only one of the three World Series they captured—oddly by the vastly inferior 1973 Mets, winner of just 82 regular-season games, who took a three-games-to-two lead in the World Series before succumbing to their spirited opponents. In the end the only thing that beat the A's was their owner, who broke them up before their time.

The A's did not lack for motivation. It came from within and without—the latter the parsimonious Finley, who could not have believed how his tight rein on his budget became a unifying force for his players.

First of the great clutch performances that comprised the trio of championship efforts was turned in by catcher/first baseman Gene Tenace, whose four homers in the '72 World Series made up for the power lost from the injured Jackson.

GENE TENACE (Athletics, Padres, 1969–79): With the talent factor and the determination factor and the unique owner we had, all those things taken into consideration, we all had a goal we wanted to achieve, and that was to win. Once we had a taste of it in '72 and all that talent, we kept it going. We were an excellent execution ball club. In the seventh, eighth, and ninth innings, we could execute with anybody. We didn't make a whole lot of mistakes. With our bullpen, there weren't too many teams that were going to beat us in the seventh, eighth, and ninth innings.

I don't think it was so much of that [players vs. Finley]. I think it was pride in ourselves. We were not going to be denied success. We worked out in the winter in top-quality shape. There was a big pride factor in everyone who wore that uniform.

Sometimes it was difficult [to put contract battles behind you]. I used to hate when December came around. It was Christmas. You still had a feeling you had to go to war with Charlie every year for something you felt you deserved, and unfortunately most of the time you weren't going to get. It was a battle with him.

There's no question we would have continued to win our division [after 1975]. The average age was 27, 28 years old.

Tenace's partner in success and roommate was Bando, the clutch-hitting third baseman. Each man used his savvy to stay in the game, Tenace as a longtime big-league hitting coach and Bando as GM of the Brewers.

SAL BANDO (Athletics, Brewers, 1969–79): I felt like as a team we'd intimidate [opponents]. We had excellent pitching, good speed, power, so there were a number of ways we could beat you. I thought we were going to win for years. But I think our biggest threat after our first year really came from the Baltimore Orioles, which were such a strong fundamental club. With good pitching and good defense, they were excellent [playoff] series we had with those guys.

I think the media made more of what went on [in the clubhouse] than anything. I think all clubs have disagreements. When you have 25 different personalities living together for seven months, you're going to have disagreements. What was said about us, I don't really think was true. The one factor our club did have was a tremendous amount of pride to win. When the game was on the line, we'd pull together. Yes, we had some differences and we came from different backgrounds. We had 25 guys whose desire to win was far greater than anything else.

All of us played in an era when you really didn't have much say in what your contract was. As disheartening as it was, I think we obviously didn't carry it with us on the field.

Arbitration was our first window of being able to get paid in a comparable manner. We all took advantage of that situation and we all did well that way. In some respects the contracts really didn't bother us. For me, I think Charlie and the way he conducted business did bring us a little closer. We were all treated the same way. It was a binding influence in the long term.

In 1975 we won our division with only two regular starters—Kenny [Holtzman] and Vida [Blue]. To add Catfish [Hunter, granted free agency after Finley did not pay an annuity due to the pitcher] into our mix, we would have continued to win our division and very well might have been back in the World Series for years to come.

Finley made some key trades to augment his homegrown core. Best was in late 1971 for lefty Ken Holtzman from the Cubs for center fielder Rick Monday. After too many disagreements with the imperious Leo Durocher in Chicago and belief that the heavy schedule of day games hurt a pitcher's endurance, Holtzman thrived in Oakland as he never did in Wrigley Field.

KEN HOLTZMAN (Cubs, Athletics, Orioles, Yankees, 1969–79): I felt after we won the first year, contrary to what a lot of people say, I honestly felt it was easier to win the second and third year. I felt our team was good at that point; there was a certain amount of intimidation whenever we played in our own league or when we got to the playoffs and World Series. The Oakland A's were acknowledged to be the best and even though [other teams] tried harder when they played us, I still felt the natural intimidation of having won so often worked in our favor. And that's why I thought we'd repeat.

We were a sound fundamental team. After all, there were three Hall of Fame players that came off that team, and six and seven really close. We were determined to win. A lot of that came from the owner. A lot of it came from our own determination. I always felt we were going to win after the first year and it was just a matter of time.

There was quite a bit more [conflict] on that team than any other team I can think of, from talking to other players. Sal was unquestionably our leader both on and off the field. He kept a lot of guys who maybe were going separate ways intact. I think all the players—Reggie, Vida, Catfish, Rollie [Fingers], myself, Geno, Joe [Rudi], Campy [Bert Campaneris]—looked to Sal to kind of be our spiritual leader both in and out of the clubhouse. I think Sal was a big instigator of a lot of fights. Me and Rollie were roommates, just like Geno and Sal were for many years. Me and Rollie called Sal "fat boy" because he wore those skin-tight uniforms. You looked like something the circus brought to town. In my opinion Campaneris and Sal, and certainly Geno and Joe [Rudi], were, I believe, the most valuable players on that team. Regardless of the Hall of Fame voting, I felt those four players constituted the heart and soul of the Oakland A's.

Finley struck gold two years in a row with the Cubs near the end of 1972, thanks in part to the Holtzman trade. Monday's veteran presence in center squeezed out top Cubs outfield prospect Bill North, who clashed with management and was thus dealt. He found a home in Oakland for his bat and legs, leading the AL twice in stolen bases.

BILL NORTH: In the locker room and the bus trips from the airport to the hotel, you had Vida Blue, Rollie Fingers, me, Kenny Holtzman, you had Reggie, Gene Tenace, Sal Bando, all these guys could talk. They talked about each other incessantly. Baseball is a game of repetition. Perfect practice makes perfect. If you have negative repetition, that will become ingrained as a habit. We were taught to play your position, don't give up extra outs, don't play anybody else's and everything will come together. My job is to play center field, throw it to the closest guy coming out of the infield. I was the leadoff man and I felt I was a pretty good one. We had a car, Reggie drove the car, but you weren't going anywhere till it got turned on. That was my job.

There were cliques, but you get 25 guys together—33 including coaches and trainers—every day for seven months with egos with pro athletes, you'll have some trouble. Every team I was ever on fought. I think we fought a little bit more because sometimes people didn't know when to turn it off. I had four rules: Don't go in my locker, don't play the homosexual act running around the locker room grabbing at each other, I don't play nigger jokes, and I don't talk about anybody's old lady. Those four things are the stuff that start the tension. I'd nip somebody if they started stuff so I didn't have to bite them later. I was glib. I said I don't play that. People try to get away with stuff unless you stop them.

We won in spite of him [Finley]. Dick Williams made that team. Then Charlie started talking crazy to Dick. Dick said I don't need this and left. When Dick left, Alvin Dark became the manager. The type of ethic instilled by a strong leader will carry over for at least one year. Then Charlie started messing with the machine in '75. He didn't know the intricacy of a Ted Kubiak. Ted Kubiak was the best two-week shortstop around. Charlie Finley, you couldn't tell him anything. Bowie Kuhn couldn't. Charlie put it together, and then he tore it apart. Charlie went against the grain. He made his money selling malpractice insurance to doctors, which nobody else wanted to touch. Charlie loved the limelight, partner.

To say Finley ran a tight ship is being generous. He ran the front office with just a handful of employees. The key underling was not the ticket manager or receptionist, but a local kid named Stanley Burrell, who was Finley's eyes and ears. In his later incarnation Burrell added his own voice and legs—as rapper MC Hammer. Having sold real estate in remote Baker City, Oregon, for three decades, former left-fielder Rudi is about as far away from the appeal of Hammer's latter-day persona as possible.

JOE RUDI: He hired good people but never let them do their job. He had to have his hand in everything. He had a very small staff in the office.

MC Hammer was his snitch. One of his older brothers was our first batboy. Hammer would just come to the ballpark with his brothers and help clean shoes after games. Finley got to know him and would have Hammer sit up in his box and broadcast the game [back to Chicago] to him. We found out that Hammer would hang out in the clubhouse, listen to the conversations, and go tell Finley everything he heard, which was unfortunate, but it was just the way it was.

Charlie wanted to be involved in everything. Here he's calling us personally to negotiate contracts. But he could be very generous. There were several minor leaguers who had medical issues and he took care of them. When it came to business, he was a tough, astute businessman. He was very generous with Christmas gifts, watches, before the Mike Andrews thing [1973 World Series roster controversy in which Finley tried to remove Andrews from the roster out of spite for a misplay], which soured him. The first year we won, he bought us all kinds of trophies—we all got the owners' trophy as a gift. He took guys, and I was one of them, he offered to invest my World Series share in the stock market. He treated his players good. He was a tough businessman when it came to negotiating contracts and not having waste with people in the front office not doing anything.

Finley was notorious for calling his managers in the dugout, à la George Steinbrenner or disturbing their sleep from two time zones away in Chicago. Well, Chuck Tanner turned the tables on Finley in 1976, taking advantage of the fact the bars had finally closed in Chicago and Finley had to retire for what remained of the night.

CHUCK TANNER: We won the game. I'm in Oakland in a motel. It's 2 in the morning. I said, "Ah, shit, I'll call Charlie." I called him in Chicago and there's [two hours] difference in time. He's sleeping. I say, "Charlie, this is Chuck. We won. Bando got the [clutch] base hit." He said, "I know, I know." Next night we won again. I waited till 2 a.m. and I called him again. He says, "Y'know, I've been sleeping." I said, "Yeah, that's really horseshit if anyone wakes you up this time of night." Because that's what he used to do to the manager. "Anybody does that is horseshit. I'll never do it again," I said. That's why I did it, to let them know how horseshit it was.

Charlie never lost money. He told me, Chuck, ever since I owned a big-league club, I never lost money. He had a girl as a secretary and general manager. He had a cousin in the front office. He had another kid from Indiana as the farm director. That was his office. He had one [phone] line. If you wanted to go to the game, there was just one line to buy tickets. That's all he had.

The A's also won in spite of their playing conditions. It was too cool for Holtzman's pitching satisfaction at night. The Oakland Coliseum was called the "Mausoleum" for good reason.

JOE RUDI: We drew twice as many people on the road as we did at home. There were many nights they said there were 10,000 people in the stands, and I counted less than 1,000. That's why we called it the Mausoleum, because it was all concrete with all those dark green seats.

It was cold and damp. All these things people don't pay attention to because they weren't around then was the huge difference in the weather. When we moved to Oakland in 1968, the population of the Bay Area was tremendously less than even in the 1980s, when I returned to coach. We had the coastal clouds coming in every day. The worst time to go to the beach in northern California is the summertime. We'd have clouds coming through our [stadium] lights. They were that low and they would actually dim the lights, and make it harder to play ball. Playing in the outfield, a ball coming between third and short, ground-ball base hit, the second it got to the outfield grass, the water was spinning off the ball. You'd pick it up and literally hope you could throw it 100 feet back to Campy [Campaneris] because the ball was sopping wet.

With the start of free agency looming after the 1976 season, Finley decided to cut his losses. He first traded Reggie Jackson and Ken Holtzman to Baltimore. Then, right at the trade deadline on June 15, 1976, Finley arranged sales of Vida Blue to the Yankees and Rollie Fingers and Joe Rudi to the Red Sox, totaling $3.5 million. Commissioner Bowie Kuhn held up approval of the deals and then on June 18 voided them in the "best interests of baseball"; he desired to prevent the rich from getting richer without just compensation in players. Finley, already at odds with Kuhn, filed a $10 million lawsuit against the commissioner and refused to let the trio of players back with the A's for almost two weeks.

JOE RUDI: We knew '76 was going to be a bear. The only thing that made it survivable was so many of us were playing our free agency out. We had a great agent in Jerry Kapstein, still one of the most honorable and honest men. He did a great job keeping our spirits up. Chuck Tanner was just a positive person. He knew it was going to be a tumultuous year. He kept our spirits up. The beginning of the year, Finley sent us contracts. We all sent it back. Mine was an offer for a three-year contract for $400,000. The best thing that ever happened to me was Finley didn't even answer it. We did a lot better in free agency.

I wasn't surprised [at the June 15 trade]. I spent so much time there. He traded Holtzman and Reggie, got [Don] Baylor, [Mike] Torrez, and a young right-handed pitcher. We were upset [at Kuhn's trades reversal]. We knew we weren't staying with Oakland. At the time, I had become sort of friends with Mr. Yawkey [Red Sox owner Tom]. I'd always get to the ballpark [Fenway] at noon, and he was out there playing pepper. I was always out there screwing around so I got to know him. Very, very nice man. Darrell Johnson was the manager. He lived not too far from me in California. He used to duck-hunt with me. It was surprising how Boston was going to make all this work—Yaz to first, [Jim] Rice to DH, me in left field. Rollie [Fingers] coming out of the bullpen would have changed history.

My wife and I both loved Boston. By far it was my best ballpark. The fans were great to me. I was excited about going there at that point in my career. She had the whole house packed up and bags at the ballpark to be shipped to Boston. She was crushed when they put a hold on the trade. We were in limbo for three, four weeks. He and Kuhn were fighting. Finally after a week he let us work out. I was very upset, I would have loved to have gone to Boston. If I had gone there, I'd probably be living in Boston.

Before the trades were voided, the A's who were left behind were in a rebellious mood. They abhorred Finley's surrender tactics and talked about a wildcat strike.

BILL NORTH: We said we wouldn't play. We were playing Boston. We gave in. Joe Rudi and them were in Boston uniforms. We were not going to play. We were going on strike. We were in the locker room, all dressed, we said were not going to play. He finally gave in to Kuhn, and Joe Rudi and them came back over to our team. We were not going to play that night.

Nobody but us and the Yankees have ever won three [in a row]. Something always happens. It's the fact that when you have people in power with egos, they always think it's them. But it's everybody. The team is a team from the owner on down. Organizations will find a way to self-destruct.

Finley lost his remaining stars to free agency after 1976. Only Blue stayed on another year until Finley traded him to the Giants. The A's quickly sunk to the bottom of the AL West, losing 108 games in 1979 before Finley himself finally sold the franchise to the Haas family, who hired Billy Martin. Eventually the A's would return to glory under Tony La Russa, but it still was not the same as the rollicking, brawling team of the True Golden Age.

THE BIG RED MACHINE: GREATEST EVER?

Presiding over the Wrigley Field right-field bleachers, Caleb "Chet" Chestnut kept the folks sitting around him in stitches at the top row above the 368-foot sign during the mid-1970s.

"My foot's gone to heaven," said Chet, a husky, ebony-skinned, white-haired gentleman near 80, his cane tapping his peg leg. Don't ever get incarcerated in Joliet, he warned everyone. "You won't be able to sit down when you come back here,"

Wrigley Field right-field bleacher fans. These fans ranged from kids to seniors in the summer of 1977. The author sat in the top row here. Leo Bauby photo collection

Commissioner Bowie Kuhn. Fans in all cities were treated to the greatest era of baseball under the stewardship of Kuhn, who was much criticized during his tenure in office. However, Kuhn instituted changes that are now an established part of the game. National Baseball Hall of Fame Library, Cooperstown, NY

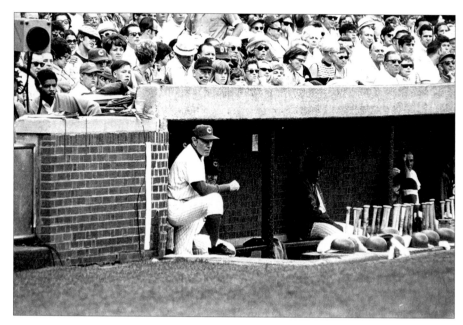

Irascible Cubs manager Leo Durocher in 1970. Durocher was the most amoral man in baseball, and his old-school handling of his team greatly contributed to its collapse down the stretch in 1969. He lost the clash of eras with Mets manager Gil Hodges. Leo Bauby photo collection

Cubs in the outfield. The Cubs players are picking up coins tossed by the rabid Left Field Bleacher Bums fan in 1969. The haul was later collected in a baseball cap. The Bums cheered on their heroes, while harassing opposition players like Pete Rose and Willie Davis. Leo Bauby photo collection

Gil Hodges. Mets manager Hodges was interviewed by Cubs star Ernie Banks for his WGN radio show. Hodges employed a five-man rotation and bullpen roles as a precursor of a new baseball era, a strategy that ended up in the wild fan celebration as the Mets won the 1969 World Series. Leo Bauby photo collection

National Baseball Hall of Fame Library, Cooperstown, NY

Brooks Robinson. Robinson was a dervish at third base and a competitive hitter, making him the most prominent third baseman of the era. Robinson almost single-handedly won the 1970 World Series for the Orioles, making third-base plays that cemented his eventual induction into the Hall of Fame. Leo Bauby photo collection

Lou Piniella. Here is the player and eventual manager in a calmer moment as a young hitter with the Kansas City Royals. Piniella was at once one of the era's best clutch hitters and most emotional players. His explosions entertained both teammates and foes. Leo Bauby photo collection

Steve Carlton in mid-delivery. "Lefty" parlayed a tiff with Cardinals owner Gussie Busch over a comparative pittance into a trade to the Phillies and status as the 1970s' best southpaw. Silent to the media, Carlton's biting slider spoke volumes on the mound. National Baseball Hall of Fame Library, Cooperstown, NY

Roberto Clemente. The heart and soul of the Pittsburgh Pirates, Clemente and Willie Stargell were team leaders who influenced their teammates. His final big-league hit was his 3,000th. Clemente's tragic death on a humanitarian mission to Nicaragua on December 31, 1972, rocked the Pirates and baseball. Leo Bauby photo collection

National Baseball Hall of Fame Library, Cooperstown, NY

Al Oliver. Oliver flexes his muscles at his favorite road ballpark, Wrigley Field, as he's flanked (below) by Willie Stargell (left) and Manny Sanguillen among other Pirates "Lumber Company" members. The Pirates often had too many hitters and couldn't keep them all in the 1970s. Leo Bauby photo collection

Harry Caray. A true 1970s Pied Piper of the airwaves, Caray dressed for the part as he broadcast from old Comiskey Park's bleachers, while also posing with the "Holy Cow" (his trademark home-run call) mascot of sponsor Falstaff beer. By 1977, Caray led fans in "Take Me Out to the Ballgame" from his broadcast booth, a promotion that got even bigger when he moved to the crosstown Cubs in 1981. Leo Bauby photo collection

Dick Allen. Allen finally found a home—briefly—at Comiskey Park. Here, he accepts his 1972 American League Most Valuable Player award, achieved with his heavy, productive war club that made him the game's most feared hitter. For several years Allen found peace in Chicago that he was unable to achieve in Philadelphia, where he used to scrawl messages in the dirt around first base.

Leo Bauby photo collection

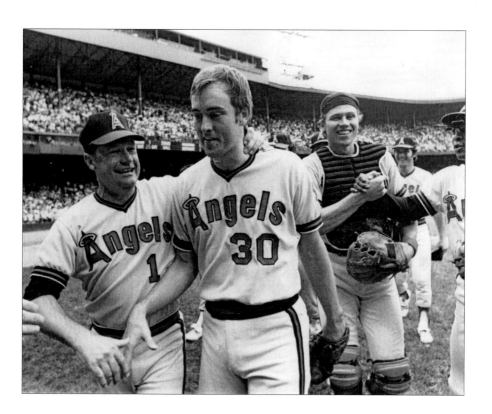

Nolan Ryan. Ryan accepts congratulations (top) from Bobby Winkles after no-hitting the Tigers in Detroit on July 15, 1973, as catcher Art Kusnyer follows him. Ryan was the subject of promotions using early radar guns to determine if he could crack 100 mph. Catcher Jeff Torborg (right) helped smooth out Ryan's mechanics. Torborg had caught no-hitters by Ryan, Sandy Koufax, and Bill Singer, displaying baseballs commemorating each hitless gem. Leo Bauby photo collection

The swing that launched Henry Aaron's 715th homer in 1974. Aaron's quest to break Babe Ruth's record was both exhausting and frightening as the Braves slugger received racist hate mail and threats. His dignity was such that he's still considered the real home-run champion after Barry Bonds was stained by steroids. National Baseball Hall of Fame Library, Cooperstown, NY

The man who loved the limelight. Put him on a national stage, and Reggie Jackson obliged. He became "Mr. October" in the 1970s with World Series heroics that culminated in a three-homer game against the Dodgers in 1977. Leo Bauby photo collection

Charlie Finley was the game's most controversial owner in the 1970s. An innovator and a promoter, Finley was always at odds with his players over his skinflint ways. But he assembled a three-consecutive World Series winner in Oakland that has not been matched since. National Baseball Hall of Fame Library, Cooperstown, NY

Tommy John delivering a pitch for the Yankees. John wouldn't have even worn pinstripes if not for the ground-breaking elbow-tendon transplant surgery that bears his name. He was the test subject for Dr. Frank Jobe. The Tommy John Surgery was a success for its namesake as well as for scores of other pitchers over the next 36 years. National Baseball Hall of Fame Library, Cooperstown, NY

Mike Schmidt. Schmidt connects for one of his four homers in an 18–16 victory at Wrigley Field on April 17, 1976. He single-handedly brought the Phillies back from a 13–2, fourth-inning deficit in the game. The all-time third baseman was a like a god at the Friendly Confines, totaling 50 homers in 18 seasons. Leo Bauby photo collection

typical **Mark Fidrych pose.** "The ird" charmed baseball in 1976 with is on-the-mound antics. He could itch a bit, too, winning 19 games. Arm roubles cut a great career short in nsuing seasons. Leo Bauby photo collection

Thurman Munson. Baseball lost a great leader in 1979 when Munson was killed in the crash landing of his private jet. Munson, like Roberto Clemente, was the man who set the tone for his team. He was an original Yankee who was the rock of stability among much turmoil around Billy Martin and Reggie Jackson in 1977.
National Baseball Hall of Fame Library, Cooperstown, NY

Phil Niekro. "Knucksie" was baseball's most prominent knuckleballer. His specialty was one of the most baffling pitches in the game in the 1970s. He was among the last pitchers to throw 300 innings in one season.
National Baseball Hall of Fame Library, Cooperstown, NY

Disco Demolition Night. Even Bill Veeck could not have dreamed how Disco Demolition Night turned out. It was a baseball game turned into a rock concert as up to 70,000 fans, attracted to a promotion in which disco records were blown up, took over old Comiskey Park in 1979. The game between the White Sox and Tigers was canceled and forfeited to the Tigers. Weeks later, marijuana plants were found growing in the outfield. Leo Bauby photo collection

The author's "wire room" at the *Chicago Tribune* on March 16, 1975. In the wee hours of the weekend, George Castle tended the old teletype machines and debated baseball with the night crew on duty. Both the hair and the collars were a bit longer in the 1970s, but the attempt at a mustache didn't quite take hold.
Author's Collection

Bill Veeck. Still making news in the 1970s, Veeck finally sold the White Sox and got out of baseball ownership in 1980. He then retired to the Wrigley Field bleachers, where the author caught up with him one day. Veeck used his peg leg as an ashtray and brought lamb chops for his fellow bleacher fans. Author's Collection he said of the special lovin' one could expect in state prison. There was the story about him working construction in Chicago in the 1920s and getting a bird's-eye view of the private goings-on in adjoining skyscrapers. Did you hear the one about the German shepherd and the woman in the window? At times Chet's benchmates would be rolling in the aisles to the ribald stories. They laughed so enthusiastically they were hardly aware of Tom Seaver taking a no-hitter into the ninth against the Cubs in 1975 before they looked up to watch the mounting drama.

But whenever the Cincinnati Reds hit town, Chet put his stories on hold. He transformed into a fire-and-brimstone preacher, extolling the virtues of Rose, Morgan, Bench, Perez, Griffey, et al. You couldn't stick up for the Cubs, because Chet would shout you down. "They're the greatest team in history," he said, and that included the Babe Ruth Yankees he watched back in the day. Chet had fodder for his claim, whether it was five solo homers against Steve Stone belted in less than three innings one 1974 afternoon, or the 11 Cincy wins in 12 tries against the Cubs in 1975. *Chicago Tribune* sportswriter Bob Verdi contrasted the Cubs as the "Little Blue Bicycle" compared to the Big Red Machine. Chet saved his loudest cackling, worthy of Lionel Barrymore in *It's a Wonderful Life,* for an August 1976 series when the Reds trotted out their finest guns.

Who could really argue with Chet? The Reds had everything save for an airtight pitching staff. And even that was maneuvered around to peak efficiency by Sparky Anderson, alias "Captain Hook." Through the decades, the Machine's back-to-back MVP is still his old team's best promoter.

JOE MORGAN (Astros, Reds, 1969–79): All I can say is I would take my team over any other team. I'm sure the Yankees would say the same thing about their team. I just think if you look at the people who were on the team I played on, I don't see how you could get a better team together.

The Reds might win the "greatest ever" tag by acclamation had they not been done in almost single-handedly by Brooks Robinson in the 1970 World Series or outfoxed by the Oakland Athletics two years later in the Fall Classic. The vastly inferior Mets upset them in the 1973 National League Championship Series, punctuated by a fight between Pete Rose and Bud Harrelson. But consider 1975 and 1976. Other than the most memorable home run post-1960 in World Series history by Carlton Fisk, the Reds were virtually invincible. With the exception of 1971, they won 95 or more games every season from 1970 to 1976.

The franchise was built slowly through the 1960s, first via Rose, then Tony Perez and Lee May, and then got lucky when Bill Capps, the Dallas-based Cubs area scout, could not persuade his superiors to take Johnny Bench in the 1965 draft. The Cubs passed over Bench twice before the Reds plucked him. The final building block to get the Reds to first place after a bunch of runner-up finishes was a 36-year-old rookie manager, whom pundits said looked 20 years older, taking over the Reds in 1970.

SPARKY ANDERSON (Reds and Tigers manager, 1970–79): [In 1970] we took a bunch of kids—Hal McRae, Bernie Carbo, Dave Concepcion—we just brought him along very slowly that year—we took a kid named Darrel Chaney, we took Don Gullett, 19 years old. We got Ken Griffey Sr. just a baby. We had all babies. George Foster was a baby. All of a sudden when the time came that they became good players, everyone said they were great players. Well, they weren't great players when my coaches started with them. They were all babies, just kids. We won over 100 games that first year after finishing third the year before. They weren't the Big Red Machine in '69. Starting in '70, they were the Big Red Machine. Carbo and McRae split left field between them. Those were kids we put in there. We got rid of Alex Johnson, who was a .300 hitter, and played those kids. We had the youngest club in the NL, even with Rose and Perez there. We had Bench at 22 years old. We had the youngest club in the NL and won it going away.

The crowning touch to give the Reds their air of invincibility was a late 1971 trade that dispatched their entire right side of the infield—first baseman May and second baseman Tommy Helms—to Houston for second baseman Joe Morgan and four other players. Pitcher Jack Billingham and third baseman Denis Menke were welcome parts coming back, but Morgan was the key while Cesar Geronimo solidified the defense in center for years to come. The trade may have been the best of the 1970s. Johnny Bench analyzed it correctly before the new players played an inning in the regular season in a spring-training 1972 radio interview with Harry Caray.

JOHNNY BENCH (Reds, 1969–79): I have to say it's going to be a good trade. Menke is a good third baseman, and move Perez to first, which is what they wanted to do for a long time. We wanted [Joe] Morgan very badly. Morgan's a very good all-around ballplayer.

Morgan's own game matured overnight, going from an also-ran in Houston to an established contender in America's Rhineland.

TONY PEREZ (Reds, Expos, 1969–79): Morgan was the last piece [of the puzzle]. We had a good ball club before, but we needed more speed, more defense. He was MVP two years in a row. You had to be there to see what he did for the ball club. He was a very smart player. Morgan made us almost a perfect ball club.

Morgan's good batting eye came in handy to complement the "chicken-wing" startup to his swing.

JOE MORGAN: The Reds already were a winning team, and I just mixed in with what they already had there.

Bob Howsam said at the end of the '76 season this would be the last team created that way, through trades and the farm system. Now you have a lot of free agents and movement. But anytime you have players with the same goals in mind, the chemistry will be there. It can be repeated, but it's not easy to do with so much turnover in the game.

We all had the same goals in mind to win a championship, and me playing alongside those guys and becoming friends with them, I think all of us grew closer together. To be perfectly honest, I learned to play baseball in Houston—no one remembers that. Not as consistently, not as good of a ball club, and I was in a bigger stadium. We all grew closer together as a group of players—friends more than anything else. To this day we're all still very good friends. We all had a special chemistry.

I had to learn that [patience] from the time I was a little kid. To be honest with you, I was always smaller than the other guys. I had to find ways of getting on base other than just getting base hits—do what I could to help the team win. My understanding of the strike zone, I learned at an early age and it just continued to get better as I got older. It's a thin line [between] being patient and being patiently aggressive. It's difficult for a lot of hitters to be patient and be aggressive. Sometimes you have guys just taking pitches. That's not being actually patient. Then you have guys being overly aggressive and swinging at a lot of pitches out of the zone.

Morgan, Bench, and soon Foster comprised an unparalleled middle of the lineup. The only thing lacking for Anderson's crew were facial hair and long hair, banned by neat-freak Howsam and his equally conservative successors. Foster's development pushed the veteran Perez farther down in the order. But there was no question the popular Cuban was the heart and soul of the Big Red Machine. He may have been their single-best clutch hitter. If you needed a two-run single in the late innings, Perez was your man.

TONY PEREZ: We got a lot of leaders—Rose, Johnny [Bench], Morgan. They said I was the leader. Everyone got along with me. I was in the middle of everything. The players were looking at me as a leader. I didn't realize that before, but after the guys said that when I left in 1977, I have to say yes. I have to say I was the big leader.

Lee May gave me the nickname Big Dawg. When I was at the plate, I used to chew a lot of gum—three or four pieces in my mouth. The way I hit, he said it was like I was attacking the pitcher. He said the Big Dawg is going to bite.

We didn't have deep pitching, but Sparky did a great job with the pitching. He used the pitchers the way he was supposed to. He was taking care of it.

SPARKY ANDERSON: Tony was a great clutch hitter, there's no question about that, but he was a greater person. Tony's greatest asset was that he was such a great person. He probably was the only guy I knew there who was totally liked by every player. Tony had a great, great way about him. He and his wife were marvelous people. I remember when Eduardo was just a baby. I was there with [Ken Griffey Jr.] and [Brian] McRae. All those kids used to sit on my lap.

The Red Sox were not cowed by the Reds in battling them to a standstill, thanks to some all-time heroics in Game 6 of the 1975 World Series that forced a seventh game won by Cincy in small-ball fashion at Fenway Park. But one of the heroes, Fred

Lynn, points out that the Reds could have been as pinched as Boston was by losing one of its stars for the Fall Classic.

FRED LYNN: We played them tough, no question. We negated some of the things they did well. And we could stand toe to toe with them powerwise, which most teams couldn't. I've had this discussion with Joe [Morgan]. If they didn't have Bench or Perez in their lineup, think they could have beaten us? That Yankees team in '78 was pretty doggone good. The early Baltimore teams were pretty good, too. What made those Reds teams really good is they played a lot of teams on their rug and they could use their team speed. Well, we didn't have any rug and that place played slow. It slowed them down, no question. That's the idiosyncrasy of our park.

On August 11, 1976, at Wrigley Field, the true comeback power and confidence of the Reds came on display, aided by their opponents' mistakes, this time by the opposing manager. The Cubs took a 10–1 lead after three innings. But the Reds whittled the score down to 10–8 going into the top of the ninth.

Chicago manager Jim Marshall elected to keep aging side-arming right-handed reliever Joe Coleman in for a third inning despite having been touched up for three hits, a walk, and a run in the seventh and eighth. Meanwhile, southpaw reliever Darold Knowles warmed up with lefty swingers Griffey Sr. and Morgan due up. But as Griffey approached the plate, Knowles stayed in the bullpen instead of Marshall playing the percentages. Coleman stayed on the mound, Griffey took his cuts and powered the game-tying homer 430 feet to the concession stand in center. Knowles later came in and gave up the game-winning three runs in the 10th. You could not make mistakes like that against the Reds.

The comeback carried over to the next day as the Reds could get into both the opponents' and umpires' heads. Cubs ace Rick

Reuschel pitched well and took a 3–1 lead into the eighth. He threw a pitch seemingly right down the middle to Morgan, the NL leader in walks. Morgan took it and plate ump John Kibler called it a ball, perhaps a "superstar" call endemic in most sports. On the next pitch, Morgan slugged his 21st homer. As Morgan circled the bases, Reuschel—enraged over the called ball to the selective Morgan—stormed off the mound uncharacteristically and had to be held back from Kibler before being ejected. Rookie Bruce Sutter replaced Reuschel and immediately served up a game-tying homer to George Foster. Foster homered again in the ninth as the Reds won 8–3. Foes had to almost play the perfect game against the Reds and not let their strength psych them out.

Only months later, after the Reds dispatched the Yankees four in a row in the World Series, the first cracks—man-made—in the Machine appeared. Management made a purely baseball move, dealing Perez to the Expos to open up first base for promising young hitter Dan Driessen, who had nowhere regular to play the preceding several seasons. In upcoming seasons the honchos saw what a mistake they had made in dealing away the team leader.

JOE MORGAN: I always felt if Tony Perez had stayed there, we would have won three in a row and maybe more. I know we would have won the next year if he had stayed there. But they had the philosophy that they wanted to get rid of a veteran a year too soon rather than a year too late, which cost us a chance to win. Tony was just as important as anyone else. He didn't win a Most Valuable Player Award like Pete and John and myself, and George Foster. But he was just as important as the rest of us.

Johnny Bench was the only Machine centerpiece allowed to continue the rest of his career solely with the Reds. The franchise stayed competitive, winning another NL East title in 1979 and missed out on a postseason berth in 1981 due to the fractured strike season rewarding first- and second-half division winners. The Reds actually had the NL's best overall record, but they finished second in each of the season's jerry-rigged halves. Soon they nose-dived, and they did not return to glory until newcomer Lou Piniella led them to an upset 1990 World Series crown.

But Cincy will always have its Big Red Machine, respected and feared for all time by anyone who came into contact with them.

THE LUMBER COMPANY THAT MORPHED INTO A UNIQUE "FAMILY"

Another team that percolated throughout the 1960s, but didn't put it all together until a new decade dawned, was the Pittsburgh Pirates. They could hit, and hit some more, and continue hitting until you waved a white flag. In fact, they had more hitters than they knew what to do with. The Pirates, run by GM Joe L. Brown, actually had to move hitters off their roster to make room for homegrown batsmen who performed even better. They came up there swinging and no pitch was out of reach. Try to throw one extra-low and a Bucco might go down and golf it out of the park.

Roberto Clemente, Willie Stargell, and Matty Alou were the core of the original group of hitters that fell short in the 1960s due to some shaky pitching. But by 1969 outfielder–first baseman Al Oliver, outfielder Gene Clines, catcher Manny Sanguillen, and third baseman Richie Hebner made sure the lineup had few holes. And those were closed up soon afterward by the arrivals of infielders Dave Cash and Rennie Stennett, first baseman Bob Robertson, and outfielders Richie Zisk and Dave Parker. By the early 1970s they were branded the "Lumber Company."

Like Mike Schmidt and the Reds, they loved hitting in Wrigley Field. The Pirates put a world of hurt on the Cubs, their left-handed hitters whacking around the Cubs' largely right-handed pitchers with ease. From 1971 to 1973, the Pirates had a composite 36–15 record against the Cubs.

And they didn't take guff. After they boarded their post-game bus on Addison Street following one 1972 game, your then-high-school-junior author decided to give Hebner some lip. "Hey, Richie, why don't you ever wear long sleeves?" I hollered at the off-season grave digger, who rarely wore a sweatshirt under his uniform, better to show off his muscles even in 35-degree weather. Hebner heard my voice and leaned out the bus window. "Hey, buddy with the big mouth, come here!" Hebner shot back with his New England accent. I quizzically pointed at myself. "Yeah, you, buddy," he hollered. With that, I turned tail and ran toward the L station.

The Pirates could outhit—and verbally outsmack—all comers. They simply drew from an organization that knew how to produce hitters better than anyone else at the time. The end results were World Series triumphs in 1971 and 1979, which virtually bookended the True Golden Age, and consistent contention throughout the decade.

AL OLIVER: I signed in 1964 as a free agent before the draft started. When I went to spring training 1965, there was so much talent in our farm system. Anybody, including myself, could have easily gotten lost in the shuffle. But evidently they liked something about me to stick with me. There were a lot of good first basemen and we were *loaded* with outfielders. A lot of those I can never forget were sent home. They were super ballplayers and I know they could have made other ball clubs.

They had a very strong scouting system. I look back at that when I came up in the minor leagues. Most of those guys were natural hitters. They saw the ball and hit the ball. They could run, hit, and throw. They were just natural athletes. Hitting was almost secondary to most of us, we did it naturally. The scouting was outstanding. They found me, and I was definitely almost overlooked. They weren't after me. I was on my way to Kent State on a basketball scholarship, not even thinking about baseball as a career.

The minor leagues had a lot to do with it [confidence in majors]. With that competition, we knew we *had* to perform, or else we might have gotten lost in the shuffle in that talent. I look back at those guys and still talked to several of them, and wished they could have come up with another ball club. They didn't get a break, but I knew they could play major-league baseball.

It was the confidence factor. We all had different styles of hitting. It was a good competition we had with each other. No one wanted to get lost in the shuffle. We were a first-ball, fastball-hitting team. We didn't believe in taking too many pitches. We were all very aggressive as hitters. We basically geared to fastballs, but could adjust to something slower. Today, you see so many hitters guessing and see so many taking called third strikes right down the middle of the plate, which is almost unbelievable. That's hard to do. We didn't do much guessing.

We just blended in so well with the veterans. We won in the minor leagues, and once we came to the major leaguers, our confidence level was high and blended into the confidence of the veterans.

We definitely had character. We were young players and we really didn't need a lot of guidance. The only thing we really needed was to see a veteran player like Roberto or Wilver [Stargell] hustle. They showed us and led us by example. We didn't have to be told to hustle or do certain things on and off the field. Luckily we were very fortunate to have Roberto, who carried himself on and off the field.

The Pirates did not need a crafty hitting coach to guide them. They often were their own coaches.

GENE CLINES (Pirates, Mets, Rangers, Cubs, 1970–79): It started out with the talent. The way we attacked the ball, being a very aggressive organization, it rubbed off on the guys who followed us. We pretty much were like our own teachers. I pretty much knew about Dave Cash's stroke, he knew my stroke. We coached each other. We spent a lot of time as players together. We talked baseball all the time. We talked strategy. We talked situations. We'd spend an hour, two hours, especially on the road, in the clubhouse talking baseball. Guys have so many other interests besides baseball they don't sit down and talk about baseball. A clubhouse now 45 minutes after a game is pretty much cleaned out.

When you're coming up and a Willie Stargell or Roberto Clemente speak, you listen. They show you how to play the game the right way, not to embarrass yourself. A lot of stuff he [Roberto] told me was be yourself, let your talent take over. The only pressure there is, is pressure you put on yourself. Let that talent shine and that's what we did.

The Pirates just kept the hitters coming through the farm system. Legendary scout Howie Haak, responsible for the Buccos' early success mining Latin-American talent, gave Harry Caray a sneak preview of two top talents in a 1972 radio interview.

HOWIE HAAK (Pirates scout): Our hitting is a matter of concentration and minor leagues. I don't think they can develop in the big leagues. For years, we had George Sisler with us. He was a fine hitting instructor. [Bill] Virdon came under him. We're using George Sisler's theories and they're pretty good theories. If I had to make a guess [on the next great hitter], it would be Zisk. He's the only outfielder who can come close to him [Clemente]. We got a boy coming up you can watch by the name of Parker. He can run faster than anyone else in the organization. He's a little man—6-foot-4.

The Pirates hitters actually ramped up their game against the game's best pitchers. They knew they were in for a challenge and were eager to meet it.

DAVE PARKER: We were a first-pitch, fastball-hitting ball club. We believed that to be a great breaking-ball hitter was to not miss the fastball. So we were a first-pitch, fastball-hitting club and adjusted to everything else with two strikes. That was the key to the Pirates organization. Most pitchers try to get ahead of the hitter and try to get ahead with the fastball. That's what we looked for.

We looked at it as a challenge, guys like Jenkins, Seaver, Steve Carlton, that magnitude. We looked forward to the challenge. Nolan Ryan, everyone raved about his fastball and curve. We looked forward to that. We didn't shy away from [facing] you because of your reputation.

Hall of Famer Jenkins in particular had trouble with the Pirates. He was 14–23 lifetime against the Buccos, oddly enough winning his final big-league game (number 284) in relief against the Pirates on September 21, 1983, at Wrigley Field.

FERGIE JENKINS: I survived down and away and after a while they knew this. They were out to get me from the first inning on—guys like Oliver, Matty Alou. They adjusted to me. I tried to adjust to them. I'd lose games 2–1, 1–0. They'd get me early. They seemed to know the action of my ball more so than any other team in baseball. I didn't have very good success against the Pirates.

AL OLIVER: Our left-handers did have an advantage. The key with Fergie is you had to wait because of his great control. It [slider] was coming into us as a left-handed hitter as opposed to going away, which made a great difference. Against Hall of Fame pitchers, you couldn't be overconfident. You knew you had to be right to have any kind of success against them.

Roberto Clemente and Willie Stargell were the Pirates' co-leaders. But after Clemente's tragic death in a plane crash off San Juan, Puerto Rico, on New Year's Eve 1972, Stargell became the unquestioned team elder and wise man. Soon he would earn the nickname "Pops." He may have been physically the strongest man in baseball, with seats in Three Rivers Stadium's upper deck painted to denote where his tape-measure homers had struck. But he had a gentle giant's personality.

DAVE PARKER: I always believe in players policing players. Stargell was sort of our silent leader, but verbally I was always the guy that got guys going and policed individuals when I felt they weren't putting out. Willie led a lot by example.

I learned a lot watching Willie go about his daily work. He was a universal personality. If you couldn't like Willie, you couldn't like anyone. He was just a very special personality.

Willie was an enormously strong guy. He would pick people up by the seat of their pants and pull them out of brawls. Willie just had to be there. He didn't have to physically participate. His stature meant a lot.

Frank Howard was known for hitting tremendous home runs. I remember working at Crosley Field in Cincinnati as a teenager. The sundeck was 340 feet and they had eight lanes of highway behind the fence. Only two guys I remember hitting it in the neighborhood there were Stargell and [Willie] McCovey. That left a lasting impression after working as a teenager.

GENE CLINES: Willie was such a down-to-earth guy. Willie never got down, good game, bad game. He was a guy who showed us if you have a bad game, it's not the end of the world. I never saw him pout. I only saw him get angry one time. We fed off that inner strength that he vibrated throughout that whole clubhouse, not only the Pirates, but visiting teams. Everyone loved being around Willie.

He had a quiet sense of humor and he could be a prankster, too. He never did advertise himself. He was a prankster, but always in a good way.

BERT BLYLEVEN: I thought Pops was the strongest man in the majors. In Montreal he hit a ball that quieted the crowd. They put a different color in the seat. It was such a shot. They just went silent for a second and pointed to where the ball went. He was the first one to hit a ball out of Dodger Stadium. When he made contact, you knew it was gone.

While Stargell walked the walk, Parker talked the talk. Called the "Cobra" for his 6-foot-5 frame uncoiling his bat, the former heavily recruited halfback was the most voluble Pirate of the era, like it or not.

DAVE PARKER: I was a Major League Baseball player not because people liked me, but because I could play. I didn't feel I had to apologize for being successful. I felt very strongly about that. I was basically telling the truth. People would take things out of context and put it in their own words. They weren't going to let the truth get in the way of a good story. If there was something that bothered me pertaining to the front office or on-field personnel, I'd speak up about it if I felt it wasn't right. I felt I told the truth and did not apologize for being successful.

I knew with the status quo for a black individual, you had to do it twice as good as a white individual at the time. I was just being me. The civil rights movement was right around the time I was in school. I felt, deal with me on my own merit. What I display and produce, that's all I ask [to be rated on].

The death of Clemente was followed by the mysterious implosion of control of Pirates ace Steve Blass, who was an All-Star in 1972 after recording two complete-game victories in the 1971 World Series. He won 60 games between 1969 and 1972. Almost in an instant, it was over, and Blass has never been able to explain his loss of ability.

STEVE BLASS (Pirates, 1969–74): I had won 19 games in 1972 and finished second in the Cy Young voting. I had a good spring training in '73. I was 3–3 at one point. It seemed to gradually slide away. It wasn't one incident or one particular ball game. All of a sudden I could not make the ball go where I wanted to. To this day I don't really know why. I spent the better part of two years making sure I pursued everything so that I didn't wonder later on whether I left any stone unturned. To this day I really don't know what caused it. I don't know with the modern analysis and scrutiny, and all the advances that have been made, whether at this point . . . they could figure out what happened.

I watched different tapes of when I was pitching well and when I wasn't pitching well. I tried to pitch from the back of the mound to see if that would help give a better feel for when you got up on the mound. I tried throwing a lot, tried throwing a day, tried to take a week off. It just wasn't there. I tried to throw in the bullpen a lot. I tried to throw in relief. It just never did come back.

I think I had a pretty good perspective on it. You don't want any career, whether it was baseball or business, to destroy you or bury you. As long as you can keep track of things when things are going particularly well, you won't get too far down when they go in the other direction. I didn't consider myself a superstar or any of that. When I went bad, I was able to keep a pretty level keel. Not to say there weren't some very, very long nights wondering what the heck was going on and why it was going on.

That was one of the real positives. I was never with any other organization. Through this Joe Brown was the GM and Danny Murtaugh was the manager. It was a mutual thing if either party wanted to shut it down from either direction. They were willing to go with me as long as I wanted to pursue things. We kind of decided in the spring of '75 that we pursued all the things that we could think of and it was time to shut it down. I never failed for support from the organization or from the teammates. I felt quite good about that. It was never a negative thing from an organizational standpoint. I couldn't have gotten more support from the Pirates.

I'm a fatalist. I think things happen because they're supposed to happen. I don't know why that happened. I never had a sore arm. I could have pitched till I was 40 years old. Whenever anyone has a control problem, I get the phone call. I invariably tell these people you're calling the last person you want to talk to that particular individual, because I never came out of it. Most of the guys who go into control slumps come out of it one way or another. I don't have any advice to offer them.

The peak of the Lumber Company's prowess came on an overcast Tuesday, September 16, 1975, at Wrigley Field. A day after whomping the Cubs 9–1, the Buccos outdid themselves in a 22–0 massacre, the most lopsided shutout in history to that point. Rennie Stennett tied the single-game record with seven hits out of the 24 the Pirates collected.

The Pirates had been a loose, talkative bunch since the '60s, but really shifted into high gear as the '70s drew to a close.

After yielding the NL East to the Phillies from 1976 to 1978 and starting out 1979 slowly, the Buccos gained momentum. A key midseason acquisition was two-time NL batting champion Bill Madlock, whose former team, the Cubs, allowed him to pass through waivers to the Pirates. They were a rollicking crew, backing up boasts with accomplishments. By late season they had adopted the Sister Sledge disco hit "We Are Family" as their anthem. That echoed through a World Series in which they stormed back from a 3-games-to-1 deficit against the Orioles with Stargell doing the Roberto Clemente hero's role with three homers (tallying the winning runs in Game 7), four doubles, seven RBIs, and a .400 average.

How loose were the '79 Pirates? The identity of this randy player will be protected because he has a veneer of respectability in late-middle age. We won't even name his position. But in one game at Wrigley Field, a high pop drifted into the stands. Propped up on the box-seat railing was an attractive woman's bare foot. The lady turned her head to follow the foul ball. While she looked away, this Pirate, well, sucked her big toe, then quickly retreated back onto the field before she realized what happened.

DAVE PARKER: I thought the teams from a few years earlier were colorful. I owe all that to Dock Ellis. Dock was a phenomenal leader. A lot of people looked at Dock in a negative way. Dock got a lot of points across through humor. He was more intelligent than people gave him credit for. It kind of carried over to me. I carried it to the '79 team. I was a verbal leader. Stargell was the stabilizer.

Phil Garner was a funny guy. Steve Nicoscia had a great sense of humor. Tony Bartirome, our trainer, was funny. Even Stargell. He liked to put shaving cream in people's shoes. Willie and I were locker mates. He had a great sense of humor. He'd catch a guy on the plane. [Back] then they'd let you take your cosmetic bag on the plane. A guy would be sleeping. Willie would put something on the tip of his hand and his nose. He'd wipe his face and shaving cream would be all over.

Garner was considered the clubhouse lawyer. Phil was definitely a guy who had a broad range of humor. He was a student of the game. He played for one of the best managers in the history of the game. Chuck [Tanner] put a lot of responsibility on the players to govern each other. He governed with one eye and one ear. He left players with a lot of rope to hang themselves. He actually put that in our hands. I can't see everything and hear everything. You guys got to govern yourself—that's what he meant by one eye and one ear.

BERT BLYLEVEN: The biggest thing was Chuck Tanner. He just let us play. He knew the personalities he had. The white guys would call the black guys the N-word. Dave Parker and Ed Ott were the best of friends and they would yell at each other. Phil Garner would do the same. It was a constant zoo day in and day out. It was an unbelievable atmosphere. The clubhouse just had a good time.

In the Pirates' system, for some reason, everyone got along. The hard-nosed play of Tim Foli created some interested rhubarbs in the clubhouse sometimes with his personality. The makeup and character of everyone on that ball club, everyone just got along. If we lost a ball game, there'd be music in the clubhouse. If we lost two or three, the music would be louder. Forget about it, go on with life. That was the era where everyone had a boom box. On the bus there'd almost be a war between Parker and Donnie [Robinson] who could be the loudest. You couldn't outtalk Parker, but he had the numbers to back it up. He was like a Muhammad Ali, but in a baseball uniform.

When we landed, we all jumped on one bus. Now you have two buses—a media and coaching staff bus, and a players' bus. There was more of a team concept back in the '70s.

Tanner indeed gave the players a lot of rope. He also let them know that they'd prefer the "good cop" side of his personality. They did not want to see his "tough cop" veneer.

CHUCK TANNER: I managed them. All you do is be on time and play hard. That's my rules. The reason I kept them in line was because I was the strongest in the room and I didn't take any crap. Wilver was my captain and if there was problem, Wilver would handle it. He was my leader. In the clubhouse he had a demeanor of calmness. He had the respect of the guys. If you have the respect of the other guys, it's going to be easy. But if you're just some donkey out there and you think you're going to do it, they'll tell you to go shit in your hat.

We took guys nobody wanted. I said I wanted them. They gave us [John] Milner, he doesn't want to play every day. I said I don't want to play him every day. I'll use him to pinch-hit, left field, first base, [because] Stargell's old.

Don Robinson was another confrontation we had. I watched him and he said he'll be on this team. They [Pirates management] said no, he has to go to Triple-A, he's been at Double-A. No, no, he's coming with me. If he doesn't go north, I don't go north, the hell with all of you. He ended up Pirates Rookie of the Year. After the way we used him, no one said anything. I was lucky I was able to get done what I accomplished.

Madlock was the key to our team. He tore the lineup card in front of the manager. Then he came to me after he arrived. He [asked if I was] glad to be here. I told him one thing: "If you ever tear the lineup card in front of me, I'll put your head in your hands." He said, "Oh, no, no, Chuck, I'll do anything you want me to do." I got him to say that.

I said you're batting sixth. He's oh-oh-oh-oh, OK. Then I said here's the reason why. He's a batting champ, and I'm hitting him sixth. You can steal anytime you want to unless I have a do-not-steal [sign]. This way, Garner and Ott are going to get fastballs to hit. They're not going to want to let them steal. I showed him how to get signs from the catcher. They're calling all fastballs. Garner hit .290, Ott hit .280.

Oh, shit, he [Dave Parker] was a piece of cake. He was the best player on the team. He belongs in the Hall of Fame—hit, run, field, throw, and power. He was never a problem. He could do it all. He had the best tools of any player I managed.

There were guys with dry humor. Ed Ott had dry humor. He was the toughest. Parker was the loudest. Blyleven was funny. Rooker was funny. He didn't like it because he didn't want to come out [of the game]. That's why I liked him because he didn't want to come out. Blyleven was pitching at Cincy—we had won two straight in Cincy—we have to win it to get into the World Series. He came up to me and said, "I'm not coming out today. I don't care what you do or what you say. I'm pitching and don't even come out to see me." That's good enough for me, and he went nine. I'm not going out there under any circumstances.

They were self-motivated [behind the Orioles 3 games to 1]. They know we're going to beat them. Garner talked, "Let me tell you something. We're going to go down there [Baltimore] and kick their ass." They don't realize it when they're behind. If we're down by three runs in the seventh, they were laughing. They said they don't know it, they're behind, but they're going to find out. In Philly they're kicking the shit out of us, 8–0 in the fifth inning [on August 11]. Madlock said to Ed Ott, "Hey, Chuck should rest some of the guys who have been playing every day." Ott says, "Why? This game isn't over." He hits a grand slam and we beat them like 11–10 [actual score was 14–11]. And Madlock says, "I'll never talk like that again."

Unfortunately for the inspired Pirates, they could not bottle their charisma and chemistry into another decade. The '79 run was the last World Series victory in Pittsburgh. But if it's fated to remain so, it will be remembered far beyond the 30th anniversary reunion of the "We Are Family" crew at PNC Park. They don't make colorful teams like they used to.

THE MOST UNAPPRECIATED TEAM OF THE TRUE GOLDEN AGE

Were the Yankees the winningest team of the 1960s and 1970s? Not by a long shot. The Baltimore Orioles take that title. Starting in 1960, when they were 89–65 and thus threw off the final aftereffects of their past as the woeful St. Louis Browns, the Orioles had 14 seasons of 90 or more victories through 1979. They stumbled into just two losing campaigns, in 1962 and 1967. They appeared in five World Series and won 109, 108, and 101 games in successive seasons from 1969 to 1971. They fielded an unprecedented four 20-game winners—Jim Palmer, Mike Cuellar, Dave McNally, and Pat Dobson—in 1971.

But baseball measures great teams by how many World Series victories they take home. The Birds won just two of five Fall Classics, losing in the seventh game twice to Roberto Clemente– and Willie Stargell–inspired Pirates teams, and serving as the final victim of the 1969 Mets' magic. To be sure, the Orioles won the World Series in 1966, 1970, and 1983, before the organization nose-dived from its generation-long tenure of quality.

The Orioles simply have taken a backseat in history to the bigger-market Yankees and other colorful or dominant teams like the A's or Reds. But the truth is no team was better overall, knocking out the trio of October near-misses, or possessed a better baseball organization. The team truly lacked for nothing, as Curt Gowdy said when Baltimore swept the A's out of the ALCS in 1971.

One memorable player who doubled as a human vacuum cleaner at third base witnessed the Orioles organization built from the ground up, playing until the very heart of its glory years.

BROOKS ROBINSON: I think it really started from the top down. We had terrific ownership and they let the general manager do what he had to do. We had a lot of smart guys. [GM] Harry Dalton, they had good people. They started signing guys. The reason I signed with the Orioles was mainly because of Paul Richards. I was told if you do fairly well, you had a chance to play here early in your career. I had a pretty good first year in York, Pennsylvania, in '55. I got to play the last two weeks of the season with the Orioles. They made the right decisions, that's what it's all about.

Absolutely [the Orioles did not get proper credit]. The name of the game in sports is to be the best. [Otherwise] people tend to rate you a little lower than you should be. We had three years where we won 100-plus games. That's only been done once or twice in the game. But going back to the '60s, we had about a 20-year stretch where we won more games than anyone in baseball. Frank [Robinson] came over and made us real good.

I look at what the A's accomplished when they won three straight championships. You still have to do it. Anything can happen when you have to win three out of five or four out of seven. We just weren't able to do it. We had a terrific team, but you never get the credit you should if you don't win.

After Robinson the Orioles' key personality was a crusty manager who joined him and several other Baltimore luminaries in the Hall of Fame.

EARL WEAVER: It was a good front office. Harry Dalton and then Frank Cashen. Then Hank Peters. They hired good scouts. They hired good minor-league managers. And they stayed within the organization developing their own players.

We had a great team. We won 109, 108, and 101 three years in a row. That signifies a great team, not [winning] four out of seven. We didn't win the seventh game of the World Series twice. That's very disappointing. In those games just give credit to the opposition. All of my teams are my favorites, because those are the guys I selected to be on my 25-man roster. Each and every one of them are there to help you win a ball game. Certainly, when [we got] to the World Series and won it in 1970, [that] has got to be my favorite team. All five of our teams that got to the World Series had good ballplayers on them.

Frank [Robinson] led by the way he played baseball. He was pretty good at that. We never had a captain, but Frank did step in once in a while and straighten a player out.

New arrivals via trades, such as Don Buford, left fielder on the 1969–71 World Series teams, quickly adapted to the Orioles way and found their games uplifted. They, too, believe the Orioles were short-changed in the esteem of the baseball public.

DON BUFORD (Orioles, 1969–72): It's kind of a shame that recognition is not bestowed on that Orioles organization. Look at the Hall of Famers on that team. The whole team played in All-Star games. Four 20-game winners in one year. I don't think you'll see [one] 20-game winner on any one ball club because the pitchers don't stay out there that long.

We lost to the Amazing Mets [in 1969], but we wanted to prove we were the best team in baseball. We came back to win the World Series in 1970. That showed what kind of players and what kind of attitude the club had. [Roberto] Clemente had such a tremendous series [in 1971], he literally kind of beat us by himself with the plays he made and the hitting he had in that series.

The camaraderie was great, from '69, all those years, it was outstanding. We had a kangaroo court with Frank Robinson as the judge. After every game we were having a kangaroo court. We'd go over little things and funny things that happened. Signing autographs in the stands to young ladies was an automatic fine. Anything the players brought up was voted on. All the players voted. If you appealed the case and lost, the fine was doubled. Nobody was excluded. Our manager wasn't excluded, our coaches weren't excluded. Later on we got the media into it a little bit.

It was fortunate Paul [center fielder Blair] could cover a lot of ground, so I could extend my ability toward the [left-field] foul line. We kind of had a gauge where I knew how much distance he could cover in left-center field to his maximum. I knew what my maximum was to get to that same gap. I just made an adjustment playing the opposite way. Naturally, if Paul called for it, it was his. We never ran into each other and nor did Frank, or [Merv] Rettenmund. He was the center fielder in charge. It worked tremendously well. The Orioles never did consistently pack Memorial Stadium and were slightly embarrassed with empty seats in some '70s postseason games. But those fans in attendance were loyal and will never forget their heroes in Orioles orange and white in their ballpark.

Louis R. "Sweet Lou" Carlozo, a former *Chicago Tribune* staff writer for 16 years, is now an editor for AOL, an author, and a studio musician. He still dreams of filling Brooks Robinson's shoes, if only for half an inning. A lot of those dreams started during childhood visits to Memorial Stadium in Baltimore.

"SWEET LOU" CARLOZO (Orioles fan, 1969–79): As a red-blooded Baltimore youth, I held a much different view of Memorial Stadium than my fellow Orioles fans in grade school. As a football coach at Calvert Hall College prep, my dad led his team against Loyola High School in an annual Thanksgiving classic played at Memorial Stadium. Standing on the sidelines with Dad—on the actual grass!—made this 7-year-old boy, in 1970, dream of someday joining my grade-school hero, Brooks Robinson, on the Orioles. I believe I once stuffed some Memorial Stadium grass in my pocket. Damn. I wish I still had it.

The 1970s saw the unfortunate ascendancy of plastic, disposable, butt-ugly Astroturf ballparks—Three Rivers in Pittsburgh, Busch Stadium in St. Louis, and Veteran's Stadium in Philly—all as interchangeable as Orwellian cubicles. Yet Memorial Stadium harkened to a more genteel 1950s era, home to Orioles teams that boasted powerhouse talent. Who could forget Jim Palmer, Dave McNally, Pat Dobson, and Mike Cuellar—the four 20-game-winning pitchers of 1971? No ball club has duplicated that feat since. Manager Earl Weaver, who truly deserves his present spot in the Hall of Fame? The great slugger [and later manager] Frank Robinson? And of course, Brooks Robinson, one of the classiest men to ever play the game, who gave the art of diving for impossible catches at third base a gravity-defying air you might well compare to Willie Mays at his basket-catching best.

The stadium itself had a laid-back air that befit Baltimore and its loyal fans. I can never forget reading game programs as a kid and realizing that most of my hard-charging O's heroes actually held down day jobs in the off-season, from selling insurance to landscaping!

Memorial Stadium, redolent with the grilled smell of Esskay Franks—"Taste the difference quallllllllity makes!!!"—a simple, utilitarian brick-and-concrete structure that framed the Orioles the way a fabulous frame surrounds a Da Vinci. While there was nothing sexy about the park per se, you must understand that Baltimoreans love their traditions. When they moved into Camden Yards, the O's brought the foul poles with them from Memorial Stadium. Not "reproduced" facades as at the new Yankee Stadium, but the real deal—the *actual poles.* Baltimoreans notice those sorts of things and hold them dear. I know I do.

It is a shame that the new park, Camden Yards, has hosted miserable Orioles teams in the last few decades. This proves that any ballpark, no matter how sexy it looks on national TV, takes second fiddle to the team that inhabits it. I love Camden Yards and have been to many games there. Yet Memorial Stadium holds a more special place. In baseball the teams and performances that take place at a park imbue it with *Field of Dreams* fairy dust. I think Camden Yards and mostly I visualize Oriole teams stinking up the joint. I know: Cal Ripken Jr. and all that. But I think of Memorial Stadium and can't help [thinking] of six World Series appearances by the O's from 1966 to 1983, three of them victorious. Two of the losing ones, against the Pittsburgh Pirates in 1971 and 1979, made me a Pirate Hater for Life.

But that last crown, in 1983 against the Philadelphia Phillies, gave the Old Gray Lady on 33rd Street one last chance to taste the champagne before the stadium closed in 1997, and the wrecking ball came in 2001. What a bittersweet gift, considering crazy Baltimore Colts owner Robert Irsay moved the Colts out of town in 1983 to Indianapolis. People in Baltimore still talk about that sneaky move, in the middle of the night no less, with disdain, a Baltimore Ravens Super Bowl win aside.

Memorial Stadium, wherefore *your* memorial? Ah . . . but the *memories!*

A FORWARD-THINKING TEAM DIPS ITS TOE IN WINNING WATERS

Another underrated team of the True Golden Age was the Kansas City Royals. Only a half-decade after their inception as an expansion team in 1969, the Royals began to stir as a contender. By 1976 they were battling the Yankees in the ALCS, losing three years in a row with Whitey Herzog showing he was a legitimate winning manager. The Royals would not make a World Series till 1980 nor win one till 1985, against the Cardinals.

But the Royals set a high standard in the era. They set up baseball's first training academy early on to groom young prospects. They emphasized pitching, speed, and defense. And they were propelled forward by a true natural hitter, George Brett, who at third base helped anchor a top-flight infield that also included All-Star second baseman Frank White.

FRANK WHITE (Royals, 1973–79): That was a good time for our organization. We had not only myself and U. L. Washington from the baseball academy, which was a revolutionary idea of the late Ewing Kauffman, but we also had a great minor-league scouting system that developed George Brett, Dennis Leonard, Al Cowens, Jamie Quirk, and Willie Wilson. The trades we made early with Amos Otis, Cookie Rojas, and John Mayberry helped.

The pitching of Steve Busby really helped us get our feet on the ground and really helped us take off in '77. We grew up a lot in '76 and lost a tough game to the Yankees [on Chris Chambliss's walk-off homer] in the last game of the playoffs. After that we grew up as a unit and went on to win a few more division championships, play in a couple of World Series, and win one. It was a lot of fun. When free agency started in 1976, all the young players signed long-term contracts and gave us a chance to stay together and grow together.

The thing that helped us a lot back in those days was we were one of the few turf fields in the American League. We drafted our players mainly based on speed. Our players could do a little bit of everything—they had speed, [could] play defense, run, steal bases, hit a few home runs. It was a great combination of athletes. Our biggest weapon early in our existence was the Astroturf and our ability to play it, where the other teams didn't really have the speed to play it and changed their format a little bit.

Designated hitter Hal McRae may have missed out on a couple of World Series rings after his trade from the Reds. But the future Royals manager and Cardinals hitting coach did not miss out on the winning atmosphere and camaraderie as Kansas City was established as a consistent franchise.

HAL McRAE: I think they did [get credit]. We had a good club and a strong farm system that produced players. We had veteran players who held their positions on the club for a long time, which gave the farm system time to develop. We were strong defensively. We were strong pitching-wise. We had a lot of speed. I think the organization got a lot of credit in that period. The organization didn't sign a lot of free agents so we got players through the farm system and trades. The Yankees beat us, but the Yankees were spending tons of money, adding players each year.

It wasn't really frustrating. I remembered what kind of club we had our first couple of years. We had a second-division club that developed into a winning club. We were in the playoffs 6 out of 10 years once we started winning. We wanted to get past the Yankees and naturally go to the World Series. I wouldn't call it frustrating because it was a lot of fun. Each time we played the Yankees, we had a chance to win that series. We did win in 1980. It was the most fun I had playing baseball, those playoffs against the Yankees.

Brett was one of the best I've seen. The guy I was with in St. Louis [Albert Pujols] for five years is one of the best also. Tony Perez is one of the best also. George might be the best late-inning player I've seen. You never knew the guy was left-handed, watching his swing.

The period proved a True Golden Age for multiple franchises striving for excellence year after year. That is not likely to be repeated anytime soon.

10

Collapses, Should-Have-Beens, and Wannabes

The Boston Red Sox and Chicago Cubs share more than just his-torical bandbox ballparks that have been nursed toward their 100th birthdays in the 2010s. And a regrettable past of conser-vative attitudes toward African-American players. And a phony connection with curses that were embellishments of a book title or the outgrowth of a barkeep's publicity stunts.

The "Beantown Dudes" and "Little Blue Bicycle," nicknames bestowed on them in baseball's True Golden Age by whimsical media types, infected their fans with mass neurosis in the 1970s through a shattering series of collapses that ruined promising seasons. One massive collapse per decade would haunt most fans, but Red Sox and Cubs rooters endured them repeatedly. The only consolation is the Red Sox made the World Series in 1975 and came away with a moral victory thanks to Carlton Fisk's dramatic homer in Game 6. At the time of this writing, the Cubs have not even been to a Fall Classic since 1945. Surely, Boston fans would not trade their team's checkered past for that of the Cubs.

Chicago's most celebrated collapse, of course, was the 1969 pratfall at season's end, an 84–52 first-place team finishing 92–70 in second while the Miracle Mets zoomed past them with a 37–9 dash to end up 100–62. But the naked truth was the Mets would have won anyway with that kind of record; the Cubs would have had to play their hottest baseball in September to stay ahead.

Much more spectacular collapses that wrecked even better Cubs opportunities for a National League East title and possible

World Series berth began in 1970. Sporting a 35–25 record and 4½-game lead on June 20, the Cubs then amazingly lost 12 in a row and 15 out of 17 to fall five games back by July 5. They were never able to get a full head of steam going the rest of the season. The Cubs finished 84–78, five games behind the Pirates, despite outscoring opponents 806–679. Their horrific bullpen coughed up one-run losses and their lack of speed made it tough to manufacture runs in tight games.

In 1973 the Cubs pulled off a real doozy of a downturn. Cruising along with a 50–35 mark, they simply wilted in the summer heat, stopped hitting altogether, and crashed (including an 11-game losing streak) to 56–64 in fourth place and 5½ games out on August 16. The magic-touch Mets, under .500 in late August, had another illogical finish at 22–9 to win the NL East with a record-low 82–79 record. The Cubs, who finished 77–84, could have played 10 under .500 from their season high point and still won the division.

In 1975 the Cubs, sporting a promising young lineup, started out 20–10, 3½ games in front, on May 15 and were still 28–21 on June 5. But they swooned in June, falling under .500 by June 20 and diving to 39–48, in fifth place, 14 games out by July 9. They finished 75–87. And in 1979 the Cubs were at a season high point of 67–54, four games out, in third, on August 20. But then they followed the '73 script by not hitting—scoring more than four runs in only five more games—and finished 80–82 in fifth, 18 games out.

The all-time pratfall took place in 1977. The NL's surprise team, the Cubs had a torrid May and June to zoom to 47–22, 8½ games in front, on June 28. "You can kiss the .500 mark goodbye," proclaimed Cubs radio announcer Lou Boudreau. But then a steady decline ensued, the Cubs finally falling out of first on August 7 while sporting a 63–45 mark. They were a still-respectable 76–66 (but 13 games back) on September 11. To defy the odds and fall to .500 (81–81), the Cubs had to lose their last five in a row—which they did.

The Red Sox may not have had such a roller coaster of crests and dips as the Cubs. But they had their share of bad spells at the wrong time with a better talent base and front office than the Cubs. Much more than the Chicagoans, the Red Sox had chances in the final week to finish first. They failed, except for 1975, in duplicating the magical "Impossible Dream" 1967 season that put the franchise back on the map and among the elite teams in baseball.

The '70s Red Sox tone was set in 1972, shortened by a week due to the first-ever players' strike at the season's start. With four games to go on September 30, the Red Sox held a 1½-game lead over the Billy Martin–managed Tigers with a 84–67 record. But then they lost three games in a row—one to the Orioles, then two more to the Tigers in Detroit. Boston won its final game against Detroit, but it was too late. They finished half a game out. Due to the Tigers having played one more game in the uneven schedule forced by the strike, the Red Sox were stuck with the inequity. Commissioner Bowie Kuhn had ruled games would not be made up to balance out the schedule evenly.

An underrated collapse took place in 1974. Despite having a grossly underpowered team for Fenway Park, the Red Sox had a 70–54 record and seven-game lead in the AL East on August 23. But an eight-game losing streak helped knock them out of first by September 5. The Red Sox's 11–18 September was no match for the Orioles' 23–6 onslaught, and they finished 84–78, seven games out.

Lost amid the daily *Bronx Is Burning* melodrama of Reggie Jackson vs. George Steinbrenner vs. Billy Martin, the 1977 Red Sox actually had a 71–45 record and a 3½-game lead on the Yankees by August 18. Ah, another losing streak, this time seven games, which dropped Boston out of the lead for good. They could not get closer than three games down the stretch—until it was too late—and settled for a very nice, but too-soon-for-the-wild card, 97–64 record just behind the Bombers.

So 1978 ends up as the all-time Red Sox red herring, ranking with the Bill Buckner–Bob Stanley faux pas in Game 6 of the 1986 World Series. Boston was 36–16 on June 3, had a season-high 10-game lead on July 8, and topped out at 37 over .500 at 84–47, with a seven-game lead, on August 30. But like clockwork, the Red Sox folded spectacularly, their hitting and pitching both in the tank in a 3–14 downturn as the Yankees—14 games behind, in fourth (the Brewers and Orioles were second and third), on July 18—surged into the AL East lead. Included was the infamous "Boston Massacre," a four-game sweep by the Yankees at Fenway from September 7 to 10 by scores of 15–3, 13–2, 7–0, and 7–4. With two weeks to go on September 16, the Red Sox were 3½ games out and seemingly toast.

Uncharacteristically, they fought back, winning 12 of their last 14, including their final eight in a row, to force a tie with the Yankees at 99–63. But then came the "Bucky Dent Game" playoff, and everyone knows about Dent's three-run homer to win the game.

Other teams had their own aspirations and problems throughout the 1970s. But no two had such a long, strange, and downbeat journey as the Red Sox and Cubs.

GREAT YOUNG PLAYERS IN AN OLD FENWAY

Little could Red Sox fans appreciate what was unfolding in front of them, with all the other soap operas—players and management—always present at Fenway Park. Starting in 1969, they had a homegrown talent flow filtering its way to Boston that would have been the envy of every other franchise.

First there was New Englander Carlton Fisk, toe-dipping in the majors as early as 1969, but established as a star behind the plate by 1972. At almost the same time was rifled-armed right fielder Dwight Evans. By 1974 all-around Rick Burleson held forth at shortstop. They were known by their nicknames— Pudge, Dewey, and Rooster. At the same time, the Red Sox also developed two other good young left-handed hitters: Ben Oglivie and Cecil Cooper. But they would go on to have their best years elsewhere.

Then Boston hit the jackpot. The best pair of rookies of the era rounded out the outfield beside Evans in 1975—left fielder Jim Rice and center fielder Fred Lynn. The Red Sox had produced two 30-homer, 100-RBI types out of their farm system in the same year. In contrast the Cubs through 2010 had not developed a 30-homer, 100-RBI type who produced those numbers for the parent club since Billy Williams in 1959–60. The Red Sox should have been in excellent shape for a decade to come.

JIM RICE (Red Sox, 1974–79): I don't go back and say how special it was. I think you had two rookies who came up, enjoyed playing the game, and went out to have a hell of a year. You may see that again. But as far as going back to the '75 series, I broke my hand a week and a half to go in Detroit. I look at it as a foundation. I came up and Freddie came up, and we were able to blend in with the ball club we had, and to go on to have pretty good careers. We just took the game as it was—two kids coming up and having fun. By having some veterans on the team, they helped you along and it made it a little easier for Freddie and me.

FRED LYNN: Frank Malzone scouted me. Someone came up to me and handed me a scouting report when I was in high school, signed by Frank. It said I could do this and do that. Said I'd accepted a scholarship to play football at Southern Cal—and it will cost a lot of money to sign him. I loved that part of it. The Dodgers and Orioles scouted me, I didn't see Frank there [El Monte, California]. Those two teams wanted to draft me in the first round, but didn't know whether I'd be an outfielder or a pitcher. When they heard I was going to USC to play football, they knew the ante was going up. I was going to go to school.

The Yankees drafted me in the second round anyway, even though we told everyone I was going to school. I played for a semipro team at 16 called the Pasadena Yankees. We had the old hand-me-down Yankees uniforms—I wore Moose Skowron's "uni." No one knew this story till I told it a few years ago. I played baseball at USC and never saw a Red Sox scout. When they drafted me, I was stunned. They were invisible. [George] Steinbrenner ended up trying to get me in a deal for [Dave] Winfield, when he was having trouble with him, when I was with the Orioles.

We already played together as a unit and were comfortable with each other. There was a real camaraderie with the core of young players on that team. It was very, very easy to play. It was predicated on the ballpark. They didn't have too many homegrown lefties. It's a hitters' park. You're going to outhit people and they did the best they could with pitchers.

The Red Sox kids were baptized by fire. They had a blood rivalry with the Yankees going back to Babe Ruth's sale from Boston to New York. Tensions were always bubbling near the surface. And when they boiled over, a volcano blew. The roughest fight might have been on May 20, 1976, at Yankee Stadium. Lou Piniella barreled home trying to score a run in the bottom of the sixth. He crashed into Fisk at the plate, the two combatants entangled in a maze of legs and spikes and a chest protector. In seconds both rosters brawled. Yankees outfielder Mickey Rivers threw sucker punches. Red Sox starter Bill Lee came out of the scrum holding a limp left arm as the Bronx crowd yelped its blood lust at the sight of the injured Spaceman. He had a shoulder injury and was out for two months.

RICK BURLESON: The Yankees had so much talent on the field. You had to respect the careers and talent they put on the field every day. In those days it was a heated rivalry.

We didn't like them and they didn't like us. We didn't have friends on the other team. There wasn't a lot of fraternization in those days. That's one of the ways the game has changed. The old-school guys are trying to get back to where it was, but it goes on right in front of your eyes. They play winter ball against each other so there are so many ways to be friendly.

It had as much to do with the fans as the players, and it spilled over to the players. I don't think there were many people wearing Red Sox garb in Yankee Stadium and vice versa. If you were going to wear a Yankee hat into Fenway, you were going to take some abuse. Once it got started, it kind of spiraled. There was a lot of tension during games. Anything could set it off.

In those days you didn't have to slide into second and reach back and touch the base. You could go after the middle infielder as far as you wanted to get him. I remember one day Reggie [Jackson] came way out after me. Obviously I'm going to protect myself with my arm angle. I threw the ball into the dugout. I was going to defend myself more than I was concerned with getting the out. Now they call an automatic double play. I was clean, but if I was hit by a pitch, I would have gone down there with a little more gumph.

The two presses in New York and Boston drove the players crazy. They put a lot of unneeded pressure on the players. One time there was a New York newspaper strike, and the Yankees relaxed. In Boston the minute you slipped, the talk shows, the press, everything became negative. In those two cities there was a lot of negative press when things didn't go good. I learned more of that getting traded in December 1980 and being traded to the Angels. There might have been two beat writers covering the club. There weren't 25 guys covering the Red Sox and 50 covering the Yankees. The fans would come in the third and leave in the seventh in the middle of a no-hitter. It was just something else you could do in the summertime, going to an Angels game—they were not living and dying on every pitch. They were not the East Coast fans I had come to know. It was hard for me to understand why they weren't into it like in New York and Boston.

If duking it out with the Yankees wasn't enough, the Red Sox had to fight themselves. There was enough internal strife to keep a gossip columnist busy. A high point was when Don Zimmer managed from 1976 to 1980. With his Popeye physique and explosive temper, Zimmer was great copy. An old infielder, he also did not relate well to pitchers, and an informal dissenting group called the "Buffalo Head Gang" formed, led by a future Hall of Famer.

FERGIE JENKINS: I had this December 1976 issue of *Playboy.* A beautiful Haitian girl was the centerfold, and I put it above my locker. When I'd leave for the field, I'd always take a peek at her. We had visitors come in the locker room while we were on the road, so I put a towel over it. I came back, it was gone. A clubhouse guy said Zimmer ripped it down.

So in midsummer there was a cartoon insert in the *Boston Globe* with Zimmer as Popeye, having a big head but a toothpick body and arms. I put it where the centerfold was. That's why we called ourselves the Buffalo Head Gang—myself, Rick Wise, Bill Lee, Bernie Carbo, and Jim Willoughby. We were in the back of the clubhouse. The four pitchers among us all got demoted to the bullpen at certain times in '77. Zimmer stopped pitching Willoughby. It got to the point where we were the rejects on the ball club.

I got traded back to Texas after that season. First game back in Fenway, I had the clubbie buy a dozen roses, and

I jumped in the dugout and presented Zimmer the roses. I said, "Let's bury the hatchet." I shut out the Red Sox that game. So when he came to visit us in Texas, he gave me one or two roses and said let's bury the hatchet. A lot of it was miscommunication. I don't think he handled pitchers correctly.

RICK WISE: Those are my buddies, and we were all in Zimmer's doghouse at one point. It was very tough to please Don Zimmer. He had a great baseball mind, but he was bullheaded. Always his way. He had views and we had views—they just differed. He was a completely different guy when he was a third-base coach than as a manager. An outstanding third-base coach and baseball man. But the pressures of being a manager are completely different than being a third-base coach, first-base coach, and pitching coach.

He wanted "Pudge" and me to shave our beards. I always started growing a beard in September.

Covering the Red Sox for the Associated Press while attending nearby Emerson College was broadcaster Tom Shaer, who had an up-close-and-personal view of Zimmer. Much of the time it was unpleasant.

TOM SHAER (AP reporter, Boston, 1977–79): The damage done to the Red Sox fan, especially in '78—four of seven years had brutal collapses, then '76 when the team finished four over .500, which was hugely disappointing—it did cause people a lot of negativity. They complained about *everything.* The Red Sox had a manager who was incompetent. The fans knew it and were all over Zimmer. He was mentally, intellectually, and emotionally ill-equipped to manage a major-league team in a big market in a pennant race. If he wanted to manage the Texas Rangers, where nobody cares about baseball, or the San Diego Padres, God bless him. The Cubs fans were a little softer than they are now. He got lucky and won a division with Dallas Green's players [in 1989].

Carl Yastrzemski did not respect Zimmer, but he never said it. Yaz and Zimmer were smart. Zimmer wasn't going to take on an icon in Yaz, and Yaz wasn't going to be accused of undermining the manager, which he had been accused of doing several times early in his career. He did not respect Don Zimmer as a manager. He said as much on October 1, 1983, if Ralph Houk had been the Red Sox manager, they would have won a lot more pennants. He was talking about Eddie Kasko and Don Zimmer.

Through all the tumult was one constant: Fenway Park. A much more basic version, without the bells and whistles the John Henry ownership added in the 2000s, was present in the True Golden Age of baseball. Shaer's suburban Chicago home is a mini–Red Sox museum, so he has no problem recalling the in's and out's of the cramped ballpark near Kenmore Square.

TOM SHAER: I distinctly recall my first game at Fenway in 1969. You walk up the ramp and everything is green and in sharp focus. Just gorgeous. My family could not afford color TV and I had seen Fenway only in black and white. This was quite wonderful, seeing all the colors, including the Green Monster, the field, etc.

Fans and management did not want to replace Fenway after 1967. When the Red Sox went to Busch Stadium for the 1967 World Series, a number of the players said it would be great if we had a nice new ballpark like this. Tom Yawkey had wanted a new ballpark through 1967. He was always complaining about the lack of parking. It wasn't until a year or two after [the '67 pennant], when they were drawing big crowds and the new stadiums turned out to be not what they were cracked up to be, Fenway started to be more appreciated.

I attended hundreds of games in the '70s. I attended every home game from 1977 to 1979. In 1976 I went to 34 games. The experience was delightful. It was always cramped, but we didn't seem to complain about it. It's still cramped. The width of the seats and the depths of the aisles the seats are in, your knees are hitting the seats in front of you for half the ballpark. Parking was always a problem. Getting to and from your seat when they had a big crowd was always a problem. It was not dirty—it was clean. It was not some grimy old dump. Fenway Park was a jewel.

You had to know when you were buying seats in the middle of the row [grandstands behind poles] so you'd be looking out between the pillars. Every section had 8 or 10 seats in it that were directly obstructed by poles.

You had to get your seats in advance after 1967. They had a few slips in attendance where you could walk up and get a decent seat, but not that often. The '75 World Series kind of rekindled the franchise—they had a few disappointing years just before then. The second half of the decade, you could not get seats. From 1970 through August 27, 1975, you had to get tickets in advance, but for certain games you could always get a ticket, like in the right-field corner. August 27, 1975, was a weekday afternoon game. I figured I'd just drive there and get a ticket. The place was sold out and had just SRO seats. That's when people started finally believing in the '75 Red Sox.

Bleachers were $1 in the late 1960s and early 1970s. They went up to $1.50 in the mid-'70s and in 1977 went to $2. They had signed Bill Campbell as the first big-money free agent—he got $1 million for five years. Opening Day 1977 there was a sign in the bleachers that said, "Sell Bill Campbell. Bring Back $1.50 Bleachers." Bill ended up meeting the guy with the sign and they became friends.

Bleacher lines were very long. The bleacher fans were tougher [than Wrigley Field]. The fans in Boston were a little more vicious than the fans in Chicago. The fans have a sharper edge. The bleacher bums weren't as organized as they were in Wrigley Field. But they were always very, very abusive toward the visiting players. In center field the front row was 420 feet away—they couldn't hear you. Right field was brutal. They'd throw stuff.

The food was always very average. Back in the day, there were two things you absolutely had to have at Fenway. Hood Ice Cream made the Sports Sundae Bar—vanilla ice cream with a thick fudge strip in the middle, covered with chocolate coating. Absolutely fantastic. They started selling those things in 1973 or 1974. You absolutely had to get the popcorn—fantastic. The lousiest stuff was the pizza—like cardboard. The hot dogs were always very average, but they had the New England Hot Dog Bun—a square piece of bread with a slit in the top. Picture a rectangle—the hot dog goes into the top of the roll.

When they put the message board in 1976, people reacted very well to it. Bill Lee ripped it and called it a "despicable ostentation." It was a nice addition to Fenway. The first replay shown on it was Jim Rice sliding into home plate against Cleveland on Opening Day 1976. It was not a close play and they wouldn't show close plays. That was a nice addition. As the decade closed, they converted some of the lower-priced seats, put in some new red plastic seats, and raised the price significantly. A lot of people complained about that.

After the big fight in May 1976, the first time the Yankees came back to Fenway, there were some fans distributing leaflets for a Monday night game: Mr. Yawkey's always been good to the fans, let's be good to Mr. Yawkey, let's not have any obscenities or any fighting. They started it at 8:30 for the ABC Monday night game and people had plenty of time to get liquored up. Fortunately, there were no incidents.

The 1970s were indeed a huge window for the Red Sox in which they did not take advantage to jump through more than once. One problem may have been the AL East—perhaps the toughest division in history. Three teams—the Yankees, Red Sox, and Orioles—won at least 97 games in 1977. The Brewers made it a quartet of big winners as four teams won between 90 and 99 games in 1978. In 1979 the Orioles won 102, the Brewers 95, the Red Sox 91, and the Yankees 89. Still, Red Sox players figure they should have won more.

FRED LYNN: No question. We had the best talent on the field. We might not have had it on the mound. That's where we lost the division championships. We averaged like 95 wins in four, five years that I was there. That's a lot of wins without winning anything. We never had that closer. We never had an [extra] starter. We had to just club our way to the top. You can only do that for so long, even with a great offensive club.

Really, the turning point was when Bowie Kuhn negated the sale of players for our ball club. We would have had Rollie Fingers and Joe Rudi. Rollie in his prime in '76. Vida Blue to the Yankees. He would have helped them, but not as much as Rollie would have helped us. [They were] the best interests in baseball. We had a commissioner then. The decision didn't go our way. If it would have, we would have been in the [World] Series, no question.

One famous story is the Red Sox's refusal to sign Tommy John as a free agent in 1978—to at least keep him away from the Yankees. In New York John won 43 games in his first two seasons.

TOM SHAER: After a game at Fenway when John beat the Red Sox, Yogi Berra was up in the pressroom—when uniformed people would go up there after the game and mix with others. Yogi asked Haywood Sullivan, "Why didn't you sign Tommy John?" Sully said our medical people said our reports said he wasn't worth signing. And Yogi said, "Gee, I'm glad we didn't see those reports," which was a great line.

The Boston contending window indeed closed after 1980, not reopening till 1986 and a fateful World Series. The ownership and baseball management was in flux while that homegrown nucleus, with the exception of Rice, left. In a game of failure, the Boston story was in lockstep. Eventually there was success, as the law of averages applied in a way it would not 800 miles west in Chicago.

AN OWNER WHO PAID HIS WAY IN, BUT DIDN'T LEARN ANYTHING

In a mid-1970s weekend wee hour at the *Chicago Tribune*, a wayward city-side copy editor complained about the Cubs' latest woes.

Enough, already. "If you don't like it, why don't you have the *Tribune* buy 'em?" your opinionated author, then a college-age copy clerk, snapped back. The walls must have had ears. The newspaper's parent company did buy the Cubs five years later.

Gum magnate Phil Wrigley, wealthy enough to own five big-league teams, held on to the Cubs literally as a family heirloom and refused to sell for 45 years until his death in 1977.

Wrigley had promised his father, William Wrigley Jr., on the old man's deathbed that he would keep the beloved team and Wrigley Field in the family as long as he financially was able to maintain ownership. The younger Wrigley knew nothing about baseball, had no passion for the game, and did little networking to meet good people to hire. The Cubs developed into an inbred, incompetent operation, made worse by Wrigley's brainstorm meddling that produced a team without a manager—the comical "College of Coaches" of 1961–62—along with an Air Force colonel named team athletic director and the game's most consistently unproductive farm system.

The Cubs desperately needed to be sold to a legitimate, passionate baseball fan. McDonald's impresario Ray Kroc, a Cubs fanatic who settled for the Padres to quench his thirst for baseball ownership, led a long line of spurned suitors, asking Wrigley to sell in 1972. By the testimony of Randy Jones, the Padres' 1976 Cy Young Award winner, the Cubs lost more than people realized when Chicagoan Kroc was unable to make the deal.

RANDY JONES (Padres, 1973–79): The work ethic that made McDonald's so good, Kroc brought with him. He brought a passion for the game. Not all of his decisions may have been right, but his heart was in the right place. The first time we drew 1 million was when Kroc bought the ball club. He got his personality involved. He turned baseball around in San Diego. In 1975 he made an offer—we hadn't won a game on Sundays the whole year—that the first win on Sunday, anybody who had a ticket stub would get a free Big Mac at McDonald's in San Diego. We had 36,000 on a Sunday, and I was pitching. I beat the Phillies 4-0 and you thought we had won the World Series the way those fans acted.

He was crazy like a fox. It would have been phenomenal. It definitely would have been a change in the history of the Chicago Cubs. It would have been like night and day with what Ray Kroc could have done if he had gotten that team. His passion for the game and the Cubs—oh!— that would have been off the wall. That would have been wonderful. Their loss was definitely our gain in San Diego with Ray Kroc as owner. He finally started that turnaround.

Bill Veeck, whose baseball career started with the Cubs in the early 1930s, wanted to buy them. So did Bears owner George Halas. Wrigley even was visited at his Lake Geneva, Wisconsin, mansion in 1964 by a rabid 19-year-old Chicago north suburban fan named Jim Anixter, who told the owner he wanted to buy the Cubs. Anixter tried again as a young businessman in 1981, was told the team was not for sale, and watched in amazement as Tribune Co. completed the purchase a couple of weeks later.

Other than a 1932 promise, why would Wrigley keep hanging on to a team in which he had marginal interest? After all, the owner was renowned for never showing up at the ballpark that bore his name. That gave the impression he didn't care. But maybe he witnessed more in person than he let on. And if the stories were indeed true, how could Phil Wrigley not have learned something about baseball—as any fan does—through osmosis when he watched games live?

The first individual to discover the owner's secret life was rookie outfielder Pete LaCock. The son of *Hollywood Squares* host Peter Marshall, LaCock strolled down Michigan Avenue one September afternoon in 1972, soon after he was called up for the first time. Spotting the gleaming white gothic-towered Wrigley Building, the free-spirited LaCock decided on a whim to walk in and ask to see his boss.

PETE LACOCK (Cubs, Royals, 1972–79): I walked into his office. I told him I was Pete LaCock, one the new players in 1972. A minute later the secretary takes me into his office. I talked to Mr. Wrigley for an hour and a half. He knew about my dad, Aunt Joanie [actress Joanne Dru], and [singer] Dick Haymes. We sat there and talked, and I asked him why he doesn't come out to the ballpark. He said writers gave him so much grief.

And then Mr. Wrigley leaned over and lowered his voice, almost in a whisper like he wanted to tell me a secret. He said he got out, dressed pretty casually, paid $1, and sat in the left-field bleachers. He loved to sit in the left-field bleachers. He said he did it often. It cracked me up.

Wrigley apparently moved around the ballpark. Around 1970, Cubs pitcher Bill Hands stood on the field and a companion pointed to the elusive owner up in the $1.75 seats.

BILL HANDS: I was told he did [attend games] on numerous occasions. On one occasion he was pointed out to me. I had met him once in my life, at Leo's [Durocher] wedding. The only other time I laid eyes on him, he was sitting behind home plate, but way up in the back, in the grandstands. He didn't sit in a box or anything. He probably dressed up as a senior citizen. I wouldn't have known it was him if he wasn't pointed out to me. I'm sure of it [wanting to avoid being mobbed by media people]. That was his own doing. I'm sure he was there many times.

Wrigley Field park operations director Salty Saltwell was puzzled by how the supposedly absent Wrigley would question him over the phone about aspects of the ballpark that could only be gleaned from personal observation. Then Saltwell pretty much confirmed the clandestine Wrigley visits when the owner's chauffeur told him he dropped him off 2 blocks from the ballpark—all the better to allow Wrigley to blend in with the crowd going to the game. Meanwhile, Wrigley paid $9,000 for an all-expenses-paid trip for 50 left-field Bleacher Bums to attend an August 29–31, 1969, weekend series in Atlanta. Why would he pop for such coin unless he sat among the yellow hard-hatted, pot-smoking, beer-swilling, guerilla-theater-in-the-ballpark gang?

Wrigley was sound asleep when David Condon wandered into the *Tribune* city room in the early morning hours. No doubt extending his waking hours after the bars emptied out, lead sports columnist Condon, a champion old-school cigar-chomper, often peeled off a $1 bill to send a copy clerk to fetch a 10-cent cup of coffee from the mailers' room—and keep the change, kid. Stories abounded that one night Condon was so drunk he mistakenly offered his runner a sawbuck and told him to keep the rest—a nice $9.90 tip for someone making $4.60 an hour.

But Condon's most impactful contribution to the times was his revival of the Cubs curse legend. The supposed curse was merely a publicity stunt by William Sianis, owner of the Billy Goat Tavern near the old Chicago Stadium. Sianis and his mascot goat were kicked out of the 1945 World Series at Wrigley Field, even though he had tickets for both. Patrons complained the goat smelled. For the benefit of the newspapermen who quenched their thirst at his bar, Sianis proclaimed a curse on the Cubs to never appear in a World Series again for mistreating the goat. Sianis tried other stunts such as smuggling another goat in a hearse into the Republican Convention at the stadium. He was warned off by Bill Veeck from sneaking the animal into the 1959 World Series at old Comiskey Park; Veeck claimed the police were on the lookout for Sianis and his mascot.

Condon, a decades-long patron of the Billy Goat, of course knew of the legend. But no Chicago writer regurgitated the 1945 curse story until the Cubs started to endure pennant-race collapses in 1969. Condon and *Chicago Daily News* columnist Mike Royko began playing the curse and Cubs follies for laughs. When Sianis's nephew and successor Sam Sianis brought a goat named Socrates in a limousine to Wrigley Field and was barred admittance, on July 4, 1973, Condon wrote a column on the attempt. When the Cubs, 50–35 and in first place two days after the goat was locked out, collapsed to 56–64 five weeks later, the original curse story gained traction and hasn't had workable brakes ever since.

While Condon and Royko used their column inches to poke fun, they ignored the rot Wrigley tolerated in his organization. Condon also was not going to take buddy Charlie Finley, owner of the Oakland Athletics, to task for continually ripping off overmatched Cubs GM John Holland in trades. The 1970s featured a constant shuttle system between Chicago and Oakland. Finley, based in Chicago and easily accessible to Holland, made 12 trades with the Cubs between 1970 and 1975, when Holland retired in favor of temporary successor Salty Saltwell. Finley continued to deal with GM Bob Kennedy, who took over late in 1976, through the end of the '70s. He snared lefty Ken Holtzman and leadoff man Bill North, centerpieces of his championship teams. In return, the Cubs often got mediocre or overage players. The Manny Trillos in Cubs pinstripes were uncommon. Four players ended up with two tours of duty each with the Cubs and A's: pitchers Jim Todd and Bob Locker, and outfielders Tommy Davis and Adrian Garrett. Locker was traded to the Cubs in 1972, traded back to the A's in 1973, and then returned to the Cubs in a third deal in 1974. Even a fired Cubs manager of little repute, Jim Marshall, ended up managing the A's in 1979.

None of the supposed newshounds got hold of a Cubs' internal survey conducted by employees who believed Wrigley's trumped-up policy banning lights from Wrigley Field was harmful to the effectiveness of the players. Mid-'70s trainer Gary Nicholson knew that the constant switching back and forth from all day games at home to night games on the road wore the team down over the long season. But as long as Wrigley was in charge, the Cubs would not have lights.

Nor did the columnists talk to LaCock about the front office's fear of a radical new exercise program he, Locker, and pitcher Bill Bonham practiced on the field. The trio performed yoga in full view of fans and other players, but then were ordered by the brass, fearing their contortions were "too freaky, too hippie-like," according to LaCock, to continue out of sight of the paying customers.

While they had a dearth of position players and sparse contingents of black and Latin players coming out of the farm system, the Cubs did manage to produce a steady stream of pitchers who were highly rated. They had some moments in Chicago, but more often they matured and thrived elsewhere with 20-win seasons and no-hitters. Starting with Holtzman in 1965 and running through 1977, the farm system spewed forth Bonham, Joe Niekro, Bill Stoneman, Jim Colborn, Joe Decker, Larry Gura, Burt Hooton, Rick Reuschel, Ray Burris, Bruce Sutter, Mike Krukow, Dennis Lamp, and Donnie Moore. Only Holtzman, Reuschel, and Burris won as many as 15 games in a season as Cubs, while Sutter became one of the greatest relievers of all time. Throttling the development of the others first was the irascible Leo Durocher's mishandling of young pitchers at the start of the 1970s. Then the resulting instability in managers and coaches slowed the development of the kids.

RAY BURRIS (Cubs, Yankees, Mets, 1973–79): We [the pitchers] were very close from the standpoint that we took our relationship from the field, off the field. We did things together as families. To me that's something I'll always remember. In the minors we did things as families. Those relationships stay longer, because you get to know someone personally. If they had kept the nucleus of those [pitchers] together, there's no telling what those clubs could have done.

But in the first six years in Chicago, it seemed like I had a different pitching coach every year. It means a lot. You learn what to expect from each other. You learn what things the manager wants to implement. When you go through a 162-game schedule, you get acclimated to that manager, then you have a new guy, it takes till the second half till you get adjusted. As a young player, when you have so many changes, it makes a big difference.

My first year, 1973, [pitching coach] Larry Jansen. Then Hank Aguirre. Then Marv Grissom. Barney Schultz. And then Mike Roarke. It got to the point I expected a new pitching coach every year. When you're learning the skill of pitching at the major-league level, it can be very tough from a standpoint of different philosophies coming in every year, after you've gotten adjusted to one particular coach.

To Krukow, now a Giants announcer, the pitchers themselves needed to take charge of much of their development. But they had a shaky supporting cast.

MIKE KRUKOW: A [pitching] coach's responsibility is to get you in shape. The really great coaches have longevity with their athletes. You see them and they don't get hurt. The best coach in regard to pitching is yourself. We were too young to be factors as we were later on in our careers. Reuschel was always a good pitcher. A lot of it had to do with our offense—it was the "Rush Street Offense," a lot of singles, not much scoring. Get 15 hits and score just two runs. And in that division, we didn't match up with the power of Philadelphia, the power of Pittsburgh. This is something you have to really point out.

Every good pitching staff must have good defense. And defensively, I don't think we were ever a good team. Guys were playing out of position, with not much range. When a young pitching staff sees the ball's not being caught, they try to strike everybody out. You try to throw your best pitches first, you get behind 1-and-0, 2-and-0 and the hitters aren't going to swing at 'em.

A generation and a half later, the schizophrenic 1977 season still sticks in Cubs players' collective craw. After four straight seasons in which they won 77 or fewer games, the Cubs zoomed to that 8½-game lead, 25 games over .500 on June 28—most over .500 they had been that early in the season since the team's glory days in the 1930s. Standing ovations were the daily norm at Wrigley Field. But the Cubs utterly collapsed from the All-Star break on.

BILL BUCKNER: We were picked to finish last and here we are eight games up at the end of June. A couple of the young guys like [Manny] Trillo and [Jerry] Morales were having career years. [Rick] Reuschel started out having his best season. And [Bruce] Sutter was the big guy, but Herman [Franks] was pitching him two or three innings a lot. When he got hurt, and other guys were hurt, we lost it. But the fans were great. It was an exciting year.

Players on the '77 Cubs looked for help in the second half when the team was still in first place, and are still upset the brass did obtain reinforcements. Washed-up closer Dave Giusti was the only "name" second-half pickup. By now the owner was Bill Wrigley, succeeding father Phil Wrigley, who died at 82 on April 12.

MIKE KRUKOW: We needed help and we didn't get it. We needed to improve our team in August and we didn't do it. In the five years I was there, that was the best team I was on. It got progressively worse after Mr. and Mrs. Wrigley died. Nineteen seventy-seven was our best chance because after that, money started leaving [due to Bill Wrigley's divorce and inheritance tax obligations]. It got so bad that in 1981, if there hadn't been a strike, we would have lost 116 games.

It's frustrating because as an athlete, and every team since, have all understood what it would be like to win a championship on the North Side of Chicago. We got a taste with the White Sox in '05 with the parade. The Cubs would be 10 times that and twice as much as Boston. When you see your chance you have to go for it.

"SOUTH SIDE HIT MEN"

While the Cubs flirted with something special in '77, the cross-town White Sox matched them in first place in the AL West, and held the lead longer. They did it going against the game's fundamentals and their own history—by outslugging opponents, overcoming shaky pitching, and defense. They were the lovable "South Side Hit Men," authors of 192 homers and the first regular curtain calls in baseball.

Impoverished owner Bill Veeck could not afford the new crop of free agents. So he devised a "rent-a-player" scheme in which he'd obtain big names in the final year before free agency. Foremost were sluggers Richie Zisk and ex-Cub Oscar Gamble. They came through magnificently with 61 homers combined. With their ugly navy-blue-and-white softball-like uniforms, the White Sox seemed as blue collar as their fans. They never won anything but are fondly remembered even today. Steve Stone was closest to a true "ace" as the Hit Men possessed, and he recalled a team built in the most eccentric manner.

STEVE STONE (Giants, White Sox, Cubs, Orioles, 1971–79): [GM] Roland Hemond wanted me back. Bill [Veeck] realized he was on a fairly limited budget and we just go out and assemble all the hitters he could possibly assemble. We had 10 players hitting at least 10 homers or more. The South Side Hit Men couldn't field very well. They didn't pick up the ball. They didn't turn any double plays. They had Alan Bannister making 40 errors at shortstop, Jorge Orta still looking for his first double play turned at second base. We had Lamar Johnson at first, Jim Spencer sometimes. A unique bunch of characters.

We weren't shut out till September, when Nolan Ryan did it. You went out there knowing you were going to get a lot of runs and hoping someone, somewhere could catch the ball and throw somebody out. I was 15–12, which statistically wasn't too bad. But my ERA was in the 4.50s because nobody could catch it. It would fall in the outfield, it would fall in the infield. We were a team, plain and simple, that would club you to death. When my agent went in to negotiate with Bill Veeck after that season, Bill said, "I'll double his salary. He pitched great for us, we didn't have anybody who could field." So that was the character of Bill Veeck and the South Side Hit Men.

GIANTS: THE KINGS OF NEAR-MISSES

Symbolically, it was like the handoff of a baton of leadership. In an NBC TV *Game of the Week* between the Giants and Reds in 1969, Willie Mays and Bobby Bonds converged on a fly near the right-field fence in Candlestick Park. Both leaped. They came down in a heap. Mays, the greatest all-around player of his generation, was tangled up with Bonds, his projected successor. The athleticism of the two was replayed incessantly over the next four-plus decades.

BOBBY BONDS (Giants, Yankees, Angels, White Sox, Rangers, Indians, 1969–79): When the ball was originally hit, neither one of us knew that we could get the ball because Bobby Tolan hit the ball and split us, probably as good as two individuals can be split in the outfield. I couldn't call the ball and Willie couldn't call the ball because neither of us were sure we could get to the ball. I arrived a little bit before him to begin a leap. He had already started his leap in the air to try to extend to the ball. Fortunately he caught the ball. We had a collision on the play and went down, and I grabbed the ball out of his glove because the ball was rolling out. If it had hit the ground, it would have been no-catch. I kind of reached over as it was going out of his hand and grabbed the ball. The mistake was they thought I caught the ball because I was the one who raised the ball up. But he had caught the ball. I just grabbed it out of the glove before it hit the ground.

Bonds was the latest great young hitter out of the Giants system, but the talent flow did not bring the team a string of championships. From 1959 on, the Giants had a core of Mays, Orlando Cepeda, and Willie McCovey. Soon Juan Marichal and Gaylord Perry would anchor their rotation. But they had only one trip to the World Series, in 1962, to show for it. They finished second five consecutive times from 1965 to 1969. In 1970 the Giants slumped, but then finally squeezed out an NL West title in 1971, the last hurrah for the Mays-McCovey-Marichal-Perry collection. The Giants would spend much of the rest of the 1970s trying to rebuild.

In 1995 Bonds, coaching his son Barry on the Giants, recalled why the Giants just missed every season. He died of complications from lung cancer in 2003.

BOBBY BONDS: When you talk about dynasties, that means you're pretty much set in every position, that you have a solid pitching staff, a solid defensive club, and a solid offensive club. The Dodgers had that with outstanding pitching, a great leadoff man in Maury Wills, Junior Gilliam could get him over, and Tommy Davis could get him in. The Baltimore Orioles had a great pitching staff. We had a fine offensive ball club. We had a good defensive ball club. We had two outstanding starters, both in the Hall of Fame. Our pitching wasn't as strong as a whole as the clubs who beat us for the division. But offensively and defensively, we compare with any ball club. We ran short on the third and fourth starter. We weren't as strong. Most of the ball clubs had three or four decent starters. It was disappointing to finish second to them, but you couldn't hang your head.

Whether enduring a near-miss season or suffering through a tailender's woes, the hardy Giants fans braved the elements at poorly located Candlestick Park in southeast San Francisco. The capricious winds froze players and fans alike at night, and caused havoc with fly balls in the late afternoon. Putting up with the cold to watch the Giants was fan Mark Gonzales of Santa Clara. Two decades later Gonzales covered the Giants at the "Stick" for the *San Jose Mercury News* before moving on to baseball beat jobs at the *Arizona Republic* and *Chicago Tribune.*

MARK GONZALES (Giants fan, 1969–79): Until I started visiting other ballparks, Candlestick Park was a palace. Little did I know what a dump it was.

My first major league game was at the Stick on July 4, 1969, a doubleheader between the Giants and Atlanta Braves. My father took me, and in those days it was not uncommon for male fans to wear slacks and white shirts. Although my dad liked to sit in the shade behind home plate [reserved seats], I believe I wore a short-sleeved white shirt and slacks.

Because I was only 8 at the time, walking up "Heart Attack Hill" to get into the park was no problem for me because of the energy I had just to attend my first game. Candlestick Park installed escalators the following year, so fans could bypass walking up the hill if they wanted to gain admittance.

There were plenty of stories about people witnessing Willie McCovey hitting a ball into the bay. Even at 8, I knew this was impossible because of the distance between the right-field fence and the bay. But it was a pretty good view to see fans in right field chase home runs, as well as those in left field who would scramble out of their seats to retrieve home runs. When Peter Magowan and Co. took over the Giants before the 1993 season, they installed portable bleachers closer to the left-field fence that should have been done sooner.

I was lucky enough to attend a game at Candlestick Park before it became fully enclosed in 1971 to accommodate the 49ers, who moved from Kezar Stadium. The view of San Francisco was beautiful, and I was too young to realize how blustery the conditions were.

My father took me to my first Dodgers-Giants game in 1970, and it was so windy that the game was stopped so the grounds-crew workers could water down the dirt infield between batters!

I saw a lot of violence and hatred at Dodgers-Giants games at Candlestick Park. Part of it was simply the rivalry. Giants fans didn't like the Dodgers and their fans wearing those satin Dodgers jackets. The Giants finished runner-up to the Dodgers for so many years in the 1960s, that I think that had a lot to do with their frustrations. Mike McCormick pointed out to me later that the Dodgers did a great job of developing pitchers while the Giants developed mostly hitters.

The fact that the visitors had to walk from their clubhouse down the right-field line to the third base dugout didn't help matters. Tommy Lasorda was a master at goading the Giants fans who waited near the clubhouse entrance doors to swear at him.

It was unfortunate that Reggie Smith went after a fan in the stands, but that was the culture in those days. My friends were security guards in those days, and one of them testified on Smith's behalf. Whenever the Giants had a semi-contending team, the intensity seemed to increase among the fans.

The concourses at the Stick weren't wide enough, and getting out of the park was even worse because there were only two true arteries getting in and out of the park. When I started covering the Giants in 1992, I would sometimes give writers a lift to the San Francisco International Airport—about a 10-minute drive south of the park—so they could get a cab back to the city! Cab drivers didn't want to come out to the park even though they could get a pretty good fare in those days.

There weren't enough seats between third and first base at the Stick, and there was plenty of foul territory that made fans feel more distant. I always thought Pat Gallagher had the toughest marketing job in baseball because he had to promote baseball at the Stick, and the Giants weren't consistently good after the 1960s until Roger Craig took over as manager in 1986, and later when Dusty Baker and his group jelled in 1997.

The concession stands at the Stick served the worst food. Hot dogs and polish sausages were usually cold. The best bargain was the malts, but who would want them on cold nights?

CARDINALS HAVE LITTLE TO CHIRP ABOUT

The Steve Carlton trade in 1972, ordered by Cardinals owner Gussie Busch in a fit of pique, set the tone for the rest of the decade in St. Louis. The Cardinals would be in true contention in only two seasons, 1973 and 1974, the latter year boosted by Lou Brock's then-record 118 stolen bases. But too often the Redbirds would be a pitching- and power-poor ball club, shifting to an emphasis on speedy players who beat the ball into the ground on the Busch Stadium Astroturf, installed in 1970. Often the hottest thing going was the turf heating up to more than 130 degrees on tropical Sunday afternoons at midsummer, with players soaking their cleats or otherwise improvising to avoid the ultimate hot foot.

GARRY TEMPLETON (Cardinals, 1976–79): Yes, I am surprised [the Cardinals never won in the '70s]. Also, I knew that back then we didn't have any pitching. One year we had five guys hit .300, and we still lost. It seemed like we had to score seven, eight runs to win. It's unfortunate to play on teams like that. We didn't have the pitching to go with the hitting.

One positive Cardinals achievement was developing Keith Hernandez in 1975–76. Hernandez brought back the concept of the slick-fielding first baseman.

KEITH HERNANDEZ (Cardinals, 1974–79): I did realize there were more first basemen who knew what they were doing [fielding] out there. It was a pleasing sight instead of seeing those old truckhorses out there that's kind of like a cow put out to pasture, but he could hit a long ball. When I came up, McCovey was there, Johnny Bench was moved over there, it was all guys to get them in a position where they couldn't make the most mistakes and hurt the ball club. But outside the catcher, first base is probably one of the most critical positions. They get the most putouts and chances. You get a ball in the dirt, you got to scoop it or if the bases are loaded, you're in trouble. [Growing up] I liked Bill White, he was a right-hander. I thought he was the best-fielding first baseman.

Busch Stadium was surprisingly a good venue for fans. Unlike the other cookie-cutter stadiums of the era, the ballpark had left- and right-field bleachers right on top of the outfielders with tickets sold day-of-game only. That was the second of three ballparks in the city patronized by lifelong St. Louisan Jim Rygelski, a baseball historian and co-author of the 1999 book *The I-55 Series: Cubs vs. Cardinals.*

JIM RYGELSKI (Cardinals fan, 1969–79): One of my more lasting memories of baseball from that era was seeing a photo of workers installing Astroturf in Busch Stadium right before the 1970 season. Baseball will never be the same on artificial turf, I lamented.

It wasn't. Gappers that might have bounced high off the wall and been triples instead went into the bleachers for ground-rule doubles, and outfielders stopped short of charging a fly ball dropping short of them for fear it would bounce over their heads. Cardinals speedsters used the concrete-like surface to their advantage by hitting high infield chops that they easily beat out. The turf's green faded. It certainly made it much hotter for the players on the field, though for us in the stands, midsummer St. Louis seemed no more sizzling than it had always been. For a few years the club's ownership brought in the outfield distances by 10 feet through temporary and very ugly walls to encourage homers; it didn't and merely obliterated the bleacherites' view of plays near the barrier.

The changes to Busch marked the turning of what had been a modern baseball stadium, part of a progressive plan for the remaking of downtown St. Louis, into a bland multipurpose athletic complex. And they heralded a decade of disappointments. In 1970 Richie [as he was still called] Allen hit 34 homers, but I was stationed in Europe with the army that season and didn't get home to see him. Next year, I promised. But the Cardinals traded him to the Dodgers after his one year in a Redbird uniform.

The Cardinals also dealt away Steve Carlton and Jerry Reuss—trades ordered by an irritated and irrational Gussie Busch that denied the Redbirds a couple of damned good pitchers for the few seasons they were contenders that decade.

Because of overseas duty, the first game of the 1970s I saw was during the last month of the 1971 season. The pennant-bound Pirates whipped the Cardinals, who'd been a contender earlier that year, on a midweek night.

I splurged and bought a box seat a few rows behind the Cardinals dugout for $4. A drunken fan, about the seventh inning, stood up and gave the finger to Willie Stargell in left field. I don't think Stargell noticed it; he'd hit a home run earlier in the game.

It was the decade before nachos with cheese and two decades before specialty sandwiches and desserts, when ballpark fare was still hot dogs, peanuts, popcorn, and beer—all at affordable prices.

At mid-decade the Cardinals' players voted to replace the traditional black cleats for red ones. Eventually, all teams did away with the uniformity of shoes as players got endorsement contracts. And uniforms became colorful, though not necessarily better looking. The Cardinals went to a pullover jersey with beltless pants. The Pirates never wore the same uniform two days in a row. Both they and the Cardinals wore those goofy caps modeled on 1876 styles during the nation's centennial celebration. The Cubs' 1978 road uniforms reminded me of a bedsheet I'd once used.

I worked in Chicago in 1974 and the first half of the next year. Thinking I'd spend the rest of my life there, I tried to switch allegiance to the Cubs. It was fun to watch games in a real ballpark again, but the Cubs were miserable those two years. I came back to the Cardinals at mid-season in 1975. I felt guilty that I hadn't been a Cardinals fan during Lou Brock's greatest season the year before.

Al Hrabosky, with his behind-the-mound meditation and pounding of the ball into his glove—plus his high, hard fastball that batters wailed unsuccessfully at—was the most exciting relief pitcher many of us have ever seen, and no one since him has replaced the electricity he generated when he entered Busch Stadium in his best years. We'd go to games hoping the Cardinals would have a late one-run lead and that he'd be summoned in the eighth, for he and other closers of that era often worked the last two or even three innings.

My favorite Cardinal team of that decade was the 1973 bunch. They started 1–12 and seemed hopelessly out of it. Yet while making only one starting lineup change—Mike "Rocky" Tyson for Ray Busse at short—they went on a 56–30 binge to take a commanding five-game lead in the NL East in early August. That season I also had my first sweetheart, a real amour named Sherry, who baked with me in the left-field bleachers at a Sunday game against the Padres in mid-August. The Cardinals, then in the throes of a slump, hung on for a 1–0 win. On that happy and typically hot day, who knew that the Cardinals would fold over the last six weeks of the season and finish second or that Sherry would dump me for someone else just a few weeks later?

//

Throwing Off the Shackles

One of baseball's biggest misdirections was painting players as a financially downtrodden lot prior to the 1970s. To be sure, they did not make Hollywood-style salaries of the modern era. But compared to the average worker, they made out all right in an era of lower revenues for the game, which was operated much like a cottage industry in much of the country.

The longtime minimum salary was $6,000 through the 1950s and 1960s. That put a rookie on a par with the baseball writers covering him. But if the player stuck around and produced, his compensation rose to put him firmly in the upper middle class. Star performers zoomed into the upper five-figure pay range, if not $100,000-plus. That compensation made them firmly among the wealthy. The old saying was "home-run hitters drive Cadillacs." In the '50s and '60s, a fully loaded Caddy went for $5,000 or $6,000, affordable to all experienced big leaguers. Players generally enjoyed privileges not available to the average working Joe.

But there was a catch. The players' actual market value was depressed. Unlike almost all other workers in a capitalist economy, they worked under a perpetual contract—the reserve clause—which bound them to their original teams unless the clubs traded or released them. The players had no way to determine their real value as free agents, unless a team willfully released them. They could retire and their original team would still hold their rights if so desired.

In the real world no contract was legally binding without a beginning and an end. The average worker was free to seek a better deal anywhere. Even actors operating in the "studio system" in Hollywood could shop their talents when contracts expired. Baseball was able to enforce its system of servitude through its status as exempt from antitrust laws, a position grandfathered in from antediluvian times and rigorously protected by the owners. Every hint that Congress might lift the antitrust exemption united the usually fractious owners into a kind of political action committee, and the legislators stopped nosing around in baseball's business.

But the onset of the '70s meant radical changes down to the core of society. The concept of attacking the reserve clause became a cause that would not go away. Longtime labor economist Marvin Miller, who had energized the Players Association as its executive director starting in 1966, knew a full-bore legal assault on the reserve clause would not work. Curt Flood's Supreme Court challenge in 1970 was well publicized but ultimately failed. Like a crafty pitcher working the corners, in and out, Miller had to chip away at the established system until the flow of history would finally provide the players the workplace rights enjoyed by almost everyone else.

In the meantime the players were compensated at the pleasure and whims of their owners. They were on their own negotiating their compensation, and the process sometimes dipped into low-comedy levels as owners tried to justify paltry raises even for top achievements.

PHIL NIEKRO: Everybody thought that was so darn out-of-sight [Sandy Koufax and Don Drysdale collaborating to hold out for $100,000 each in 1966]. That maybe set the standard of getting the value higher. One time I won the ERA title and got a $4,000 raise, maybe $6,000, and I had to fight for it. If there were three doubleheaders in a row, we had no control over it. We didn't feel we had the backbone as an individual player or a team. Marvin [Miller] wasn't very liked by the owners much. He was the backbone when players look at how the game was played.

I wasn't personally interested in being a free agent. I was born a Brave and threw my last game as a Brave. I knew the game was going to change. There would be new rules and regulations. I really wasn't into that. My part was to go out there every five games and pitch.

Some players were lucky to play for generous owners, as White Sox third baseman Bill Melton did with John Allyn. Others, like pitcher Bert Blyleven, dueled for every nickel with penurious moguls like Calvin Griffith.

BILL MELTON: You don't get paid for elegance, how handsome you are. I did have an accountant who later became an attorney and is now an agent. Let's call him my agent. All he did was take care of my books and give me a quarterly report. When it came to negotiating with Roland Hemond, I did it. I never had him [the agent] approach him. At that time you could be friends with the general manager. You didn't have a whole lot of leverage starting out. I started out at $10,000, which was the minimum. I went from $10,000 to $14,000. I just accepted it. There was no negotiating.

I made good money. I made [more than] $100,000 after six years in the big leagues and it took Brooks Robinson 16 years. Sal Bando was on three world championships making $40,000. I was $85,000 or $90,000, and he used me in arbitration in 1976. Contracts were four pages. Covenants and conditions. They had a little area six inches wide where you type in—you get a room by yourself or you pick up my incidentals. That's as far as it went. Ours weren't complicated at all. Either they wanted you or they didn't.

Up until 1976, salaries were secret. Who would I compare myself to? It was my word against my general manager's. There wasn't arbitration that dictated numbers. It was how your team did.

I went from $14,000 to $30,000, from $30,000 to $80,000, from $80,000 to $110,000. That was plenty. There was nothing to argue about. At $80,000 I had the two homes, all the cars, you name it. That was good money. I was in the top 5 percent of the American and National League.

Players were grossly [underpaid] before free agency. A lot of my friends were in the $25,000s and $30,000s. I was one of the fortunate ones and made good money—I had all the bells and whistles. When my career was over, I had to get a real job because my income stopped all the things I had. I couldn't go back to the minor leagues for $16,000 or $12,000 for six months. I'd have to give up my family, my house. That's why I had to exit the game. That's why they lost a lot of good ballplayers that were in the $80,000s, $110,000s. A lot of the guys making $20,000 or $30,000, who went back to the minor leagues making $16,000 or $20,000, that's working wages. You had all these things, you couldn't support them, you had to give them up.

BERT BLYLEVEN: The saddest thing for me is when Harmon Killebrew had to play his final year at the major-league level in a Kansas City uniform. What I had heard is Harmon wanted to play one more year, but Calvin felt Harmon's career was done. Calvin was a good baseball man. He took care of his family first. He had a totem pole and the players were down on that pole.

Every player would love to do what Cal Ripken did, wear one uniform. To see Harmon not be able to do that— probably the low point of the '70s. Calvin over the years is probably turning over in his grave with the salaries today. He said free agency took all the love out of the game he had, because he had control of it.

You had to go in and talk to Calvin face-to-face on a contract. I was 19 years old [in 1970]. His secretary gave me a call and said Calvin would like you to come in. He sent me a contract, and I sent it back. I was not happy with it. The minimum in 1970 was $11,000, and he sent a contract for $11,000. I remember walking into his office. He had a big desk and a big chair in which he sat behind the desk. He said, "Have a seat, son." I sat on a couch that basically had no springs. I was basically sitting on the floor, looking up at this giant of a man.

It was pretty scary. I was probably more nervous then than at any game I pitched at the major-league level. He asked what I wanted. I figured I'd go high. If I could get $15,000 in my first full year, I'd be happy. I think [when I asked for that] his head came off his shoulders. His head spun around a couple of times: "My God, son, you want to double your salary? I don't even give Harmon Killebrew double his salary. Last year you made $7,800 [after coming up June 1] and you want to double your salary. C'mon, son, what's wrong with you?" I settled for $12,000. I moved him up a little bit.

He wrote on a separate piece of paper that if I won 15 or more games, he'd give me a $2,000 bonus. It was not part of the contract. He signed it. In my first full year I won 16 games. At the end of the year, I informed the secretary I have a $2,000 bonus. She'd get back to me. When she did, she said Calvin doesn't remember signing anything like that. Thank goodness, I kept that piece of paper in a folder. I had to personally come in and show him he had signed it, and I got my bonus. But if that paper had been misplaced or lost, I wouldn't have received that bonus.

I don't think under Calvin you ever felt you were the ace. I signed a two-year contract, which was unheard of, after my first full year for $16,000 and $20,000. After I won 20 games in 1973, I jumped up to $35,000. What ended our relationship is after [free agency started], I was making $66,000 in 1975. He gave me a 20 percent cut after winning 15 games. He never had any intention of signing me. He never talked contract. I was going to test the market. I basically played for the 20 percent cut, and later that summer I got traded to Texas, where [owner] Brad Corbett basically tripled my salary and gave me three years—$150,000, $175,000, and $200,000. My top was $2 million for one year with the Angels.

From the fans' point of view, they'd probably say [free agency] hurt the game. But from the players' point of view, there were only 500 major leaguers at the top of the field. TV contracts started to go up and clubs were receiving more money other than the gate receipts. The Players Association wanted a bigger piece of the pie. In the early 1970s players were only getting about 25 percent of the pie.

In 1971 Cardinals lefty Steve Carlton and Phillies right-hander Rick Wise were their respective teams' aces. But their efforts to get fair compensation for a cumulative 37 victories were summarily rejected by management. Carlton and Wise were traded for each other as spring training 1972 began. Carlton gave his side in a 1972 radio interview with Harry Caray.

STEVE CARLTON (Cardinals, Phillies, 1969–79): I think it shocked everybody. It came kind of unexpectedly. It came early in the morning. I was still asleep when it came. We were $10,000 apart and Rick was asking for the same amount of money. We signed at the same time [after being traded for each other]. It's kind of a funny deal. I guess they try to keep the people happy they trade for. I didn't want to be traded from the Cardinals— that's my home. I was very happy with the Cardinals, it's a good organization. I've got to go with the money. I wasn't making money over there. I had good years, I should be making money. You compare my talents with other ballplayers who were making a greater amount of money. I was more or less spinning my wheels. I'm a lot better off in the Phillies organization right now. We didn't score a lot of runs with the Cardinals. There were some lean years and we won.

Wise ended up signing with the Cardinals for the salary Carlton had demanded. He had been underpaid as a Phillie.

RICK WISE: I was in a big contract hassle. That was my seventh year in the big leagues, I had 75 wins, and I was only making $25,000. You had nothing. I wanted $50,000. I was the ace of that staff, won 17 games, threw 272 innings, and had 17 complete games, represented the club at the All-Star Game, and threw two no-hitters. He [Phils GM John Quinn] offered me a $10,000 raise. That was ridiculous. Guys today have no conception of what went on. I went to spring training, but I hadn't signed. Steve was at odds with Gussie Busch. When we both got traded, we signed for what we wanted with our new teams. I got more than $50,000. They wanted you to know who was boss.

Players of the era are forever indebted to Marvin Miller's stewardship of the Players Association that first brought arbitration, then free agency by 1976.

When he wasn't massaging a sore elbow that resulted in the groundbreaking surgery named after him, Tommy John remembered how Miller engaged the players.

TOMMY JOHN: I was a player rep then. Arbitration didn't come from the players, it came from the owners. Guys were holding out into spring training. Owners needed to get players into spring training in a timely manner. Marvin was so smart. What we have today is as a result of Marvin Miller. He told us different scenarios that will happen. The owners will win arbitration cases, but won't win [overall]. If they win, they will lose. They will pay out more money than they normally would. The owners win, but this guy will receive this much more money. They had to give reasonable salary figures.

Free agency did not ruin the salary structure of baseball. It's the guys who played two or three years making big money. Arbitration was the root of all the salary problems. Marvin Miller should be in the Hall of Fame. Two gentlemen changed the face of baseball—Jackie Robinson breaking the color barrier and Marvin Miller for what he did for the players. They should get him into the Hall of Fame before he dies. He left his mark on baseball, good and bad.

I think Marvin kept talking about it [free agency]. It just wasn't going to work. Curt Flood tried to sue baseball because he didn't want to be traded from St. Louis to Philly. That wasn't going to fly. Marvin knew you just started chipping away. Marvin found the perfect guys in Dave McNally and Andy Messersmith to test the reserve clause. I had a contract with Rawlings Sporting Goods. They gave me shoes and gloves every year. I wrote them that I'd like my name on a glove. They said they had no interest in having my name on a glove. I wanted out of my contract. I gave my contract to Marvin. I was with the White Sox then. He looked at it and just turned and laughed. When did you sign this, he asked. I said when I signed in 1961. He asked if I wanted out. Two days later, I got a call from Rawlings that said you're out of your contract. There was no ending date—they signed and it just went on and on. Marvin said it was illegal. I signed with Wilson and I was with Wilson up till the end [of my career].

He was such a smart man. People said Marvin ruled the players. No. Marvin would come in and said this is what I'd think. I'd tell what Marvin said and we'd take a vote.

Marvin never twisted anybody's arm. Marvin would say the closer we are to unanimity, the better it is as a whole.

The dam broke after arbitrator Peter Seitz declared pitchers Dave McNally and Andy Messersmith free agents on December 23, 1975. Players henceforth would become free agents after playing a year without signing a contract. A court appeal went against Major League Baseball, and the owners finally gave in. A score of major leaguers played the 1976 season without signing a contract, preparing for their eventual freedom after that season.

The first form of free agency was a "reentry draft." Teams would draft the free agents in which they were interested, then the player would go about fielding offers. Reggie Jackson led the first free-agent class after the '76 season, going to the only stage big enough for him—the Yankees. Subsequent seasons resulted in even more player movement and the axiom of then and now—the rich will get richer.

TOMMY JOHN: I was in the draft after the 1978 season. I was drafted by 12 teams, 9 of which offered me contracts. The first contract offer I got was from the Texas Rangers. They offered me five years at $1 million total, $200,000 a year, which was three times what I was making from the Dodgers at the time. I was making $72,000 with the Dodgers.

The Braves offered me a very good contract. The Brewers, Royals, Cardinals, Yankees, too. The Red Sox had drafted me but chose not to offer me a contract. Their team doctor, Arthur Pappas, was part of the ownership group. He concluded my arm was not sound enough to draft and that it would break down after a few years. When I went over to the Angels, Rick Burleson was my team-mate, and he had been with the Red Sox. He asked me if they had offered me a contract. I said no. He asked why wouldn't you get Tommy John. Arthur Pappas said his arm would go bad. Here it's 1983 and you're still throwing well. Burleson said if we had gotten you, we would have won in 1979, 1980, and 1981.

I just looked at what the city could have done for me. St. Louis would have been great. Kansas City would have been good. The Brewers would have been good. I asked Tom Paciorek, a teammate with the Dodgers who had gone to the American League, "Wimpy, who has the best infield that can help my sinker?" He said the Brewers and Yankees. He said Yankee Stadium is death for right-handed hitters; it's a lefty hitter–lefty pitcher ballpark. So that weighed on me. Steinbrenner and Al Rosen gave me an offer I couldn't refuse. It was four times as much as the Dodgers. My yearly contract was not as much as I thought because I got a lot of deferred money. I thought New York could do more for my career. It was five years plus an option.

The onset of free agency benefited the core of key young Red Sox stars—outfielder Fred Lynn, catcher Carlton Fisk, and shortstop Rick Burleson. But in the long run, the new system hurt the franchise, which did not want to keep up with the rising salaries when the trio's first lucrative contracts expired.

RICK BURLESON: Our agent, Jerry Kapstein, foresaw free agency coming in. So all three of us were holdouts [in 1976]. We signed five-year contracts with the Red Sox in August 1976. No one had ever held out in Red Sox history. He advised us to hold out, you'll get a lot of money if you don't sign the one-year contract now.

Minimum salary in 1974 was $15,000. I was runner-up as Rookie of the Year. I got a raise to $30,000. When I signed in August of 1976, I signed a five-year contract. I got a $100,000 signing bonus and my [prorated] salary was $80,000. Then the figures were $100,000, $110,000, $120,000, $140,000, and $160,000. Halfway through that, though, I was underpaid again. Our walk season was 1981. You're going to have to re-sign them again. They offered me a contract in the winter of 1980 for half of what I signed with the Angels. Being a player and paying attention, I knew what good shortstops were making. They tried to get me cheap. Instead of letting us walk after '81, they traded Fred Lynn and me to the Angels, and by not tendering Fisk a contract by a certain date, he ends up walking to the White Sox. They got nothing for him. If that had happened in modern baseball today, the GM would have been hung.

[Red Sox GM] Haywood Sullivan was upset we all played without our contracts in 1976. He said that would never happen again. He held a grudge and broke up the team in December 1980. We would have all played another 5 to 10 years there. A top shortstop was going to make $600,000 to $800,000 a year.

These 1970s salary figures seem quaint by today's mega-millions standards. Yet the fact that the game's financial system did not collapse under the weight of nine-figure contracts proved free agency was good for the game in the long run. The free movement of players stimulated fan interest and revenue. Unfortunately, admission and concession prices, always the biggest attraction for baseball compared to pro football and basketball, also skyrocketed. For the players, the time was a True Golden Age for their pocketbooks. But the appeal of waking up the day of a game, packing a lunch, and paying $1 or $1.50 for a cheap seat was about to change. Progress unfortunately is never casualty-free.

12

Baseball Finally in Living Color

In roughly two decades after Jackie Robinson broke baseball's color line in 1947, African-American and Latin players were welcome in the game—basically as guest workers.

Their on-field skills were prized, and enough stars were soon developed, particularly in the National League, that the NL's most valuable player award was dominated by African Americans starting in the 1950s. But in management jobs, front-office positions, and other adjuncts of baseball, the barriers still stood. Players of color were acknowledged for their physical prowess but not their mental acuity or leadership potential. Most black players would not have been surprised by how they were referred to by longtime stalwarts in the game. In 1959 Hall of Famer Rogers Hornsby, then the Cubs batting coach, picked out Billy Williams and Ron Santo as the only hitters worthy of promotion to the big leagues among all the organization's farmhands. But he confided a man-of-his-time opinion of Williams to then-Cubs announcer Vince Lloyd, who in turn recalled the anecdote in the late 1990s.

"He's a nigger," Hornsby said, "but a *good* nigger."

Meanwhile, Robinson himself busted another barrier—the first African-American baseball announcer on network TV, via ABC's one-year stint airing the Saturday *Game of the Week* in 1965.

Minority players were just that on rosters. For nearly the first decade after Robinson's debut, an unwritten rule suggested that no team would field a majority black-Latin complement of position players. The Dodgers reportedly let prize prospect Roberto Clemente go to the Pirates in the minor-league draft late in 1954 to avoid fielding five minorities, plus the pitcher in Don Newcombe. If so, they jumped the gun and lost out on a Hall of Famer. The Dodgers' Opening Day lineup on April 17, 1956, at Ebbets Field had Newcombe, Robinson, second baseman Charlie Neal, catcher Roy Campanella, and left-fielder Jim Gilliam. Black Cuban Sandy Amoros pinch-hit. Three days later at Wrigley Field, the Chicago Cubs probably were the second team to field five African Americans in the lineup via shortstop Ernie Banks, second baseman Gene Baker, left fielder Monte Irvin, center fielder Solly Drake, and pitcher Sam Jones. They produced 10 hits, including two homers, and six RBIs, while Jones threw a four-hitter in the 12–1 win over the Reds.

But the Dodgers and Cubs were uncommon in their full integration. Scores of franchises held back promoting black and Latin players. The Phillies did not integrate their parent roster until 1957. The Tigers had Latino Ozzie Virgil Sr. in 1958, but their first African American wasn't until a year later with Larry Doby, who had integrated the AL with Cleveland 12 years previously. Pumpsie Green, of course, is renowned as the man who integrated the Red Sox, the all-time laggard team in crossing the color line, in '59. For another decade, some teams were fine with few players of color. Playing in a city with a large African-American population, the Tigers were content with a stable threesome of outfielders Willie Horton and Gates Brown and pitcher Earl Wilson in the mid- and late-1960s. A black or Latin player had to be at least of near-star quality. They could not easily hang on as a backup or utility player, or reliever. "The average run-of-the-mill player is likely to be paid less than his white teammate with comparable skill, coached less attentively, given less opportunity to play . . . and disciplined more sternly for an infraction than white teammates," stated a 1970 report on "Blacks in Pro Sports" compiled by the Nashville-based Race Relations Information Center. Meanwhile, recruitment of Latin players was spotty, seemingly confined to a few enlightened teams like the Giants and Pirates.

Worse yet, their big-league status could not shield players from off-the-field discrimination. Those who followed Robinson had to stay in segregated, inferior quarters, particularly in spring training in Florida. Even in the first-class hotels in major cities, they had unequal access. The Dodgers' Newcombe was told he was welcome to stay at the Chase Park-Plaza Hotel in St. Louis but was discouraged from using the swimming pool. In 1962 Houston, Billy Williams protested the team hotel's dining room's refusal to serve him. Other slights and insults are too numerous to catalog.

In an environment where players were first-class superstars but suffering through second-class status in many ways, careful behavior was mandated. Players had to watch what they said and who they were seen with. While the civil rights movement began in earnest and constitutional rights of free speech were exercised, baseball fell behind. A savvy outfielder like Lou Johnson was a Negro League veteran whose organized-baseball career began in the Cubs organization in 1956 before he finally gained notoriety with the Dodgers in 1965. But he knew he had to hold his tongue to feed his family.

LOU JOHNSON (Angels, 1969): Back in those days, most African-American ballplayers couldn't speak freely as we could [in the present time]. I always spoke freely. There was something I believed I could do. What happened in the 1960s was the civil rights movement. How were we as African-American ballplayers going to be able to participate with what was going on? You'd play your ass off on the field. We all knew it [discrimination in the game] went on. Sometimes as an individual you're more free than when you have a family. You've got mouths to feed now. I had kids. So sometimes I had to bite my tongue and go on, but I tried to take it out with my performance on the field.

If African Americans had to watch their tongues and possess eyes in the back of their heads, imagine the frustration of the trickle of Latin-American players signed in the 1950s into the 1960s. They had both color *and* a language/cultural barrier to overcome.

Thus Orlando Cepeda faced odds as tough as Robinson's in his stellar career and enshrinement in the Hall of Fame. Teams dispatched many of their prospects of color to Southern minor-league affiliates, where Jim Crow otherwise held forth outside the ballparks. These scared young players had little or no backing from the parent clubs. Puerto Rican native Cepeda felt "lonely" in the minors in Virginia, "but someone had to do it," in the Giants' chain in 1955.

ORLANDO CEPEDA (Braves, Athletics, Red Sox, Royals, 1969–74): It was very hard. There were maybe five [Latinos in the majors]. You had to struggle to communicate. I looked at it as a challenge to learn better English, learn the American way. They don't want to know what we're coming from. There was a big difference from Puerto Rico to the States, in food, language, everything. I sat down with Del Crandall. Many times they don't know where we're coming from. Sometimes we got lost and confused. So many coaches and managers, they labeled us hotheads, hot dogs, and we were lazy. We were just confused.

The Latins were treated as poorly as African Americans by fans and Jim Crow adherents more than 15 years after Robinson's break-in. The Deep South was a far cry from Luis Tiant's native Cuba.

LUIS TIANT: It was easier in the '70s than in the '60s when I came in, no question. We used to play in the minor leagues, in the South. We had no chance to do anything. We can't go nowhere. We can't stay in the hotel. The fans called you names. They called you everything. Words I never heard in my life. They treated you like dogs. Charleston, West Virginia, in 1962. Burlington, North Carolina, in 1963. These people were horrible. On the road the white players had to bring the food into the bus. That's the only way we could eat.

Tiant still faced challenges when he was called up by the Cleveland Indians. The lack of understanding of Latin players by the established baseball folk extended to their very language.

LUIS TIANT: The problem was, when I come into Cleveland, was Joe Adcock, the manager [in 1967]. We had seven Latin players on the team. You put us all together, we're not speaking too many words in English. They're telling us if they find us speaking Spanish in the dugout or the clubhouse, he will fine us $200. And we're not making crap. Because he thinks when we're speaking Spanish, we're talking about him, that we don't like what he does. He doesn't want us to speak Spanish. I tell him fine me anytime you want, English is not my language. We got a bunch of guys here, you put us together, we don't speak three words of English between us. I tell him you got to be out of your mind. How stupid can you be? Orlando Peña was also mad as hell. He said you can fine *me*, too.

You heard about managers. You hear about Alvin Dark in San Francisco. They don't believe we have any brains, that we're baseball players only from the neck down. My father played in the Negro Leagues for 14 years. What Jackie Robinson went through was what we went through. I have to take whatever is coming to me, whatever it takes to get to the big leagues. He showed he could make it, why can't we do it? That kept me fighting, it kept me strong. I know he was going through hell.

But with the civil rights movement having been established for several decades and some of the changes it wrought slowly filtering into even the more conservative sectors of society like baseball, players of color in the 1970s did not have to carefully practice self-censorship in the same manner as Johnson. "At that time, you felt you were able to say things and express yourself more than in the '60s—especially when I first signed [1966]," outfielder Gene Clines said. The trend for players of color was upward. Yet they realized life was far from nirvana and often still had to fight dug-in attitudes about their color and culture, depending on where they played.

DUSTY BAKER: It's not real conducive to speak your mind now. There was more control over the players [then] than there was now. The money wasn't the same as it is now. What's the difference now? There's no difference now? Look at the guff I got for the things I said [as a manager] in Chicago. There's not a whole bunch of freedom of speech. You have to monitor what's said. Anybody who says anything about politics, religion, race, there's not a whole lot of difference. There's only a few minorities who can really get away to say what they want to say—maybe Charles Barkley and Ozzie Guillen.

I got called into the office when I was with the Braves. I was a generation after Hank [Aaron] and those guys. They warned me all the time about hanging out in certain parts of town or hanging out with certain color of men and women. Just [for] being from California and being open-minded on a number of things: I'll put it like that. Oh, hell no, that [interracial relationship] was taboo.

The Braves didn't like my collection of clothes. I had a shoulder-bag briefcase. They asked me if that was my sister's purse, my wife's purse. I don't care what they thought. The game was conservative. I don't start no shit, but I don't take no shit.

It was a lot better in parts of California than it was when I was in Atlanta or other parts of the country. Hey, there are people in parts of the country who think people out here are kind of weird. I hung out in Haight-Ashbury, Berkeley, Golden Gate Park in '67, '68, '70, and the whole country was in a spiritual, economic, and racial revolution. All I know is [the upheaval in] our country between racial unrest, between anti-Vietnam, anticonformity of any kind by my generation. I watched on History Channel on Veteran's Day about the Tet Offensive, how the North Vietnamese were pleased by demonstrations here. And then there were urban riots. That's one reason why I joined the Marine Reserve instead of the National Guard. I didn't want to be in the National Guard out there squelching riots. I was going to be construed as a traitor and be shot first. The Guard was called out against the rioters. Being African American on riot duty was not conducive to me. The Marines were a better option and possibly being called to Vietnam than being called out to [riot duty].

Outfielder Bill North, a Seattle native, seconded Baker's remembrance that open-mindedness often depended on in which part of the country you worked.

BILL NORTH: I love America, especially California. It was a whole different culture. I was with a team [Oakland] that was a world champion with all these guys who had never held their tongue. I fit right in there. It was 900 percent better.

Atlanta was a different thing. Dusty never had any trouble talking, but he was tactful. He was brought along real good by Hank Aaron. Billy Williams brought me along. We had mentors—guys who kept us out of trouble. Gary Maddox and Gary Matthews out there had [Willie] Mays and [Willie] McCovey. That's how we were brought along, we were protected. I couldn't talk more smack than Reggie [Jackson], but the difference was he was the straw that caused the swirl.

If I had said the stuff in Chicago I said in California, they'd have gotten rid of my ass far sooner than that. You might have found me in the Chicago River. Boston was the most racist city I've been in. Chicago is a segregated city. The Polish live with the Polish. The Jews live with the Jews. The Italians live with the Italians. The further east you go, the more that happens. California was liberal. The further away you get from that bastion of conservatism. You get people raised in Nebraska, Iowa, and Ohio who want to get away from there because it's so much conservatism.

I was raised in the '60s and president of the black student union in college. I still kind of kept myself to myself. I tried not to [flaunt romantic relationships]. In California you could do anything you wanted to, there were so many people doing the same thing.

While lesser-talented African-American players benefited by the moderate liberalization, true progress was still years off in the future, according to another prominent player in the 1970s.

ANDRE THORNTON (Cubs, Expos, Indians, 1973–79): Norms were being challenged in our society. Those norms as well in baseball, as more and more young African Americans got an opportunity to play. The status quo was no longer acceptable. Undoubtedly there was some tension and conflict in that period. There was still old-line managers who still managed with their own particular biases. It was moving beyond just the star players. Other African-American players who were not star players, who were role players, got a chance to be a part of 25-man rosters that probably didn't take place in the '50s or '60s.

One shining example of progress in attitudes is the manner in which outfielder Jose Cruz was accepted in Houston. A product of the Cardinals organization that finally recruited Latin players, Puerto Rican native Cruz found a home in the Astrodome in the mid-1970s and became one of the most popular Astros of all time.

JOSE CRUZ: As a Latin player, it was more easy for me. Those guys had a hard time coming up in the '60s. I had it easier coming up in the '70s. I talked about Vic Power. He had a lot of problems, sit in the back of the bus, stay in different hotels. I don't think we had that problem. Everyone stayed at the hotel. It was easier for us, because there were a lot of Latin players with the team. With St. Louis, there were a lot of Latin players.

I was lucky when I first signed with St. Louis in 1967. My manager was Ron Plaza, who spoke very good Spanish. A lot of coaches spoke Spanish. I was a pretty lucky guy. When they called me up in 1971, they had Matty Alou, Orlando Peña, Diego Segui. In '71 Joe Torre was MVP, he really helped take care of the young guys. We learned from Lou Brock. When I came to Chicago, they threw me apples or ice from the stands. They holler, "Go back to Mexico" or "Get your green card." I don't take that thing personally. They're just messing around with me. I never did anything to embarrass myself. They paid for a ticket, and I just concentrated on the game.

I only had a problem in my first year, 1967. We went to a restaurant in Florida and they didn't serve us. About five guys sitting at the table, me, Willie Montanez, and three Dominicans. Plaza talked to the people and we had to eat at the bus, it was ready to go.

Tal Smith was there [as Astros GM]. He signed me for five years. I got to stay there the rest of my career. I had a chance to be a free agent, and Tal wouldn't let me be a free agent. I could have signed with the Yankees. But I had loyalty. The Astros gave me a chance to play regularly. I loved St. Louis, but my team is Houston. My two kids were born in Houston. I'm happy and people were happy with me. I thank God that I stayed in Houston and people treated me like a king.

The best thing that happened to me was when I got traded to Houston. I was there for 13 years. I hear Rusty Staub talking about hitting in the Astrodome. It was a big ballpark so I decided to spray the ball around and hit .300 seven times. I think because I was loyal to the fans and stayed a long time, the fans liked me.

Outfielder Ron Swoboda believed he had a greater under-standing of African-American culture being around enthusias-tically verbal black teammates on the Mets in the late 1960s. Old stereotypes died quickly as he interacted with them as teammates.

RON SWOBODA: It showed an intelligence that white baseball was not quite ready to admit to when I first came into the game in 1965. There was this simmering sense that black athletes are great ballplayers, but they're not all that smart. But I'm around Al Jackson, I'm around Cleon Jones with his Deep South accent, almost a patois that if you weren't around him a lot, it took a little while for your ear to be tuned in to him. These guys are smart, they're not stupid. You played against Bob Gibson and Curt Flood. Lou Brock. These are smart guys. Willie Mays was a smart guy.

THE FIRST TO BREAK THE SECOND COLOR LINE—MANAGER

The concept of a black manager had been advanced since almost the time Jackie Robinson first integrated the game. Robinson himself had been touted for such a role. An October 27, 1951, *Collier's* magazine devoted its entire issue to a "future history" of a 1952–55 nuclear war with the Soviet Union and the world's rebuilding through 1960. In connection with a fictional '60 Moscow Olympics, *Collier's* referred to "Brooklyn Dodgers manager Jackie Robinson." Still, the black-manager issue remained in the talking stage for another generation.

Organized baseball did not even witness a manager of color in the *minors* until ex-infielder Gene Baker, who had helped integrate the Cubs in tandem with Ernie Banks in September 1953, was named to pilot the Pirates Class A New York–Penn League affiliate in Batavia, New York, in 1961. But at the major-league level, an African American was not even hired as a coach until the legendary Buck O'Neil was promoted from scout to the Cubs on May 30, 1962, obviously to assist with five black players in the lineup at the time. O'Neil's elevation came with a caveat—he would not be rotated into the "head coach's" job in the Cubs' wacky College of Coaches scheme nor be allowed to coach third base. When head coach Charlie Metro and another coach were tossed out of a game later in '62, O'Neil was not moved up to fill in. Metro claimed in 1999 he had left instructions that O'Neil was to take over, but was run from the field by the umpiring crew before he could make that dictum clear. In 1963 Baker was promoted to the Pirates' coaching staff. In the next decade a handful of blacks, such as the Dodgers' Jim Gilliam, the Yankees' Elston Howard, and the Montreal Expos' Larry Doby, became big-league coaches—but none at the crucial third-base slot.

In a fluke event that took place while the majority of the nation slept on the night of May 8, 1973, Banks, coaching first for the Cubs, actually took over as the first-ever black manager—for 1½ innings. Manager Whitey Lockman was ejected in the top of the 11th for arguing a third-strike call on Billy Williams in a night game at Jack Murphy Stadium in San Diego. Third-base coach Pete Reiser and pitching coach Larry Jansen, who ordinarily would have filled in for Lockman, were not with the Cubs due to personal health issues. So Banks, in his second season as a Cubs coach, shifted from first to third and directed the club to a 3–2 win over the Padres in the 12th. But there would be no second act for Banks or anyone else for the better part of two seasons.

As the 1970s began the eventuality of a black manager was a given. But who and when? "The coaches with the Cubs told me, 'You're a college man, they'll have black managers one day, why don't you start coaching?'" ex-catcher John Hairston, one of a record five members of his family over three generations to play in the majors, said of his days at Triple-A Tacoma in 1969. The Race Relations Information Center in 1970 predicted that the majors would have a black manager within the next three years, with the best candidates being Banks, the Giants' Willie Mays, and the Dodgers' Maury Wills.

The Race Relations Information Center also said a baseball executive informed them that Commissioner Bowie Kuhn had instructed all 24 teams to recruit minorities for executive positions. If such an order had been issued, it apparently was not enforced for years to come.

Jackie Robinson had been the most vocal critic of the game passing over qualified African Americans for executive and managerial positions. In his final public appearance on October 15, 1972, nine days before his death, Robinson—with Kuhn looking on—spoke at a Riverfront Stadium pregame ceremony during the World Series that marked the 25th anniversary of his break-in with the Dodgers. He used the bully pulpit to make a famous appeal. "I'm going to be tremendously more pleased and more proud when I look at that third-base coaching line one day and see a black face managing in baseball," Robinson said.

Less than two years later, Frank Robinson was that face, named Cleveland Indians manager only a few weeks after he had been acquired in a waiver deal from the California Angels. Robinson had prepped for such a job with winter-league managing positions in Puerto Rico. Yet players of color at the time were divided on whether they thought Robinson would be first or others were even better candidates. Several went on to become managers or coaches themselves.

DUSTY BAKER: It took some intestinal fortitude for whomever was the boss to make that first step. Nobody really knew at that time. It wasn't only the person that was going to be chosen, but it had to be the right town to accept who that person was. If there was a right town, it had to be Cleveland, who had the first African-American player [in the AL], and first black mayor [Carl Stokes]. It's about as far north as you can go. In the AL that was probably an even greater step, because the towns in the AL weren't as conducive to having African-American players as the NL.

A better choice by the establishment? Who knows what the criteria were? Robinson wanted it. You had to have someone who was kind of tough and thick-skinned and able to handle the player-manager job. Guys of that generation had to be thick-skinned.

CECIL COOPER: I never gave that a lot of thought back then. But now, looking back, you kind of think an Ernie Banks or someone would be the guy to do that. Back in the day, when [Frank] Robinson played, he was a kind of different personality than most. Very intense. You wouldn't think that he would have been the guy. I think so, that it gave a lot of hope there would be other opportunities down the road. Here we are, how many years later, and here we are. They look more at your abilities rather than your color.

GENE CLINES: Right off the top of my head, the person who came into my mind right away because of his character and demeanor was Vada Pinson. Vada was a very laid-back-type guy. Another guy who was a leader by example. I thought he had the right temperament to handle that job. The personality difference between him [Robinson] was like night and day.

By no means whatsoever [did I think Robinson was the leading candidate]. Because of his demeanor and because of his fiery spirit. The way he led that Baltimore ball club, I didn't think Frank had the makeup to handle everybody.

I don't think Roberto [Clemente] wanted to do that. He never gave me any indication, never even talked about managing. He never brought it up and never gave you an idea he wanted to manage at the major-league level. He probably was last on the list of those I thought of as a major-league manager.

There was so much going on in Hank's [Aaron] life and all the stuff he had to go through, coming up as a player and being there in Atlanta. I don't think Hank wanted to be in that situation again. He was chasing the home-run record and to be a manager, at that time, Hank wasn't ready for that. I was surprised [at Robinson's appointment], but I was very happy.

Longtime Braves teammate Phil Niekro seconded Clines's analysis that Aaron did not want to manage.

PHIL NIEKRO: I never looked at Henry as wanting to manage. Most coaches and a manager voice their opinions a lot. I never saw Henry do that. He'd sit down and help the players when they came up and asked him. He never pushed himself on anybody, as great of a ballplayer as he was. Not, "Here's how you hit it, here's how you catch it." It was "Watch me and I'll show you how to play the game."

As Clines suggested, Robinson's fiery, take-no-prisoners personality became a bigger issue than internal racial tension with the Indians, for whom Robinson made a dramatic debut as player-manager on April, 8, 1975, before 56,715 fans at Municipal Stadium. Serving as DH and batting second, Robinson stunned the huge crowd and assembled national media corps by slugging a homer off the Yankees' Doc Medich in the first inning. Cleveland players at the time were impressed by such a feat and Robinson's personality, but they realized living up to his standards was difficult.

ANDRE THORNTON: The subtle tension that is around a situation like that is no different than [that which] existed in the first months of President Barack Obama's presidency. There's tension, whether people want to mention it or not. We still weren't winning. There were some personalities on Frank's team that disagreed with him. He certainly knew the game. The only knock I remember hearing on Frank was he had very little tolerance for guys who weren't as good as he was. That was 99.9 percent of everyone else. We had a couple of issues between the front office and Frank.

ALAN ASHBY (Indians, Blue Jays, Astros, 1973–79): Speaking as a young player at the time, I didn't much think of him as the first black manager at the time. I was a big fan as a kid and he was one of the biggest names in the game. He was a man we all respected. I didn't think about the color barrier, although it was constantly in our face from the media.

Frank was a very intense man. He tried to squeeze out every bit of talent from his players he could. He demanded that guys give their best on the field, and as a player I respected that. For me, it came down to respect. Speaking for myself and many of the other guys on the team, there was so much respect. Everything he asked for, he gave on the field. If he was asking for something he wasn't willing to give on the field, then you might have argument with it. He was very fair. I don't know if he was the odds-on favorite to be the first manager to break the color barrier, but I couldn't see any better than Frank, and to this day I respect him immensely.

I'm sure there were some human beings, and they were players, who might have had some [race] issues. But I never saw anything inside. I saw a player or two I played with under Frank who had issues with Frank, but it had nothing to do with race. They didn't see eye-to-eye because of some of the demands.

Robinson himself always is reticent to talk about his past. Approached several times with historical questions during his final managing job with the Washington Nationals in 2005–6, he declined comment, saying he prefers to dwell in the present and future. So the next-best viewpoint of his 2½-year managerial tenure in Cleveland comes from his closest aide, then-coach Jeff Torborg, who ended up succeeding Robinson.

JEFF TORBORG: When we got to that [1975] spring training, it was one of the most rewarding spring trainings I ever had. We only had four coaches—me, Dave Garcia, Tommy McCraw, and Harvey Haddix. We were really close on the staff with the first black manager, with all the publicity and interest in what was happening. We really ran spring training for him. We ran great meetings. He would be the first to admit, I don't know much about the pitching and catching side and the signs. I want you to do that and want you to teach me. In turn, he's teaching us. He didn't miss a trick on the field.

I thought Maury [Wills] would have been a great manager. I've taken Maury with me when I managed the Mets. I had him with Montreal. I thought I was going to manage Houston and I called him. Frank was unique. He was legendarily tough, a fighter.

The organization wanted him badly. Phil Seghi had been the [Reds] farm director when Frank was there. [Cleveland president] Ted Bonda was a very open-minded guy. Frank had a run-in with Rico Carty. He had a run-in with Gaylord Perry. Other guys who played for Frank loved him. It's true with every manager. In Frank's first game, the home run, we win. How does a guy do that, it's his first managing position, socially a happening? He hits a home run and he almost hits a second one. We were in awe of him.

But managers are hired to be fired, even a trailblazer like Robinson. Even though he had guided the Indians to a cumulative two-games-over-.500 record in his first two seasons, a vast improvement compared to their lowly standards, a 26–31 start to the 1977 season gave the brass an excuse to cashier Robinson, with whom they'd had some clashes. They turned to a reluctant Torborg as his replacement.

JEFF TORBORG: I was talked to before his firing by the ownership, by Ted Bonda and GM Phil Seghi. I turned down the job five different times. I told them they were making a mistake. I don't understand why they fired him. They never really told me.

I thought he was a great manager. The morning this happened, I'm in his office early. I told him I don't want your job. The tears are running down both of our faces. He said it's not my job anymore, they're taking it from me. He said if you think you can do it, take it and continue what we were trying to do here. Add to that, the first day I managed, it was a doubleheader against Detroit. We had two complete games by Wayne Garland and Jim Bibby. Ralph Houk said congratulations and good luck—I think. We won eight in a row. Every day Frank called me and helped me lay out my game plan for that day. The unbelievable thing was here's one of the greatest competitors ever in the game. What would make him think I wasn't working behind his back to get his job? That happens a lot. For him to call me 10 days running on the road on how to be successful in his job is an unbelievable story.

Only one other African-American manager logged service in the 1970s. Just as Bill Veeck made Larry Doby the second black player, after a Robinson, in 1947 with Cleveland, Veeck anointed Doby the second black manager, after a Robinson, for the last 87 games of the 1978 season with the White Sox. Doby, who went 37–50, did not return for '79. Another color line had been crossed along with the appointment of the short-term Bill Lucas as general manager of the Atlanta Braves. But baseball still had light years' worth of improvement to go in hiring minorities for management and front-office positions.

PIRATES SHOW THEIR TRUE COLORS

Despite Jackie Robinson patron Branch Rickey assuming control in the early 1950s, the Pittsburgh Pirates were no pacesetter in integration. Infielder Curt Roberts broke the Buccos' color line in 1954, but few other minorities joined Roberto Clemente on the roster throughout the rest of the 1950s. Behind the scenes, though, Rickey successor Joe L. Brown had strengthened Rickey's farm system and backed ace scout Howie Haak's expeditions into the Caribbean in search of fresh talent. By the early 1960s a bumper crop of minority players began to work its way through the Pirates system. Soon the franchise would overtake the Dodgers and Giants, the original integration pacesetters, and become baseball's leaders in minority numbers on the roster in an era when most of the old informal quotas had fallen. By 1972 some 20 percent of major-league rosters were comprised of African Americans, rising to a peak of 27 percent in 1975.

DAVE PARKER: That's [credit to] Joe L. Brown. He kind of felt that way. If you could play, there was a position for you in the Pirates organization. Give Joe credit for having blinders on. Not seeing black or white, Latin American. I give the credit to Joe L. Brown.

A lot of it was [Willie] Stargell, [Roberto] Clemente, those two guys were leaders. They emphasized leaving something for those coming behind you. That was something Stargell always said. The leadership of the Pirates made the team so cohesive.

GENE CLINES: If you came to a Pirates spring training camp in the 1970s and you saw as many blacks and Latins as we had, it would scare you half to death. They'd sign them in abundance, and there was always competition. In 1970 we had Bill Mazeroski as the veteran second baseman, and coming up behind him was Dave Cash, Rennie Stennett, and Willie Randolph. When I came up, they had to trade Matty Alou to make room for me. They brought up Mitchell Page, Tony Armas, Angel Mangual, and John Jeter, and they had no room for them. The talent just kept coming and coming. They put a lot of resources into signing these players.

Without a doubt, there were probably more minorities in the Pirates organization at that time than any other organization in baseball. That team was color-blind. We did everything together. There was a party, everyone showed up. With our ball club, there was no color [no cliques]. The combination of what Joe L. Brown had done and knowing we had a very talented ball club, you didn't look at color, you looked at talent and ability, who could win. Color never came into the picture at all.

The Pirates' integration took hold so quickly that by June 17, 1967, manager Harry "the Hat" Walker could field an entire lineup of minorities other than the pitcher in a game against the Phillies at Connie Mack Stadium: Matty Alou in center, Maury Wills at third, Robert Clemente in right, Willie Stargell at first, Manny Mota in left, Jose Pagan at shortstop, Andre Rodgers at second, and Jessie Gonder catching. Then the Buccos truly made history, also against the Phillies, on September 1, 1971, at Three Rivers Stadium. For the first time ever, the entire nine-man lineup was African-American or Hispanic. Normally with left-hander Woodie Fryman on the mound, the white Bob Robertson would have started at first. But Robertson was ailing. So without regard to the ethnic composition of his lineup, Pirates manager Danny Murtaugh wrote down this order: Rennie Stennett at second, Gene Clines in center, Clemente in right, Stargell in left, Manny Sanguillen catching, Dave Cash at third, Al Oliver at first, Jackie Hernandez at shortstop, and Dock Ellis pitching. Bob Veale came in later as one of three relievers in the 10–7 victory.

GENE CLINES: It started that afternoon. I got to the ballpark and one of our batboys made the comment, "The Homestead Grays are playing tonight." That thought stayed in my mind and it didn't dawn on me until they were playing the National Anthem. I looked to my left and I saw [Willie] Stargell and I looked to my right and I saw [Roberto] Clemente. I turned around and I started looking at all the positions. I said, "Now I understand what the batboy said earlier that afternoon." When you got to the ballpark, you knew if you were playing or not.

It felt good. I didn't know the magnitude or if it had happened before until after the game, when all the sportswriters began flocking in there and they went to Danny's office. When they asked Danny if he knew he had made history by having the first all-minority lineup, he said, "Hey, it wasn't planned that way. I put the best nine guys I thought could win that night, and it just happened to be nine [minorities]."

AL OLIVER: I was not aware of it early in the game. Not until the third or fourth inning. I just looked around and thought about it. I remember asking Dave Cash, Dave, we got all brothers out there. He kind of laughed. It just wasn't that noticeable to me because we usually had five or six out there anyway. Not knowing I'd be part of history, I felt good about it. You've got to give Danny Murtaugh credit about it. Odd thing about it was Bob Robertson didn't play that night. Usually [against a lefty] I'd play center or be on the bench.

BOB VEALE (Pirates, Red Sox, 1969–74): It was a historic event at the time. We didn't really care about it at the time, but we knew what we had done that day. That's as far as it went. The name of the game was to make money, not to see how many blacks or whites you could put on the field.

Either the all-color lineup was not considered newsworthy across the country or the Pirates already had set a standard for roster integration. Wire-service accounts of the game in Chicago and New York did not mention the racial angle in the lead. Just the facts, ma'am—the score and the major contributors. Progress in a way had been made.

THE CUBS TURN BACK THE CLOCK

The yawning chasm between the Pirates and Cubs, competitors in the NL East starting in 1969, can never be better illustrated than the contrast in each team's view toward race. The Pirates embraced players of color. The Cubs gingerly tolerated them. No wonder the Buccos typically beat the Cubs like a drum through much of baseball's True Golden Age.

As the 1970s progressed, the Cubs seemed to turn back the clock toward the early integration days of the game rather than advancing with the times. Consider this was a franchise that signed black players as early as 1947 and signed Jim Gilliam (and then released him in 1950). The Cubs fielded the first African-American coach in Buck O'Neil and had the first black manager, albeit for just 1½ innings, in Ernie Banks, who then and now ranks as the franchise's greatest and most beloved player.

But just below the surface, out of view of a usually soft Chicago sports media, were racism, intolerance, and fear that far undercut the Red Sox's reputation on race. The main culprit was a nondescript general manager named John Holland, in over his head but kept on the job for 19 seasons from 1957 to 1975, some of them incredibly bad, by his fealty to owner Phil Wrigley, who prized loyalty over ability in most cases.

Holland rolled back whatever progress on race was made by predecessor Wid Matthews, who worked under Branch Rickey in the Dodgers front office when Jackie Robinson was signed. Matthews not only integrated the Cubs with Banks and second baseman Gene Baker in 1953, but had five African Americans on the roster three years later. Unfortunately, that was Matthews's only accomplishment—the Cubs never had a winning season in his regime. A native of Wichita, Kansas, Holland was an organization insider, having advanced team-by-team as an executive in the minor-league system.

In 1999 Chuck Shriver, who had served as Cubs' media relations director for Holland's final nine seasons as GM from 1967 to 1975, painted a picture of a front office not up to big-league standards. Shriver went on to the same job with the White Sox and a women's pro basketball team before returning to the newspaper business. He recalled a Holland who spread out his prejudices liberally beyond blacks and Latins.

CHUCK SHRIVER: The front office was pretty prejudiced. They were out of that 1930s and 1940s mold. They were careful which black players they selected. Our scouting staff tended to be the old-boys school, older guys, very few who had played major-league baseball. A lot of old

Southerners who had played in the minors down there. They thought along John's lines. Buck [O'Neil] was an excellent scout. He'd talk about certain [black] players, and the front office didn't even want to take a look at them.

[Holland] kept making comments about our "Italian third baseman" [Ron Santo]. He wasn't enamored of Jewish players, either. Kenny Holtzman proved to be such a good pitcher, John couldn't say no to that.

And when O'Neil did sign players, Holland did not want to use too many of them beyond an established core of Banks, Billy Williams, and ace Fergie Jenkins. He worried about Phil Wrigley's reaction to negative letters from fans abhorring the aggressive integration of the Cubs. O'Neil's signees over his 33-year Cubs scouting career included Lou Brock, Oscar Gamble, Lee Smith, and Joe Carter, but Holland did not care about his record of quality.

BUCK O'NEIL (Cubs scout, 1969–79): I got all these players, but they weren't playing them at the same time. I told Mr. Holland we'd have a better ball club if we played the blacks. Then he showed me a basket of letters from fans saying, "What are you trying to do, make the Cubs into the Kansas City Monarchs?" We weren't appealing to black fans anyway, playing on the North Side of Chicago.

The end result was condemnation of the Cubs to mediocrity. Holland did not bring up one African-American player originally signed by the team between Brock's first call-up in September 1961 and the elevations of pitcher Jophery Brown and outfielder Jimmie Lee McMath in 1968. A similar drought would take place between 1976 and 1980, when Lee Smith finally made the majors.

Holland also was suspicious of Latin players and the scouts that would sign them. As a result, the Cubs did not promote any homegrown Latin players until Puerto Rican infielder Dave Rosello first hit Wrigley Field in September 1972. They fell far behind other teams in Latin scouting and never caught up until the millennium had passed.

CHUCK SHRIVER: John was mistrustful of Latin scouts. The feeling was that Latin scouts would say anything about a player to get him signed. This was another example of just being behind the times in the 1960s, operating like it was the 1940s.

Holland circumscribed a careful code of conduct for minority players. They basically could not talk out of line or act out. When Holland did permit the drafting of Bill North in 1969, he became the team's top outfield prospect, with more speed than anyone in the organization. But North's protests about an apparent promise on playing time that was broken in 1972 netted a directive for the rookie to get help.

BILL NORTH: Mr. Holland sent me to a psychiatrist in Arizona. He said he wanted me to be ready for the big city [even though North was from Seattle]. I was from the Northwest and relatively smart, and that threatened the Cub. Ability wasn't the only criterion for playing with the Cubs.

Holland also directed Ferguson Jenkins to a psychiatrist after he heaved a slew of bats onto the field after the Braves bombed him out of a game on August 15, 1973. No white players were sent to a shrink after they threw a tantrum, though.

But the one act Holland could not countenance was interracial relationships. That was deserving of severe punishment for any black Cub.

CHUCK SHRIVER: John Holland was a person of his time. That was a big deal [dating white girls]. John was as much concerned about what the public would say. He wanted to avoid a scandal. Someone in the public would raise a hue and cry, and that would get [Phil] Wrigley's attention.

Thus the popular outfielder George Altman found himself bench-bound in 1966 when his wife, of Native American and Hispanic descent and thus light-skinned, was spotted at he ballpark. Three years later, Holland set up outfielder Gamble, then the Cubs' top prospect, to run afoul of this attitude by the GM's own impatience. Gamble was barely 19, had never been away from home in Montgomery, Alabama, before he signed, and was less than a year out of high school, but manager Leo Durocher called him the "next Willie Mays" in spring training 1969. On Opening Day, Holland told Cubs announcer Lou Boudreau in his pregame WGN radio show that Gamble could be on the fast track to Chicago, despite his youth and inexperience.

JOHN HOLLAND: Certainly this boy Gamble, don't be surprised if he isn't up here in the next 30 to 60 days, because he's going to be a great one.

Continuing his impatient style of promoting players prematurely (and then dumping them when they failed), Holland called up Gamble in the last week of August from Double-A. He was thrown right into center field with the New York Mets breathing down the first-place team's back. "No, you do not bring him up, not in the heat of things," said then–Cubs pitcher Bill Hands. Gamble played decently in his first few weeks, but took full advantage of the after-hours pleasures afforded a major-leaguer. Publicized as a hotshot rookie, the women lined up at his door and he partook of their favors. Durocher caught wind of his overactive social life. "He told Oscar to stay away from a certain girl," North said of the Lip's lecture at a team meeting. After the season, Holland heard Gamble was dating white girls again in the Arizona Instructional League. "That was the straw that broke the camel's back," Shriver recalled. Holland and Durocher worked feverishly to railroad Gamble out of town in a November 17, 1969, deal with the Phillies. He'd go on to a decent career with 200 homers and notoriety for baseball's biggest Afro.

By now the word was out among Cubs that interracial dating was forbidden. When North was called up in September 1971, he was warned by black teammates Brock Davis and Cleo James to steer clear of white baseball Annies hanging around. But even an innocent conversation could draw a rebuke from management.

That's what happened to soft-spoken, religious right-hander Ray Burris one day in the mid-1970s. He was spotted talking to a white woman outside Wrigley Field. The word came down to never be seen talking with her in public again. The woman was merely president of Burris's fan club. To cut down on such meetings, innocent or not, on the road, a front-office type traveled to monitor the minority players' activities. At the same time, Burris's teammate Wayne Tyrone, a black infielder, found himself benched when his white girlfriend began showing up at Wrigley Field.

By the time Gene Clines arrived with the Cubs in 1977 to serve as a platoon left fielder, he heard about the team's policy on relationships. The entire attitude compared to the Pirates was "the difference between night and day," he said. Clines's low-key, off-field style came in handy when he struck up a friendship with female usher Joanne Budka.

GENE CLINES: I came into contact with Joanne in '72 and '73. We didn't get together till I start playing with the Cubs. We just kept it under wraps. There was no public display of it. Without a doubt [he heard of Cubs black players' problems]. It would have been handled quite a bit different in Pittsburgh.

We weren't married at that time. She was working at the ballpark. We just kept it low-key. We didn't go, say, out on the town where you would be seen or you'd be exposed. A lot of guys who come through Chicago, the nightlife has killed a lot of guys. When you went to Chicago, you knew what to expect. The number one priority, it was a great city to go play and visit, you had to keep things under perspective, didn't let the nightlife kill us. We knew there was a job to do with the day games.

For me, it wasn't management's business and it sure wasn't my character to go out and flaunt it, and go out and have a good time. You learn how to just deal with it. You're not going to please everybody. Whatever I did, I did it in a respectful way. Management didn't find out, management didn't need to know. All they're going to do is use that as a weapon if you have a bad game, and you're not going to be around a lot.

JOANNE BUDKA-CLINES: Gene and I always have been low-key. We really didn't date [seriously] till much later. We were always pretty discreet. Personally, Gene has always been a very private person. He keeps his business and matters to himself. Going back into the '70s, that's probably because he became much more of a private person.

Aggressively demanding fair wages or flamboyance were still other ways black Cubs were sent away after productive Chicago stints. Third baseman Bill Madlock wanted a good payback for his two consecutive batting titles after the 1976 season and said so publicly. The Cubs claimed he wanted an astounding $1.5 million over five years. So he was traded to the Giants for outfielder Bobby Murcer, to whom the Cubs paid more than Madlock had demanded—$320,000 per season. In spring training of 1977, three weeks after Madlock was dealt, young pitcher Jeff Albert, a new arrival from the Dodgers, was stunned at the players' reaction to the deal: "That [Phil] Wrigley said he was not going to pay a black man $1 million."

Rodney Scott did not want anywhere near $1 million after a sparkplug of a half-season in 1978: 27 steals in 78 games for a traditionally slow-footed team. But after aggravating blustery manager Herman Franks at times in '78, third baseman-outfielder Scott, nicknamed "Cool Breeze," compounded the problem by sending agent Abdul Jalil, dressed in traditional African garb, to talk contract with GM Bob Kennedy after the season. The gruff Kennedy did not like his appearance and negotiating style. "Life's too short," he huffed as Kennedy packaged Scott and defensively skilled outfielder Jerry White in a deal to the Montreal Expos for outfielder Sam Mejias. Scott stole 39 bases, then 63, in 1979–80, while White hit .297 in '79. Mejias was 2-for-11 (.182) in cameo Cubs appearances before being sold to the Reds on July 4, 1979.

GENE CLINES: Rodney Scott was a free spirit, a very talented player. They looked at him as being cocky. But it was a cocky-confident. He was confident in what he was able to do. Chicago was not ready for a Rodney Scott. Without a doubt [they'd accept a white player with the same attitude]. That doesn't mix with Bob Kennedy, didn't mix with a lot of people in Chicago. I was pretty pissed [trading Scott], knowing the talent and what he could do to help us win. I just couldn't understand their thinking. It bothered me a lot. When Dave Cash was traded from the Pirates to the Phillies, bringing that winning attitude, cockiness with confidence, he taught a lot of those guys how to win, do it the Pirates way.

If a minority player wanted a trip back in time in the '70s, all he had to do was get exiled to the Cubs. But he could quickly punch a quick trip back to the present—and baseball civilization—by acting, well, human. No wonder the Cubs' last pennant was stuck back in 1945. That's where their understanding of racial issues dwelled. Progress was perceptible for minority players in the True Golden Age, but it left the most popular team in the nation's third largest market far behind.

13

Characters

They didn't need to wear the most garish leisure suit or sport the most luxuriant Afro to be true characters. Crew cut or shaggy-haired, characters have been a staple of baseball since the beginning, and the period from 1969 to 1979 was no exception.

They entertained or outraged—or both. These men are eminently human but put on a stage that only baseball can provide.

SWEET LOU IN HIS PRIME

The home movie shot at old Comiskey Park in memorabilia collector Leo Bauby's massive audiovisual archive in Wilmette, Illinois, is classic Lou Piniella. It's 1973, Piniella's playing for the Kansas City Royals, and the man who did not tolerate failure for himself hit a routine grounder to short. As Piniella passed first, he slammed his helmet on the bag.

Piniella could do better than that—and did, often. His tantrums were the most entertaining of any player in the '70s for teammates, foes, and spectators alike. A self-admitted "red ass" during this era, Piniella admitted in 1979 to his Boswell, the *New York Times'* Murray Chass, that his explosions were part of his winning-ballplayer persona.

> **LOU PINIELLA:** At times I need something to get me going. If I become passive, I don't play as well. I need an outburst to get my adrenaline gong. Some players, if they have an outburst, lose their train of thought. I think better because of my outburst.

Three decades later a calmer Piniella entered his senior-citizen years determined to turn over a new leaf as Cubs manager, limiting his agitation to playful barbs directed at the media and misdirection-play admonitions to "talk to the pitching coach." Wife Anita likely advised "Sweet Lou" that he was too old to roar at umpires and uproot first base and heave it into right field.

LOU PINIELLA: The new hierarchy in baseball would rather have no arguments and no fights on the field, and just play the game. I would rather be recognized as a good baseball man as opposed to just a colorful baseball man.

Oh, that color does not fade through the decades. The Piniella rear-end-on-fire stories brighten up the memoirs of the True Golden Age. Start with original Royals announcer Denny Matthews. He broke in with Piniella in Kansas City's first season in 1969.

DENNY MATHEWS (Royals announcer, 1969–79): There was a little commode right around the corner of the dugout in the runway to the Kansas City clubhouse. It was a phone-booth-sized commode for the convenience of the players. The story goes that Lou grounded into double plays twice in two at-bats. Frustrated, he threw his batting helmet into the toilet and flushed it. Of course the helmet was spinning around and didn't go anywhere. He took his bat and started to plunge it [again to no avail]. The guys in the dugout were waiting for the next explosion, they were rolling around. They loved it.

Bert Blyleven, a worthy pitching opponent of Sweet Lou for the majority of his career, witnessed Piniella putting his leg into his act, while also jawing at him over a too-close pitch.

BERT BLYLEVEN: Lou got so frustrated he drop-kicked his glove over the [Kansas City] fence. They didn't have any bleachers. The game was delayed because Lou had his tantrum. We all signaled field goal. He took every at-bat like it was his last. I would love to have a guy like that play behind me.

He was the only one who made a couple of steps out toward the mound on me. I threw a fastball up and in, and then came back with a breaking ball that accidentally went over his head. He said something to me. We exchanged words and I told him if I'm going to hit you, I'm going to hit you with a fastball.

Right-hander Rick Wise was amused by Piniella's antics. That is, until he got a clutch hit against him during his Red Sox and Indians days. He was almost anal about practicing his batting stance anytime, anywhere, which Wise witnessed.

RICK WISE: He'd run by you on the mound and say, "I'll get you next time. I'll get you next time." He'd go ballistic and everyone laughed at that. But he came to play, he played hard, and had great knowledge of the game. He hit to all fields. Especially with two strikes, he was one of the tougher outs. It sets apart a lot of the hitters.

They're all laughing watching him tear up that dugout. Everyone would get away from him, throwing that helmet. It would be ricocheting all over the place.

He'd sometimes practice his stance in the outfield. Just before the inning started, he'd change his hands. A lot of guys do that.

Piniella warmed up for his 21st-century roasting of Chicago writers on his own 1970s Yankees teammates, according to that team's traveling secretary.

MICKEY MORABITO (Yankees media relations official, 1974–79): He was just so quick. Some of the best lines you'd hear on the bus would be from Lou. It's a famous story—he and Mickey Rivers went back and forth. They talked about your IQ. Lou said, "Mickey, you couldn't even spell IQ." Lou also told Catfish Hunter they'd give away construction helmets to all fans in the outfield to protect them from the home runs Catfish gave up.

In the end Piniella had the respect of an entire league for his clutch-hitting skills.

BERT BLYLEVEN: He was a very good breaking-ball hitter. He sometimes sat on the curveball. A lot of them sit on it, but whether they hit it is another issue. Lou did.

He could stay with my curveball, he could go the other way or if I hung it, he could hit it a long way. Lou had a very good eye at the plate. Lou knew what a strike was and what a ball was. You watch a guy like Joe Mauer, who has so much patience and knows the strike zone. Lou was a lot like Joe—as far as knowing the strike zone, not going out of his element to chase a pitch. He had a short, compact swing, didn't like to extend his arms. He was quick inside and covered both sides of the plate.

JIM PALMER (Orioles, 1969–79): He could use the whole field. He was capable of hitting home runs. But he was a line-drive hitter, right-center, left-center. Occasional power. Knew how to hit, he was very smart. He was a student of the game. He could hit it over the first-base bag. If you hung a breaking ball, he could hit it over the left-field wall.

Low and away, you could get most guys out. Lou could hit quality pitches, that's why he was such a great hitter. He didn't like to give away at-bats. He might have taken it to an [emotional] extreme, but for him, that worked. He understood the game. He was smart enough to be able to take that game plan to home plate. A lot of guys are fog banks between the on-deck circle and home plate. He was able to skirt around that.

"THE BIRD" TAKES BASEBALL FOR A FLIGHT OF FANCY

Out of nowhere the antithesis of the hard-bitten Piniella arrived in 1976. Mark "the Bird" Fidrych charmed the country with his antics on the mound, doing landscaping, talking to the ball, and gesturing to his fielders. He could pitch, too, winning 19 games as a rookie for the Tigers and starting the All-Star Game for the AL.

But good things often come to an end too soon. Fidrych's run was cut short by arm trouble. The Bird, no doubt a kissin' cousin of Big Bird on *Sesame Street,* then blossoming in popularity, still made an impression with his gentle-soul character long after retirement. Sadly, he was found dead after an accident apparently caused while repairing a vehicle on his farm in 2009.

The fond memories, though, cannot be stifled by Fidrych's death.

ALAN TRAMMELL: He treated everyone the same. He was the kind of guy, you go over to his place, he'd cook you a steak, chicken, whatever. He loved to interact with his teammates. He just wanted to be a regular person. When I came to the Tigers as a youngster, we kept our mouths shut and just watched and learned. He was ahead of us already and established himself as a good major-league player. As the time went by, he opened his arms to all of us. When I look back, when I retired and our paths crossed, the bonds we had as teammates never left. He was one of those guys who you thought would live a lot longer. It doesn't surprise me that he wouldn't be afraid to get his fingernails and arms dirty—that's just the kind of person he was.

That's a good description of Mark [taking joy in life]. Some guys can do things internally. He had to do it outwardly where he was talking to himself. That's all he was doing—motivating and talking to himself, reminding himself of a pitch or where his arm slot was. Obviously the people loved it.

My first Opening Day was 1978. We were playing Toronto, it was the ninth inning, he was going to have a complete game and we were going to win. It was a cool day as they normally are. There was a gust of wind that took a wrapper right in front of the mound. As he went to get the sign, it bothered him. So he stepped down to pick it up. As he went to bend down, another gust of wind took the wrapper toward the third-base line. And he was determined he was not going to stop till he got the wrapper and put it in his back pocket. As he was going after the wrapper, the crowd was going crazy. I was at short, and I was smiling and laughing. I'll never forget that.

It's one of those things where you can't choreograph these things. It has to be natural. That was him. I think we all like to see some personalities like that. We all can't be the same. Mark Fidrych was a little ahead of his time. It was the time when teams still drew just 1 million. When he'd pitch, the attendance would increase by a dramatic number. The game is so great there will be some more personalities like that after we're done.

Fidrych's antics were just one of thousands of memories for Chicago sportscaster Les Grobstein's Ripken-like streak of attendance at All-Star Games. Grobstein, working the overnight shift at all-sports WSCR-AM, has attended every Mid-Summer Classic since 1970. He got his share of laughs at the sights and sounds of the Bird starting the 1976 All-Star Game at Veterans Stadium in Philadelphia.

LES GROBSTEIN (Chicago sportscaster, 1970–79): Fidrych probably had his worst outing in that game. The National League didn't flinch at his antics. I remember the news conference the day before. It was held at the same hotel where Legionnaires' disease cropped up a week later. Fidrych spoke like the true almost-hippie type he was. He was way out there. He had everyone in stitches, he was pretty funny. So he finished. Then it was Randy Jones's turn to speak. He got up there—he says, are you kidding me? I've got to follow this? I've got to follow what Mark would say?

During the game the Bird would get on the mound and pat it down with his right hand. He'd smooth down every little rough spot and then he would grab the baseball and start talking to it. He did so many other weird, strange things. Unfortunately, that night, the National League hit him very hard.

Indeed, Padres lefty Jones, the NL's starting pitcher, found Fidrych a hard act to follow in that All-Star press conference.

RANDY JONES: When I first met him, talking to him, he was a simple country boy. I'm in a three-piece suit, in a tie, and I'm right on time. Here comes the Bird, bursting through the door. He had slept in. He was late for the luncheon. His long hair was a mess. He had a pair of shorts, flip-flops, and a T-shirt on. Would you expect anything less from the Bird?

GAYLORD PERRY: ME AND THE SPITTER WERE A GOOD TEAM

A different set of on-the-mound gyrations was sported during the True Golden Age by Gaylord Perry, a savvy country-boy pitcher. See, it was baseball's worst-kept secret that he doctored up the baseball with greasy stuff. But Perry hardly ever was caught red-handed while pitching for the Giants, Indians, Padres, and other teams. More than actually making the ball dive and dart weighted down with Vaseline, Perry developed his spitballer's character into a big psychological act. He'd touch the back of his neck, tug at the side of his uniform pants, rub the baseball. Was he or wasn't he loading up on this particular pitch? Only Perry knew.

In contrast to the solemn outrage over steroid accusations three decades later, Perry never faced a congressional committee. He was a sideshow to which the umpires were his foils and everyone used a "wink-wink" posture to him. Perry was never ejected from a game for throwing an illegal pitch until August 20, 1982, near the end of his career. At times Perry would turn the tables on hitters, accusing them of corking their bats. He reveled in his reputation for fun and profit, even authoring a 1974 book entitled *Me and the Spitter*. Despite the fact that he threw an illegal pitch 50 years after it was officially banned, Perry easily made the Hall of Fame in 1991. No pundit or baseball official ever suggested his 314 wins were tainted because the pitches were slicked-up—hence the difference in attitudes in a more libertine era toward cheating.

GAYLORD PERRY: The umpires, I knew them by their first names, I knew them better than anyone else because I had a visit every four days. I never tried to show any umpires up. I did touch my hat and the back of my head, stuff like that, because it was upsetting hitters so much. I had half the battle won. I needed some help.

I learned by sitting on the bench in San Francisco watching Don Drysdale pitching against my teammates. He'd strike 'em out and they'd come back to the bench, "He's got it on his hat today." Next guy comes back, "It's on his belt." Next guy comes back and says, "It's on his pants leg." I was 1–6 in '63, so I started to touch myself all over. I won a couple of games and said I was putting stuff on the ball. So I just kept doing it. If they would have a committee meeting and change the rules and allow that pitch, I'd make a comeback tomorrow.

I've seen many, many corked bats. In my home ballpark the opposing-team bats would be put out before they came out. I'd always go over to check them out to make sure who might be grooving their bats, who was corking their bats. Even in an Old-Timers Game, one player said take this bat. It was corked.

Figures that Perry would celebrate the moon landing in his own special way. Shortly after *Apollo 11* landed on the moon on the afternoon of July 20, 1969, Perry won out on an old dare by launching his own shot into space in the third inning of a 7–3 Giants victory at Candlestick Park.

GAYLORD PERRY: I was taking batting practice in Forbes Field. In BP I could hit it out. It was half-speed. This kid will hit a lot of home runs for you, someone said. [Giants manager] Alvin Dark turns around and says there will be a man on the moon before he does that. The day the man landed on the moon, I was on the mound when there was a moment of silence for the people on the moon. We were playing the Dodgers. In the bottom of that inning, Claude Osteen was pitching for the Dodgers and I hit my first home run.

THE MAD HUNGARIAN IS REALLY A BASEBALL FUNNYMAN

Want more mound histrionics? You just needed to watch Cardinals lefty Al Hrabosky and his alter ego, the "Mad Hungarian," during the late innings in the mid-1970s.

With a mean visage and luxuriant Fu Manchu mustache, Hrabosky turned his back on the hitter, walked to the back of the mound, and appeared as if his head would explode. He steadily psyched himself up, pounding his left hand into his glove, mumbling to himself, before he turned around and set himself to face the hitter. Sometimes, hitters would step out of the box to counter Hrabosky. And once in a while the confrontation would escalate into a brawl, as it did one 1974 afternoon in St. Louis when Hrabosky's histrionics triggered a brawl between battery-mate Ted Simmons and Cubs third baseman Bill Madlock.

AL HRABOSKY (Cardinals, Royals, 1970–79): It [Mad Hungarian character] did evolve over time. It was a by-product of all my successes and failures as a young athlete. I didn't make three Little League teams, at age 8, 9, and 10. I didn't make an eighth-grade junior high team. I didn't play in 9th and 10th grades. I didn't start pitching till my senior year. All the time I thought, when I was in high school, I thought I was the best athlete our school had ever seen. I was a tremendous football player. I had it down to a science, when to hit a runner a split second [after] he relaxed after the whistle. Just proceeded to take that football mentality onto the baseball field.

What had to happen to me was what happens to a lot of young athletes. I got to the big leagues based on my physical talents. I was young and immature, first arriving at age 20, not having a lot of pitching background. When I started getting roughed up in a few games, instead of believing in my own ability, I started doubting myself—what do I have to do to change—getting real negative.

It was around the All-Star break in '74, it was brought to my attention that if I didn't straighten up my act—and I didn't have an act then—but if I didn't straighten up my pitching, I'd be going back to the minor leagues. So I realized I had to do something to get myself back in gear. That was the advent of walking off the back of the mound, trying to be this mental giant and this physically intimidating person. There were factors there of playing with Bob Gibson. He was a great, great competitor I saw intimidate certain hitters. On the other side, I watched a guy like Willie Stargell swinging his bat around, standing in the batter's box, and I saw how some young pitchers would visibly become shaken. So I decided I would present this very, very positive, outward, aggressive image of myself through the Mad Hungarian. Whether anyone ever got to me or not, outwardly you would never see any kind of intimidation.

That was the beginning of it. At the same time, I started letting the long hair grow and the Fu Manchu and try to say this is the image I wanted to become—it would be invincible. The beauty was all of a sudden I started pitching better. It was all mental what I was doing, rather than the physical with the long hair and mustache. I was doing these things for myself, walking off the back of the mound. I started having some immediate success because I had much more concentration, locating the ball where I wanted to and going through a mental process back behind the mound. Once I started having some success, the media made the fans aware of what I was doing.

Then it evolved into a threefold effect. It immediately helped me. Two, it got a crowd reaction—people liked it at home, then I'd go into Wrigley Field and be greeted by a standing boo. Third, there was a small percentage where it bugged the hitters. Some guys like Al Oliver, it motivated. A great hitter, he [feels the pitcher] can do whatever he wants, he eventually has to throw the ball. Others, it got into a mental game, "OK, if he does this, I'm going to do that. If he does that, I'm going to do this." All of a sudden, they weren't prepared for when I threw the pitch.

First and foremost it was done for my own personal concentration. Nobody could tell you what kind of effect it would have on the crowd or the hitter. I did find there were a certain amount of hitters who would go to the plate 500, 600 times, maybe face me five or six times a year, but in those five or six times they would change every rule of their mental preparation of going to the plate. They never thought about situational hitting, all they wanted to do is knock my head off—hit the ball up the middle and knock my head off.

DAVE KINGMAN—JUST LEAVE ME ALONE

Dave Kingman wasn't quite as close-mouthed as Steve Carlton. But he had the same attitude—just leave me alone.

Marching to his own drummer, playing on four teams in one season in 1977—the Mets, Padres, Angels, and Yankees— the long, lanky, powerful slugger simply did not want to talk about himself to inquiring media even though he was a public figure. But the strongman couldn't hide his accomplishments, even amid his prodigious strikeout totals. Kingman slugged the longest homer ever at Wrigley Field as a Met off Tom Dettore on April 14, 1976. The ball landed on Kenmore Avenue four houses past Waveland Avenue, with an "X" marking the spot on the sidewalk visible for the next three years. And when the product of northwest suburban Mt. Prospect came home as the Cubs' first-ever free-agent signee in 1978, amassing a slew of tape-measure shots, of course everyone wanted to know what made him tick.

No dice. "Private person" Kingman would rather go fishing than talk about himself. That led to a contentious relationship with the media and some interesting antisocial behavior, even as he stunned baseball with a breakthrough 48-homer, 115-RBI season in 1979.

DAVE KINGMAN (Giants, Padres, Mets, Padres, Yankees, Angels, Cubs, 1971–79): I'm still on the quiet side, I guess. Once people get to know me, they realize that the Dave Kingman the press portrayed never was and certainly isn't today. My close friends know the person they tried to portray never existed. We're all different. We all put our pants on different, I guess. Everybody goes about their business in their own way. Avoiding the press was the way that gave me peace away from baseball.

Sportscasters on radio and TV can tell it like it is. They have no way of misinterpreting or inserting their feelings into the report. When they ask you a question, the public can make up its own mind. In print a writer will interpret his feelings toward an individual. Sometimes it's unjust and unfair. The reader at times comes away with a tainted feeling toward an athlete. I wasn't out there trying to be in a popularity contest. There are quite a few writers who I respect and enjoy reading and who have become close friends. But there are many, many bad writers out there who will write their columns, never venture into the clubhouse, and never make the effort to really get to know somebody before they write their articles. These are people I don't have time for.

Indeed, Kingman preferred fishing, and got up before dawn on game days to go out on Lake Michigan. His 1978–79 Cubs manager, Herman Franks, witnessed the aftereffects of his angling activities.

HERMAN FRANKS: He never drank or smoked, but Dave would get up at four or five in the morning to go fishing. When he came to the park, he was tired as hell. He'd go in the training room to take a nap. He's a great guy but did certain things I didn't agree with. . . . We just didn't agree on how to handle baseball. Baseball was kind of secondary to him.

Surprisingly, Kingman's teammates at worst tolerated him and at best liked him. Pitcher Mike Krukow found out Kingman, dubbed "Ding Dong" by columnist Mike Royko, was the best party planner on the team.

MIKE KRUKOW: I loved him, when he played for the Cubs. Every time I pitched he hit a home run. Kingman was an honest player, he was an honest teammate. He was a good teammate. He really was the face of that club.

The very first spring training, he had a party for the team. He was living out in Scottsdale close to Camelback Mountain in a nice condo. We went over there and he was running around like Hazel [1960s sitcom maid], making sure the glasses were filled and the ashtrays were empty. He never sat down.

He was quiet, especially in the morning. He sat down by his locker, went through the mail, had a cup of coffee. Willie Hernandez, who had a huge Afro, used to mess with Dave. Kingman liked his peace and quiet. Willie walked up behind him and shouted, "Watch out, Dave." That spilled the coffee over his hand and he'd get pissed, chased Willie around the clubhouse. Quite sophomoric, but very humorous. It happened again. One particular day he wrestled Hernandez—a big man himself at 6-2, about 210—down to the ground and picked him up by his ankles. He held him out straight-arm and walked him over to the two stalls in the bathroom, we thought he was going to scrub the toilet with his Afro.

One more example of his strength was on Kingman's boat in San Diego, where he lived in the off-season. It was a 40-foot boat. We came back from the game off the team bus on the boat. He had some friends from the FBI down there already there. There were 40 to 50 people on the boat. Here's Hazel walking around making sure everyone's glass was full. Dave had a keg of beer in a 33-gallon trash can full of ice in the back of the boat. As he sees the boat full up, he's got to make more room. He lifts this thing by himself over the back-ass end of the boat and reaches out, straight-arms this thing with the distance from the dock to the boat about 2 to 3 feet, and reaches out and sets it out on the dock. On top of the boat were Reuschel, Sutter, Dick Tidrow, and myself. The four of us looked at each other and said that's impossible. Later we all walked over to the trash can full of beer and we couldn't budge it. It would have taken all four of us to lift it.

Kingman's long, long-ball feats inspired a youth player in a family of baseball and softball fanatics from Peoria, Illinois, three hours from Chicago. Nine-year-old Jim Thome idolized and even had an "obsession" for Kingman. He assumed Kingman's role in Wiffle-ball games. Little could he project that three decades down the line, when Thome would both far exceed Kingman's power numbers and absolutely contrast his personality around the game. But at this point of his life, he simply wanted to meet Kingman while on a family outing to Wrigley Field. He slipped away from his parents in the ballpark, and they couldn't find him at first. Young Jim had sneaked onto the field in search of Kingman.

JIM THOME (Cubs fan, 1975–79): [Cubs catcher] Barry Foote ended up carrying me out [of the dugout]. It was a great story. It's like any kid—when they have a player they admire, they'll do anything to get their favorite player's autograph. That's how I was.

BILLY "THE KID" NEVER TRULY GREW UP

Need a manager to give a team an immediate jolt? Hire Billy Martin. Need to get rid of a manager who quickly grates on teammates and management soon after that revival? Fire Billy Martin. Want constant controversies and an overload of personal peccadilloes? Follow Billy Martin, in and out of uniform.

Martin was the constant generator of news, good and bad, through his managerial tenures with the Twins, Tigers, Rangers, and twice with the Yankees within the True Golden Age. Quick with his fists and mouth, even faster to down his shots of booze, and constantly on the prowl for female companionship, Martin inspired strong feelings from everyone he touched, including some verbal counterpunching from a prominent Red Sox left-hander of the time, responding to Martin's criticism in a 1977 radio interview recorded by then–AP reporter Tom Shaer in Boston.

BILL LEE (Red Sox, Expos, 1969–79): That's really remedial. The poor guy like that after he's been buried so bad. I feel sorry for him. He's always been a bad judge of character. He comes here and he has to find some way to stroke his ego now. He's got much bigger problems to worry about. Poor guy like that, with the 15 brain cells he's got left, he burned two of them out in the fight with [Reggie] Jackson and lost three others in the gutters of the streets of Boston. We all start out with a couple billion. It's not vicious. I couldn't play for Steinbrenner, let alone Martin. He's just going fade away as the Last Angry Man. It's a shame.

Interestingly, Martin had his devotees. One who could be classified as a protégé was Lou Piniella during his Yankees clutch-hitting days. The Boss, George Steinbrenner, told Martin to basically start preparing Piniella to manage in the near future. Sure enough, Piniella's first stint running the Yankees dovetailed with Martin's final tenure as manager. Piniella sifted the good things from Martin while rejecting the worst of his character flaws.

LOU PINIELLA: Billy was a really good field manager. I thought he ran a baseball game as well as anyone in that era. He was sharp. He knew when to pull a pitcher, when to steal a base. He knew when to squeeze in a run. He had a great sense for the unexpected. I learned a lot of baseball from Billy. I played for Bob Lemon, Yogi Berra, Dick Howser. . . . I played for some real good managers. I played for Joe Gordon. You learn something from everybody.

The guy I probably manage more like than anybody else is Billy. I like an aggressive style of play. I like to take chances. I play my entire roster and pitch everyone who's available. I differ from Billy in one regard. Billy used to pitch the hot reliever, where I tend to try to pick and choose a little bit more and try to keep everybody fresh.

Off the field, Billy had his problems, obviously. It's a shame, because he was a good person. He couldn't control one of his vices, and that was really his downfall. But he was a good man. We won a lot of games. I played for him three different times. I coached for him [while he was] manager. I replaced him as a manager, he replaced me. I was his general manager. I knew Billy really well. A good person with one vice that caused him problems. It's a shame. If it hadn't been for that, he'd have won a lot more ball games and he'd be in the Hall of Fame.

Imagine working as an Associated Press reporter while in college and coming face-to-face with Billy Martin twice only hours after his famous nationally televised dugout confrontation with Reggie Jackson at Fenway Park on June 18, 1977. Chicago broadcast personality Tom Shaer had just such an experience, and recalled the Martin-Jackson incident and its aftermath in which Martin tried to cool down in the Fenway press box.

TOM SHAER: Reggie loafed on a ball. I was in the first-base side of the press box with a perfect view into the Yankees dugout. He pulls Reggie off the field and Reggie says, "What, what?" Reggie says something and Billy goes after him. Elston Howard is restraining Billy and it was a mess. Two or three were restraining Billy. It was unbelievable.

I went into the locker room afterward. Billy faced the press. He said I'm not going to let anybody show up this ball club. He didn't hustle on the ball. If he shows up the ball club, I will show up him. Reggie had left. Leigh Montville of the *Boston Globe* figured Reggie might leave early. So he went outside and followed Reggie up the sidewalk, but Reggie hopped into a cab and left. Steve Jacobson of *Newsday* asked Billy, "Will this fuck up the team?" Billy asked him to repeat the question, which he did. Billy said, "I don't think so, we've got a lot of professionals on this team."

Afterward, Billy went up to the pressroom. I was sitting at a big, round table with Billy, [AP sports editor] Dave O'Hara, [Red Sox GM] Dick O'Connell, and two other people. For a little guy, Billy had huge hands. He held them up and made fists, saying, "I can't let that guy get away with that shit. He didn't hustle on that ball. Who does he think he is?" Then he went down in the Yankees broadcast booth to use the phone. "I have to call the front office," he said. Billy was down there on the phone at least 20 minutes, half an hour.

Dick O'Connell liked Billy Martin and wanted to hire him as manager, but the timing was never right. In 1975 Billy was managing the Rangers. He got fired in July. Darrell Johnson was manager of the Red Sox and Dick decided he was going to have to fire Darrell, the team was not doing well. But they went on a road trip and won 10 in a row and never looked back. If he had reached a decision and stuck with it to fire Johnson, he would have hired Martin. The team took off and Johnson stayed.

In another side of Martin, he gained the respect of opponents for his baseball savvy and knowledge of the game—but not necessarily for his bench jockeying, which got creative in the case of a future Orioles Hall of Famer.

BROOKS ROBINSON: I really liked Billy. I played against Billy late in his career and when he managed. It was not middle-of-the-road with Billy. I had that little short brim on my helmet. Every time I'd see him he'd say, "Robinson, you look like a German tank driver with that hat. Where'd you get it?" I don't know where he came up with that. I had a good relationship with him. Talking with guys who played with him, they loved him and they hated him, too.

Martin was most closely related in style to Leo Durocher. Fergie Jenkins had the privilege of pitching—and winning—for both irascible managers, Durocher from 1966 to 1972 with the Cubs, and Martin in his 1½ seasons in Texas during 1974 and 1975.

FERGIE JENKINS: They're pretty much the same. They were old-school managers who trusted your ability. They gave you the ball and didn't want it back unless he walked out there to take you out. When I look at the two years I had with Billy and the six years with Leo, they were two peas in a pod.

Billy hated excuses. If you went out there and performed and things didn't work out the way you wanted, he hated for you to alibi. The nucleus of the ball club played most of the time, the bench was that, the bench strength. He was about the same as a handler of pitchers as Leo. His pitching coach was Art Fowler, who had one order: Just throw strikes.

His drinking didn't affect him around the ball club. We'd see him around hotel bars and he'd get angry at people. He always had good first years—Detroit, Minnesota, Texas, the Yankees. That second year, I'm not sure if it was something that had to do with something he had to accomplish, he'd have a problem. He lost the mood of what he was supposed to do.

THE EARL OF BALTIMORE

Every bit as combative as Martin on the field, Earl Weaver was a paragon of stability compared to Billy the Kid. Instead of being fired every other season like Martin, Weaver had a 15-year run as Orioles manager during the franchise's best days. Martin may have been a thorn in the side of the arbiters, but Weaver was a serrated-edge dagger. He was combustible, with a knowledge of the rule book equal to theirs. Knowledge, as you know, is power.

No way was Weaver "working" the umpires like a politician. He was too direct and opinionated for that kind of style.

EARL WEAVER: You'd never get an edge, and they'd never take anything away from you on purpose. My disputes with the umpires—and I was there for quite some time—were because I felt they missed a call. The great thing about the umpires I was associated with, if you had an argument Wednesday, you come out Thursday and everything was clean. They're hoping to have a good ball game, I'm hoping my team has a good ball game, and you go from there.

Now you see with all the technology that they have in baseball and how you can see where they can miss a play, they're human. They're going to miss it. And when that happens, you're going to argue and you're going to try to get your point across. There were no personalities involved. They missed 'em and you were going to let them know they missed 'em. Maybe once or twice [an ump admitted he missed it] and that ends the argument just about all the time. But you're liable to say something like,

"You cost me the game," and you're liable to try to get in the last word, which is the wrong thing to do. I knew it was the wrong thing to do, but I did it a number of times.

But there is far more to managing than jawing with the umps. Weaver said his strength was evaluating talent and not misusing it.

EARL WEAVER: It's recognizing the fact there aren't too many Willie Mayses and Frank Robinsons or Brooks Robinsons. If you want a ballplayer on your club, you've got to accept his incapabilities, things he can't do. I didn't ask Boog [Powell] to steal some bases when it wasn't possible. I didn't ask somebody to go up and hit against a pitcher that I knew he couldn't hit and the hitter himself knew he couldn't hit. Like our platoon system, with [Gary] Roenicke and [John] Lowenstein later on, you recognize what a fellow can do and can't do and try to use him in situations where he's going to be beneficial.

I used all of it together [numbers and evaluation]. The more information you get, the better manager you're going to be.

Brooks Robinson was with Weaver longer than any other player. Within a few years he got to know the great manager's style inside-out.

BROOKS ROBINSON: When we were winning, he was barking. When we were losing, he was telling us how great we were. That's one of the things he was very good at. He practiced a little psychology. The good thing about Earl is he never had a doghouse. He utilized all 25 guys. No one sat for very long. Everybody played. He put some funky lineups out there. The 25th guy on the team would be playing. He had some great coaches.

He never liked to hit-and-run. He never liked to steal a lot of bases. He prided himself on three-run homers, and you had Boog and Frank, that helped out a lot. I really appreciate Earl simply because here was a guy who never wanted to do anything in his life but be a big-league ball-player. He didn't have the talent. He was an MVP in a couple of the leagues he played in. So he started in managing. He went up, through D, C, B, A, AA, Triple-A, Major League, Hall of Fame. He set out to do something spectacular, and he did it.

He was cracking us up [with umpire disputes]. We got a lot of humor out of it. The reason some of them didn't like him is he knew the rule book better than the umpires. They were afraid of him in that respect. We were playing in Cleveland. There was a pickoff or balk. They're barking back and forth on the mound. Bang! He runs back to the dugout, runs up that long hallway into the clubhouse and comes back with the rule book. He starts barking again at the umpires. Finally he ends up tearing up the rule book on the mound and pitching it up in the air. Of course they threw his ass out of there. He was a lot of fun.

In 1977 I sat on the bench most of the year [in Robinson's final season] and it was just unbelievable. He was the funniest guy I ever played with. I got more laughs out of him than anyone else. I think the umpires have a little shorter fuse now. They don't take a whole lot, you're out of there. I don't understand it.

GENE MAUCH DID EVERYTHING BUT WIN

Gene Mauch could dish it out, but could he take it?

Renowned as baseball's most assertive bench jockey and cerebral manager in the 1970s—"just as radical as Leo Durocher," said Rick Wise, one of his Phillies pitchers—Gene Mauch drove players to the point of distraction. He got into Cubs third baseman Ron Santo's head—and Santo wanted to wring his neck. But on September 20, 1972, at Wrigley Field, he accused Cubs right fielder Jose Cardenal of calling him a "vile" name. After the Cubs finished off Mauch's Montreal Expos 6–2 for Milt Pappas's 200th career victory, the little general led 20 members of his vanquished team all the way across the field to the home clubhouse entrance in the left-field corner in an attempt to confront Cardenal. Cubs manager Whitey Lockman met Mauch at the door and defused the situation. Minutes later, the talkative Mauch refused to elaborate about Cardenal's comments.

Mauch was a complicated, multidimensional man, always haunted by the most famous collapse in baseball history over which he presided. His Phillies gave away a 6½-game lead with 12 games to go in 1964, losing 10 in a row in the process. Although the last team he managed, the Angels, finally finished first in 1986 in the AL West, they in turn pulled off an all-time playoff pratfall in coughing up a sure ALCS win to the Red Sox. A World Series berth, let alone a championship, always eluded Mauch.

He was a man who sometimes tried to outsmart the game with small-ball, trick plays and five-man infields. Mauch died in 2005 at age 79. Ten years before his passing, while bench coach for the Royals, he reflected on a baseball life that included a managerial stint with the Twins.

GENE MAUCH (Expos and Twins Manager, 1969–79): Baseball is like malaria. It'll go away for a little while and quit bothering you, but pretty soon it will crop up again. There's a great deal of satisfaction. I had no problem with my career. I'm satisfied I contributed here and there. I had great cooperation from people. A lot of things were said about the penurious attitude of [Twins owner] Calvin Griffith, but that was necessary. He had no choice. If you can't afford to pay 'em, you have to let 'em go. Consequently, the manager has to make an adjustment.

I think of the years I spent in Montreal in a rehab program, taking players and putting a new set of tread on them. Getting some years out of them, guys who were deemed washed up or done with other clubs and came to us, and we put together a little well-oiled group. That might be the most fun I had as far as accomplishments were concerned.

People who didn't see Ron Santo play didn't realize what a dominating player he could be. A wonderful third baseman aside from being an outstanding hitter. He was an emotional guy. I figure, what the hell, he's killing me anyway, I might as well try to get him thinking about me instead of thinking about my pitchers. Sometimes it worked.

Outfielder Ron Swoboda could compare Mauch with Mets manager Gil Hodges, also a baseball chess master, when he moved on from New York to Montreal in 1971. He'll take Hodges, though, in a battle of wits.

RON SWOBODA: I played for Gene Mauch, who was more cerebral than anybody. He did some things that were inscrutable. He was trying to outsmart the game of baseball. Hodges was just trying to take the obvious play a step further. If you're going to gamble, put some more chips out there. Put five players in the infield. The difference in Gene Mauch and Gil Hodges was you understood what he [Hodges] wanted to do. When you fool your players, you've started to turn the strategy back on itself.

Original Expos radio announcer Dave van Horne had a different view of Mauch.

DAVE VAN HORNE (Expos radio announcer, 1969–79): I thought he really did a good job with not only minor-league veterans who suddenly found their way into the big leagues via expansion, but also these veteran players made available to the expansion teams via the expansion draft. He communicated well with both of them. I remember Ron Hunt, who said when you played against Mauch, you hated him; when you played for him you'd run through a brick wall for him.

Gene Mauch could look at a box score in the morning of a Cubs-Pirates game the night before and re-create the game inning by inning. He was a master bridge player, he had his masters points. On his off-day he'd organize three or four bridge tables. It was terrific to break in during those early years because I learned my major-league game from Gene Mauch. To his credit, as much pride as he had, he really went after the job in Montreal as a great challenge to make this expansion team better than he should be. I think he succeeded. They were for the most part a competitive team. He was a fierce competitor and had a great wit about him.

He was a neat, well-groomed man, impeccably dressed. He didn't like long hair or facial hair on players. He told [pitcher] Steve Renko, your sideburns are getting lower while your ERA is getting higher.

TOMMY LASORDA: TERRIFIC AT TEACHING KIDS TO BLEED DODGER BLUE

Tom Lasorda is one of those baseball legends whose oversize personality obscures almost everything else he accomplished.

Buddy to the stars of Hollywood, his Dodger Stadium office was a gallery of Tinseltown photos. A pasta gourmand who stocked the office with a garlicky buffet of catered and donated food. A bombastic preacher man who extolled the virtues of his team and as a result was tabbed as an ambassador for baseball.

But who remembers Lasorda the teacher, an incubator for the talent that stocked a string of successful Dodgers teams for which he'd coach or manage?

Lasorda's deepest contribution to the Dodgers was as its Triple-A manager at the dawn of the 1970s, counseling and shepherding the bumper crop of homegrown talent, much of it from a bountiful 1968 draft crop.

BILL BUCKNER: He was the biggest factor in the Dodgers organization. They had some good people and a great minor-league system, but if you were to pick one guy, Tommy influenced a lot of players—guys who went on to have 10-, 15-, 20-year major-league careers.

He was a good instructor, but more what he did was he taught the young players to love the game and compete at the highest level. That was his biggest strength. He made the game a lot of fun and exciting. You felt like when you were playing in the rookie leagues that you were in the big leagues. He made it a special thing. He always had it directed toward the big leagues. That's what he pushed us to do.

The first week I was in the rookie league, he made me write a letter to [Dodgers first baseman] Wes Parker that you better start looking for a new job. That fall, when the season was over and I was going to USC, I went to Dodger Stadium and Tommy took us in the locker room. Wes Parker goes, "You're the guy who wrote me that letter." Two years later, I took his job.

We spent hours and hours on the practice field, way beyond the time anybody else was there. He was a good judge of talent. The guys he felt had a good chance of making it, he made sure they [worked out more].

At least one Lasorda trait rubbed off on Dusty Baker, who joined the Dodgers in a trade from the Braves in 1976, just before Lasorda was promoted to manager to succeed 21-year warhorse Walter Alston. Baker's Wrigley Field office from 2003 to 2006 was the Midwest version of Lasorda's photo museum, with images ranging from Hank Aaron to John Lee Hooker.

DUSTY BAKER: I learned how to handle people being the oldest of five in my family, from my dad, who was a coaching figure in my town, and being in the Marines. Going to an all-white high school [in Sacramento], and being in the South, where segregation was still alive. Growing up in Riverside [California], which was mostly black and Mexican. The thing I learned most from Tommy was the power of belief and the power of positive thinking, and the power of faith.

For a while [I believed in LaSorda's preaching]. After a while you kind of accept it. You're going to get it anyway. You're going to get it whether you want to hear it or believe it. Tommy was a great scout of player talent. That's the biggest difference between then and now, in that the manager had more control over who was on his team, to affect the outcome of his job. The power and influence of scouts and GMs is greater now in helping to pick the team. The manager is not as conscious and aware of payroll as much as ownership and the GM have to be.

THE MOUTH OF THE SOUTH TRIES TO MANAGE

Of all the colorful owners in the True Golden Age, Ted Turner was first among equals in outlandishness when he assumed stewardship of the Braves in 1976.

An active participant in team promotions, the "Mouth of the South" cable TV entrepreneur and champion yachtsman could be found on his hands and knees, pushing a peanut forward with his nose. He defied convention and baseball rules, running afoul of commissioner Bowie Kuhn with his improper contact with potential free-agent Gary Matthews in 1976. Turner ended up signing Matthews. But the wildest image of Turner was on display on May 11, 1977, in Pittsburgh, with his Braves having lost a shocking 16 in a row. Ted Turner believed in being a hands-on company manager, and he took that role literally, suiting up in a Braves uniform while sending manager Dave Bristol on a leave of absence.

The most interesting inside-out view of Turner was offered up by his resident Hall of Fame knuckleball pitcher, who lost to the Pirates 2–1 for setback number 17 in a row. That preceded a dictum from Kuhn that an owner cannot also manage, bringing the end of Turner's second career with the Braves.

PHIL NIEKRO: I pitched that game in Pittsburgh. Dave Bristol was managing. Ted was the skipper of the *Courageous.* He put instructions down as captain and if something went wrong, he knew it. Being an owner in the stands, he couldn't see what was going on in the clubhouse, he couldn't see what was in the dugout. When we lost 16 in a row, he said I got to find out myself, I'm writing these paychecks, I got to see what was going on in the dugout, find out what the hell was wrong.

I had just gotten through taking my batting practice and Ted came walking out of the dugout, walked over to the batting cage, and he didn't look any more like a manager than I would have. Ted came up and stood right next to me. I said jokingly, "Ted, what spot you got me hitting in today?" He said, "You want to lead off?" I said, "Keep me in the ninth spot." We lost the game and Bowie Kuhn said you can't do that anymore.

He really didn't know the whole in's and out's of how the game was played. He was leaning on Vern Benson and the coaches. He just wanted to see the makeup of the club, their demeanor, if they don't give a shit. I don't know if he would have managed the whole year.

He was interested in your family and life and your future. I don't care if we won or we lost. He'd come down into that Atlanta clubhouse every night with us, sit back and pull up a chair, have a drink and talk about the game. He wasn't a heavy drinker. He was just into the game. He sat right near the dugout. He was our biggest fan. I don't know how many owners today would walk in the locker room after the game to talk to you. He wanted to let all his players know just because you're losing, I'm not giving up on you. [Braves GM] Bill Lucas was like that. He came in and patted you on the back.

We weren't very good in those days—in fact, we were horseshit—but it was a good feeling seeing Ted come in every night and talk with you and say I'm with you, guys. Never talked about the won-lost record, who made bad plays, just guys, I'm with you. How many owners did that then, and how many today?

His clowning aside, Turner actually was one of the transformative figures of the True Golden Age. The Mouth changed the way baseball was presented on TV. Televising almost all Braves games and putting his Atlanta station on satellite brought the game to millions around the country—around the world, in fact—who otherwise had scattershot video exposure to baseball. Now baseball is very heavily a cable-borne sport. The increase in costs of watching the game, via cable or satellite fees paid by subscribers, is offset in the massive increase of accessibility of the sport. No longer do teams go weeks with just a handful of games televised. Combined with the hiring of top baseball people and giving them free rein to build up baseball's best player-development system of the late 1980s and 1990s, Turner's trailblazing should merit consideration for the Hall of Fame.

PHIL NIEKRO: No question about it [being a positive] as far as letting the whole world see baseball. It was us and

WGN. I remember when the game was over, he'd replay it at 11:30 or 12 at night. He had a double game every night. I remember going to different places, they said they saw us on WTBS. We were America's team. You don't just have to be a Red Sox fan or Giants. Let everyone watch it.

That's a great idea [the Hall of Fame for Turner]. I've never heard anybody talk about it. That's good food for thought and I'm glad you mentioned that to me. I'll keep my mind open.

Similar open minds advanced the game at all levels in its True Golden Age. And in the hippie-turned-disco era, if you were a left-handed thinker in a right-handed world, finally you were not automatically cast out if you proposed something new and different. We take the end result of their groundbreaking efforts for granted these days.

14

Bread and Circuses;

Hot Dogs, Hair, and High Jinks

"Papa Carl" Leone had a rote answer for frisky behavior between the sexes in Wrigley Field's right-field bleachers. He'd take out his wallet and point. "My wife's picture is in there!" protested Papa Carl. The septuagenarian and successor to Caleb "Chet" Chestnut as sage of a group of fans at the top of the bleachers, above the 368-foot sign, tried to keep a sense of decorum and old-fashioned propriety amid increasing breakouts of ribald and anarchist fan behavior that took over Wrigley Field and other ballparks as the 1970s wore on.

The baseball world of his retirement hardly had any resemblance to his childhood. Leone would recall watching a high school kid named Lou Gehrig belt a homer in 1920 in a special exhibition at Wrigley Field. Fifty-seven years later, Papa Carl prided himself on being first in line for bleacher seats each morning, arriving at 6:30 a.m. "Force of habit," he explained from his days as an early riser to work as a paint sprayer. Papa Carl purchased tickets for later arrivals of the group on weekends, when block-long lines down Waveland and Sheffield Avenues formed for the sale of bleacher seats for weekend games against such popular foes as the Cardinals and Reds. At a designated time the spry senior handed the tickets through the iron gates to his buddies, who could then walk right in without taking their place in the queues. Upstairs, Leone literally roped off two sections of bleachers so the accustomed seats always would be available. What a prince of a man, his dignity intact except when Bobby Murcer unaggressively pursued a fly ball near the vines. Papa Carl let Murcer have it, joining other fans wondering why the Cubs traded two-time batting champ Bill Madlock for Murcer.

Leone shook his head when a teenage couple took their places in the first row below, by the wall, one weekend afternoon. The boy, shirtless and in cutoffs, faced his girlfriend while he stood with his back against the wall. The girl kept rubbing her lover's crotch through his shorts, the couple apparently oblivious to their surroundings, which was not exactly a secluded beach. After an inning the couple stopped their foreplay and got up to leave. Immediately, the entire section of bleacher fans rose to give them a standing ovation as the couple appeared thoroughly embarrassed by their notoriety, but not their carnal inning.

The old man thus saw and heard things in the stands unthinkable even a decade earlier. In some kind of strange extension of Woodstock and tougher rock concerts, the fan experience of the True Golden Age got bizarre in a heavy R- or even X-rated fashion.

The Pirates' Dave Parker spoke for a bevy of big leaguers when he said a woman flashed her breasts at him from the Wrigley Field bleachers. A few other players over the years got even more eye-popping female anatomy views as they ran in the outfield before or during games. Extending the early-1974 fad to ballparks, streakers paraded—in the same manner as at the 1974 Oscars telecast—onto the field, including a proud full-Monty fella in the left-field corner in 35-degree weather at the White Sox home opener at old Comiskey Park.

Language, of course, got much coarser. It was a break-through of sorts on April 22, 1973, when in the fifth inning of the nightcap of a Sunday doubleheader at Wrigley, the Cubs took a 9–0 lead on the Pirates, who had beat the Chicagoans like a drum the previous two seasons, and would do so again. "Pirates suck! Pirates suck!" came forth the bleachers' chant. "Go to hell, Pirates, go to hell!" was the next refrain, and the fans felt good about venting.

In almost the same breath, the emboldened ticket buyers sometimes became one and the same with the field and the players. Instances of fans storming the field by the hundreds or more became common at Wrigley Field and other ballparks. Fans lowered themselves from the bleachers and other parts of the Friendly Confines throughout 1969: on April 13, when an Ernie Banks RBI single capped a three-run ninth-inning rally to beat the Expos 7–6; on August 19, after Ken Holtzman no-hit the Braves without a strikeout; and on October 2, in the meaningless season finale against the Mets. Bleacher bums danced atop each dugout in that game to mark the Cubs' amazing season ride that ended up in September collapse. They also threw a smoke bomb onto the field, stopping play in the second, and carried catcher Randy Hundley off after the final out while waving Confederate flags in honor of the Virginia heritage of Hundley, nicknamed "Rebel." On July 13, 1969, a man slid down from the bleachers and pranced about the warning track in the second game of a doubleheader with the Phillies. Good sport Willie Smith, the Cubs left fielder, gave the gent a boost on his shoulders to climb back into the bleachers before the ballpark gendarmes arrived.

Finally, Cubs management had enough when a group of anti–Vietnam War protestors who moonlighted as baseball fans stormed the field after the Cubs' home opener on April 14, 1970. The Cubs barely survived a four-run Phillies' ninth in a 5–4 win, prompting another swarm of humanity onto the field. The dissenters got too rough bumping into a couple of players, so after the home stand was completed, the Cubs installed a basket—getting the idea from St. Louis's Busch Stadium—protruding on an angle outward from the top of the bleacher wall to prevent future fan incursions. Thus a famed big-league ground rule and the chance to get an incredibly cheap homer was born.

Wrigley Field, though, caught a break. Not hosting a World Series or even a playoff game, the old ballpark and field still stood. Any kind of postseason celebration and the fans would have taken the place apart and carried it off. Shea Stadium's field got a nice workover when thousands of fans dug it up to celebrate the Mets' World Series victory. Almost two years later, on September 30, 1971, the first game result altered by the rule of the mob took place at RFK Stadium in Washington, D.C. After an entire game of demonstrations from the 14,460 marking the Senators' final game before moving to Texas, the fans burst forth onto the field with two out in the ninth and the Senators leading the Yankees 7–5. Play could not be resumed, so American League history in the capital ended fittingly with a loss, this time via forfeit. The Yankees themselves were rushed by thousands in the Bronx when Chris Chambliss's walk-off homer against the Royals clinched their first pennant in 12 years in 1976.

Amazingly, throughout the 1970s owners actually encouraged the rule of the mob via promotions that got out of control. You'd figure "Barnum" Bill Veeck, in his final incarnation in baseball, was involved with one. Also highlighted was the hiring of a beer-soaked announcer who was the ultimate rabble-rouser and started a seventh-inning sing-along that continues today—also with Veeck's hands all over it. Meanwhile, the game endured the crossing of the clean-shaven line as facial hair sprouted all over, prompted by an owner's promotional bent, along with outlandish uniforms that rank as the ugliest in history. Combined with player high jinks that would not likely hold up in future decades, fun and frolic were a regular feature of baseball in its True Golden Age.

10-CENT BEER NIGHT ADDS TO CLEVELAND'S LEGEND

The landmark baseball comedy *Major League* (1989) wasn't pulled out of a scriptwriter's wildest fantasy. It was a truth-is-stranger-than-fiction scenario. The sad-sack Cleveland Indians depicted in the movie were absolutely factual most of the previous two decades. And the bottom of the barrel took place on

June 4, 1974, at Municipal Stadium, when a "10 Cent Beer Night" promotion turned into baseball's greatest fan riot.

Another woeful edition of the Indians wasn't drawing fans to cavernous Municipal Stadium, so team brass, headed by Ted Bonda, approved the discount-brew promotion. It worked . . . kind of. Some 25,134 passed through the turnstiles on a Tuesday night. But if you mix all-you-can-drink with holdover tensions from a beanball war between the Indians and Texas Rangers from a week earlier in Arlington, you might as well have lit a Molotov cocktail. And that might have set another fire to the nearby Cuyahoga River, a chemical-filled estuary famed for bursting into flames numerous times.

From almost the first pitch, fans tanked on brew ran onto the field. Shameless exhibitionists stripped and streaked. Eventually batteries and other objects were heaved onto the field. Several people were struck by objects, including a thrown chair. The umpiring crew, headed by Nestor Chylak, managed to keep the game going. But when a fan tried to grab the cap of Rangers right fielder Jeff Burroughs in the ninth inning, with Burroughs tripping and falling seconds later, first the Rangers, led by manager Billy Martin, then the Indians—all wielding bats for self-defense—went out to rescue Burroughs as more fans surged onto the field. The teams escaped to the relative safety of their clubhouses, and eventually the game was called and forfeited to the Rangers.

Texas's starting pitcher, who would make the Hall of Fame for feats other than this night, was not around for the finish. The crazy night potentially robbed him of a statistical milestone.

FERGIE JENKINS: The first inning we had streakers, and a few female streakers. They dropped their tops. I got hit with a line drive by Leron Lee in the fourth inning. I got up and got a standing ovation. In the sixth [teammate] Lenny Randle stepped on the back of my leg, I had to leave the game. Then the riot started.

When I left the game, it was 5–3. I was sitting on a gurney in the hospital. [Clubhouse manager] Bill Sheridan told me to stay in the hospital until someone phoned me— don't come to the stadium, there's a riot. There's guys running on the field. I should have won that game. I should have won 26 games that year. They gave the team the win, 9–0. A tough way to lose a victory.

They were all over the Rangers. When the streakers started coming out on the field and they threw seats out of the stands, that's when it started. Joe Lovitto hit this guy in the outfield. They [the players] were angry because of the situation that they could not retaliate.

Cleveland rookie Alan Ashby was the second-to-last batter of the game in the ninth, contributing an infield single as part of a game-tying rally that preceded the dual-team rescue of Burroughs and the fans' takeover of the field. He has never experienced anything remotely similar in several decades as a baseball play-by-play announcer.

ALAN ASHBY: The irony was I was [the second-to-last] legal hitter in the game. I was on first base [at the time of the forfeit]. It was a night that saw a bunch of streakers on the field. The players were getting worn out with it. It had gone over the top. There were even some moments of laughter with the streakers, including one who jumped up on the fence in center field to avoid the security. He eventually got grabbed by one leg and the other as he was straddling the wall. He was grabbed by security on both sides of the wall. The crowd was moaning and groaning.

As I was on first base, a fan came out to grab Jeff Burroughs's hat. For a moment Jeff looked like he was going to let it go. The players had just had enough. Jeff went over and grabbed this fan. Other players, including Dave

Duncan, sprinted out there. They started giving it to this fan. The fans started coming down.

It looked like an old cartoon where a wave of people was flowing into the dugout onto the field. They overtook the field and it became dangerous. There were old folding chairs that they had in that stadium that started flying and landing, and in some cases hitting people. I saw a broken bottle or two in the hands of people. Tom Hilgendorf had one of the folding chairs hit him and he was bleeding. When I saw that, I dashed into the dugout and into the clubhouse. It was really induced by this continuum of fans streaking on the field and delaying it. It was just an overbearing night and finally resulted in the brawl. I was scared. It was not a good time to be out there. It was a dangerous situation.

Lenny Randle has footage of 10-Cent Beer Night from a crew he had hired to film his games. He was part of the Martin-led contingent out to rescue Burroughs.

LENNY RANDLE: We have film of the guy running out to take Burroughs's hat. There were 20 fans ready to attack Jeff in right field. Everybody had a bat coming out of the dugout. Billy says, "Guys, let's go help Jeff." It was a mob scene. A chair flew out onto the field and hit their own guy [Hilgendorf].

DISCO DEMOLITION ROCKS OLD COMISKEY PARK

If 10-Cent Beer Night was like a pro-wrestling event gone amok, then Disco Demolition Night was more like a straight-on rock concert with a mosh pit. It gets a little rough, but it's all in good fun. And every five years its anniversary is comically remembered.

Obviously, Bill Veeck's efforts to get folks to talk about his White Sox worked too well on Thursday night, July 12, 1979.

Veeck signed off on the idea of son Mike, handling team promotions, to let popular young Chicago deejay Steve Dahl—who led his "Insane Coho Lips" army as one of the country's first "shock jocks"—blow up disco records between games of a twi-night doubleheader between the Chi-Sox and Tigers at old Comiskey Park. Fans bringing in disco records would be admitted for just 98 cents—in honor of the 97.9 frequency of WLUP, Dahl's station. But Dahl was like a pied piper. As the afternoon progressed, tens of thousands of young people swarmed around 35th and Shields. Some eschewed the bargain-basement admission and slipped into the old ballpark by scaling the outside walls like Spiderman.

As the Tigers arrived in their bus, their young shortstop realized he would not play in front of an ordinary baseball crowd, based on the sights, sounds, and . . . smells of cannabis.

ALAN TRAMMELL: We knew it was going to be a different night when we got off the bus. There were [lots of] people outside and it was a different crowd. It was like a rock concert. There was a little aura, a little aroma already. It was an eerie night.

As the first game drew to a close, Veeck and his small staff realized they had a potential situation on their hands. They had brought in enough security to handle a crowd of 35,000. But estimates have put the actual crowd count, filling every nook and cranny of Comiskey, its ramps, everywhere, at more than 60,000, maybe even 70,000. Another 35,000 milled around outside, unable to squeeze in.

Dahl, dressed in military fatigues and helmet, went out to center field to preside over the disco-records demolition. He was the man of the hour, as White Sox pitcher Steve Trout discovered while serving as the between-games guest for Harry Caray on the game telecast.

STEVE TROUT (White Sox, 1978–79): I was giving him this great, important answer. When Harry saw Steve [Dahl] walking by with two girls in bikinis, he forgot about me. I think they ran out of beer in the fourth inning. It was a pacifier for the masses.

Dahl gave the go-ahead to blow up the records. *Boom!* And then thousands of additional records came sailing out of the stands as fans began storming the field. At least one brash youth, risking his neck, shinnied down the right-field foul pole to get to the field.

STEVE TROUT: All of a sudden I hear a swishing sound by my head. An album landed by my feet. I said, "Oh, damn, almost killed by the Village People."

Sox lefty Ken Kravec, who went on to a long career as a major-league scout with the Cubs, was ready to warm up to start Game 2. He soon found his pregame routine relocated, then aborted.

KEN KRAVEC (White Sox, 1975–79): Going into warming up, I came out into the dugout and everybody said it was a nice crowd. Nobody really said how big it was. As I'm looking out toward center and left-center, I see masses of people. I couldn't see runaways or aisles. It was just masses of people. The ballpark maybe held 50,000 [tops]. It looked like [at least] 60,000. It was pretty impressive.

But from the time I walked out from the dugout to the bullpen, you could tell it was a different crowd. It wasn't a baseball crowd. It was like a rock-concert crowd. It smelled a little [of marijuana]. I finally get down to the bullpen with [pitching coach] Ron Schueler. The bullpen was so tight to the stands, you could reach out and touch the fans. After a few minutes of warming up, shoes come down from the upper deck. All of a sudden, they start Frisbeeing the disco albums. I said, "Schu, it's starting to get a little dangerous here." I said we ought to cut this thing off. He said let's go to the main mound. We get there and I threw about 10 pitches. They stormed the field. I just walked off the field. Nobody hassled me, everybody was doing their own thing. It was a happy crowd, but it was unfortunate it turned out the way it did. It worked too well.

The crowd seized control of the batting cage as Bill Veeck, peg leg and all, vainly tried to appeal for calm on the field. The merriment spread all over. Future *Chicago Tribune* Cubs and Sox beat writer Paul Sullivan, then a University of Missouri journalism student, practiced his slide into home plate. But when Sullivan and several friends wanted to refresh themselves from a bottle of Jack Daniels while encamped in the visitors' dugout, Tigers coach Alex Grammas firmly asked for the fifth while asking them to leave.

ALAN TRAMMELL: Our mouths were open, we couldn't believe it.

A lot of us initially were in the dugout, but security asked us to go upstairs. We came back out after everyone left, somehow get mentally prepared [for Game 2], but that didn't happen. It was a sight to be seen. Whether you were proud of it or not, you could say you were there.

White Sox players also were asked by security to retreat to their clubhouse. But even that did not prove to be an airtight sanctuary.

KEN KRAVEC: I went into the clubhouse. This is how the game has changed—within 15 minutes there was a fan who sprinted down the hallway into our clubhouse. He got in the middle of the locker room. He was like a lost puppy, trying to figure out how to get out. Someone just pointed to the side door, and he shot up the staircase and went out. Today, that would never happen.

In hindsight if they had a better grasp on it, they would have had more security. The walk-up was just so great. With the staff they had, they just couldn't be everywhere.

As with 10 Cent Beer Night, the unplayed second game was forfeited to the visiting team. Eventually mounted Chicago police cleared the field. Miraculously, no one was hurt. But Disco Demolition Night had literally left its mark on Comiskey Park, for the rest of the '79 season and beyond.

Left to clean up and somehow repair the battered field was Roger Bossard, now known as the "Sodfather," baseball's most renowned groundskeeper. In 1979 Roger, a third-generation groundskeeper, assisted father Gene in taking care of Comiskey. That was the only day in 46 years as a groundskeeper that the younger Bossard wishes he didn't do what he did. The rioters had made off with second and third base, home plate, and sod in front of the mound. Bossard ordered replacement sod at 1:15 a.m. and his crew was at work four hours later. Somehow they patched up enough of the field to play the rest of the series Friday through Sunday. Still, large chunks of outfield sod that they could not immediately replace were simply spray-painted green for the rest of the season.

But three weeks later Bossard had one last surprise as he tended to the patchy field.

ROGER BOSSARD (White Sox groundskeeper, 1970–79): We found 9 or 10 places in the field where little marijuana plants were growing. Fans had dropped [seedlings or residue] from what they were smoking.

HARRY CARAY: THE BROADCAST BOOTH PIED PIPER AND CROONER

Comiskey Park also was the center of other controversial bread-and-circus stuff throughout the '70s. As in his later, even bigger incarnation with the crosstown Cubs, Harry Caray often over-shadowed the team.

Hired by the Sox to help juice interest in the sagging franchise that had drawn just 495,000 in a 106-loss season in 1970, Caray worked on a jerry-built collection of suburban AM and FM stations. In spite of his bombastic broadcast style and trade-mark "Holy Cow" home-run call being carried on weak signals, Caray busted a $30,000 attendance bonus in his first contract as the Sox crowd count went up dramatically in 1971. He quickly became the man of the people, picking up the nickname "Mayor of Rush Street" for his nighttime bon vivant style. Caray broad-cast some day games from the bleachers armed with a fishnet in case a home run came his way; the net snared a couple of foul balls in its normal home in the broadcast booth. A decades-long beer pitchman, Caray did not care about FCC rules regard-ing drinking alcohol live on the air. One '70s night in Comiskey Park, he quaffed a Falstaff live and in color in between innings in the booth. And he was politically incorrect. Caray referred to one overweight female National Anthem singer at Comiskey as a "hefty gal."

But there was a price for his popularity. Caray's brutal can-dor, carried over from his St. Louis radio days, won over fans, but also rankled key Sox figures, who felt his criticism was unfair and sometimes below the belt. He even nearly came to blows with third baseman Bill Melton, a frequent target, at the Pfister Hotel in Milwaukee.

BILL MELTON: The only thing that bothered me is we had an organization we're trying to sell to the public. Harry was tearing it down. That bothered [GM] Roland Hemond and [manager] Chuck Tanner, not so much me as a player except when he got on the bandwagon to get Bill Melton out of town. I'll say one thing about Harry—he was a great broadcaster, can't take that away from him.

In my era we needed the media. But after a period of a year listening to this every day, I said I didn't need this anymore. I thought the best thing for me to do was ask Roland Hemond to [let me] leave the city of Chicago. It was the last thing I wanted to do; it was the only thing I could do.

Decades later, Tanner will still not give Caray credit for boosting the Sox from near-irrelevance in Chicago.

CHUCK TANNER: None, whatsoever. Dick Allen was the factor. Dick Allen brought the people into the ballpark. Dick Allen is the guy people wanted to see play. Harry announced the games and I had a few confrontations with him. I told him you just be the announcer. They're not here to hear you and see you. I told this to the owner, John Allyn, and Allyn told it to him. That's why he got fired. Dick Allen was the reason. Don't tell me an announcer brought the people. That's a bunch of baloney.

I went and told him, You can't do that." He wasn't going to hurt my team. He said, "Hmmm, there's something not right with this ball club. I can't put my finger on it." He was trying to get me. It didn't work. I was told to be there the next morning. John Allyn said, "You saved the franchise." He offered me a 10- or 20-year contract. We lost 10 of 11. I said that's not right. He told the girl, "Give me a five-year extension." I go to the clubhouse, Harry says how 'bout coming on TV? He said to what do you attribute getting a five-year extension? You guys have lost 10 out of 11. Well, two things, Harry—loyalty and ability. He said, "Oh, that's good."

According to future Caray broadcast partner Steve Stone, these confrontations were wasted off-camera. He recalled how Caray felt he and Tanner could have aired their conflicts for fun and profit.

> **STEVE STONE:** Harry had no problems being controversial with anyone. Harry was sniping at Chuck, and then Chuck would use the newspapers to snipe at Harry. Harry went down on the field and said, "Look, we're wasting a golden opportunity to get some great ratings. Instead of me talking about you on television and you talking about me in the press, let's just go head-to-head before the game every day. You can air your grievances, I'll air mine, and it will make for great television and radio." That's the kind of guy Harry was. Always had an eye for the ratings and never dodged controversy.

Sox owner John Allyn actually fired Caray live on Johnny Morris's early-evening sportscast on Chicago's WBBM-TV after the 1975 season. But the Sox were virtually bankrupt and within weeks were rescued by Bill Veeck in his final ownership tenure. Veeck rehired Caray. He became bigger than ever, thanks both to his teaming with the unpredictable, certifiably nuts Jimmy Piersall in the booth and Veeck's idea to pipe Caray's informal seventh-inning stretch singing over the public-address system.

When Caray and Piersall were paired, the fans doubled their pleasure in hearing announcers take off after ballplayers' foibles. Like the time Alan Bannister ran into an out at home plate in 1977 and Caray got his dander up on his broadcast on WSNS-TV.

> **HARRY CARAY:** What's going on? . . . We are having in the last two days absolutely atrocious baserunning.

Days earlier on WSNS, Piersall narrated an instant replay of Tigers second baseman Tito Fuentes's seemingly nonchalant throwing style.

JIMMY PIERSALL (White Sox announcer, 1977-79): The ball is hit sharply to Fuentes. . . . He has the notion [to throw home]. Watch him hot-dog this thing now. . . . OK, that's it, atta boy, sure. . . . He's hurt them in about eight ball games, I was told by one of the Tigers players.

If anything, Caray and Piersall created a kind of guerilla theater of the air. They often were more entertaining than the action on the field. Veeck cringed at much of the on-air criticism, but couldn't go back on his own philosophy of providing the most entertainment for the least coast.

JIMMY PIERSALL: I was just myself. He always told me, say what you think. The players create the situation. They made the error. The poor baserunning you saw in those days, you get tired of seeing that stuff. I was a fan. You feel they have to correct those mistakes. If you have poor instincts running the bases, you're in trouble because you wind up insecure and not knowing what to do. Many times they pin too many things on the [third-base] coach where they're supposed to be reading the play themselves.

We had so many replays come up and we had to report. I think Harry and I enjoyed the work. I think Harry knew the game as good as I did. That made it tough working with him at first because I knew nothing about broadcasting, and how to go in and out. He had patience with me and we had a pretty good ball club in 1977. When they're not a good ball club, they're listening to the broadcasters.

Caray was infamous for plugging his buddies' bars and res-
taurants while announcing every group in attendance, anniver-
saries, and birthdays. He'd do his carnival barking in breathless
style with the game serving almost as a backdrop, sticking in
ball and strike calls in between the endless plugola. Anxious to
get in an on-air word or two edgewise, Piersall tried to intercept
the names from the usher before Caray could read them, earning the announcer's ire.

Interestingly, the one Sox official Caray defended was
Mike Veeck, under fire for Disco Demolition Night. Through the
decades of exile from baseball and then ownership of a series of
minor-league teams, Caray's actions were not forgotten.

MIKE VEECK (White Sox promotions director, 1976–79):
He knew that to get 65,000 into Comiskey Park and
another 35,000 outside for a twi-night doubleheader on
a Thursday night with Detroit was a pretty good hustle. I
think, though, that he was embarrassed because Jimmy
attacked me and the promotion during the broadcast.
Piersall was relentless, and I think that Harry, being the pro
that he was, began to soften it and cover. That is one of
the reasons why I have always been appreciative of Harry,
because very few people came to my defense.

When it was all over, Harry said, "I can't believe that
many people hate the Village People."

In 1977 one of the baseball's ongoing traditions was born
when Bill Veeck piped in Caray's informal sing-along with "Take
Me Out to the Ballgame" during the seventh-inning stretch.
Contrary to popular belief, Veeck did not at first use a hidden
microphone to pipe Caray's warbling to the rest of Comiskey
Park.

MIKE VEECK: My Dad, who had a voice that made Harry
sound like Perry Como, would look over at Harry during

the seventh inning and notice that Harry, like himself, was always singing. So Dad called the station one day and said, "Do you have a copy of Harry singing?" They went back and edited it out of a previous ball game and sent him a copy.

Then Dad said, "Harry, why don't you sing?" Harry refused. And Dad said, "Well, I got a copy of it, so they are not going to know if you sing anyhow." The sound system at old Comiskey all came from center field. So we ran everything through the eight horns that came off the green wall out in center. That is where the sound would come from. Dad kept asking Harry, begging him for a full week. He finally told him, "We will play the tape; they won't know. They'll look up, see you just standing there swaying, think you are singing it."

So Harry finally agreed to it, and he was absolutely thunderstruck at the reaction of the crowd. They went wild. And, of course, Dad's theory was the crowd would love it because Harry is Everyman. The fans reacted so well with him.

Caray's singing in the seventh directly transferred to Wrigley Field when he jumped from the Sox after the 1981 season. His stature simply exploded, with many fans claiming the main attraction for buying tickets was to see Caray sing and direct the crowd like the off-key maestro he was.

UNIFORMS THAT WERE WORSE THAN LEISURE SUITS

Worse than economic stagflation in the 1970s was men's fashion. Garish and gaudy, huge collars and lapels, shirts open to the waist, leisure suits, and peacock-like colors. Baseball picked up on the trend to vary from the usual home whites and road grays as all teams switched from heavy, hot, woolen uniforms to more comfortable, form-fitting double-knits starting in 1970. But they went overboard.

No team wore uglier "unis" than Veeck's Sox, who cavorted in a navy-blue-and-white design reminiscent of dead-ball-era players' togs. One variation of these uniforms, worn from 1976 to 1981, was one with shorts. There's a good reason the shorts were worn only once, in the first game of a doubleheader at Comiskey Park on a temperate, 70-degree day (August 8, 1976) against the Royals. A player could skin his knees and shins pretty good in shorts. Even teams playing in tropical climates always have worn long pants for game action, with shorts limited to pregame workouts. Royals first baseman John Mayberry did some bench jockeying, saying the Sox looked "sweet" showing their knees. And everyone knew what that meant at the time.

KEN KRAVEC: The uniforms weren't very attractive. They didn't look very good, but they were comfortable. You could get dressed very quickly.

The shorts felt great. I wasn't playing in them [I wasn't pitching that day]. You couldn't slide properly, you'd tear yourself up. Back in the day, it was an innovation. You're swimming upstream with them and that's why the players had a problem with them. It was just the tradition of the game. The players weren't happy wearing shorts in the first game and they changed [to long pants]. They just decided we didn't want to wear them anymore.

Sometimes you have to throw stuff out there and see what happens. He [Veeck] had a lot of [other] ideas that worked.

The Padres tried to vie with the Sox for ugliest color scheme with all-yellow uniforms or a combination of brown and yellow. The Indians sometimes wore all-red double knits. In 1977 the Pirates varied their pioneering white-home and gray-road double-knits with wild yellow-black-and-gold combos, with pinstripes and stars on the caps awarded by team elder Willie Stargell. A big guy like Dave Parker could appear as the world's biggest bumblebee. A player and fan could be overwhelmed with color when the Astros, with a mustard-and-ketchup design on their jerseys, played the Pirates.

DAVE PARKER: I thought it was unique. We were unique. We had 17 African-American players in the '70s. That was unique in itself. The uniforms added to what we were as an organization and as a team.

The Astros—their name—led to them having those wild uniforms. When the Astros and Pirates got together, it was one of the most colorful games you could go to.

BERT BLYLEVEN: That was pretty cool. We had those jail hats with the stars Willie Stargell gave out. Kent Tekulve displayed every one that Willie ever gave to him. His cap was full of stars. They were given for contributions to a victory. Sometimes they were from a loss, if you hit three home runs. I lost a star, it fell off my hat. I went back to Willie for a [replacement], and I was upset. He said, hey, you lose it, you don't get another one. I always put one star near the *P* on my cap and I put the other stars in my locker—I didn't want to lose [them]. There'd always be argument over who deserved stars. It became another fun time in the clubhouse.

JOSE CRUZ: I saw we were different than every team in the NL. We're the Astros, we have a lot of rainbows. I love it. People say you have ugly uniforms, but I say I'm proud of my uniforms. To me I was proud to have the uniform.

RANDY JONES: My fondest memory was when we [the Padres] wore the gold sanni's [sanitary socks], brown socks, white shoes on the road. We were colorful with the orange-and-brown hats and we were playing the Astros with those tutti-frutti uniforms. I remember playing them in the Astrodome and with all those guys running around there, it was a horrific sight, that's all I can say.

I inherited it when I got there in '73. When you saw Nate Colbert and Cito Gaston in those butt-ugly, gold-banana uniforms, it was scary. Brown shirts—you bring back some fond memories.

The goofiest-looking hats were the red-white-blue versions with the curly M symbol worn by the Montreal Expos, which according to original team announcer Dave van Horne, came under ridicule from Game 1 in franchise history.

DAVE VAN HORNE: [Manager Gene Mauch] was told after the first Expos game on April 8, 1969, [Expos won 11–10] that some of the writers had been from the Mets clubhouse and let him know Seaver said those tricolor hats Expos wore are really funny. Gene, without hesitation, without a moment's pause, said you can tell Seaver he remembered when they laughed at the entire Mets uniform.

I thought they needed a propeller. I think one of the [ad] agencies that did a lot of the work for Seagram's came up with the tricolored design. Charles [Bronfman] always said he wanted his team to be distinctive and different. And the tricolored cap certainly was.

HIRSUTE IS IN

Charlie Finley beat Bill Veeck to one novel idea simply because he owned a team in 1972 and Veeck, living on Maryland's eastern shore as a retired squire, did not: breaking baseball's clean-shaven line.

Reggie Jackson tried to do so in spring training '72, reporting to Athletics camp with a full beard and mustache. Rather than confronting Jackson on his grooming or lack thereof, the promotion-minded Finley decided to try to make a buck over facial hair. He offered every Athletics player $300 to grow a mustache by Father's Day, which Finley would designate as Mustache Day at the Oakland Coliseum. Reliever Rollie Fingers quickly raised his trademark thin handlebar mustache and negotiated a year's supply of wax, costing $150, from the normally thrifty Finley.

By late summer 1972, the facial-hair revolution spread throughout the game as a number of big names grew their first-ever mustaches, with full beards not far behind. Several franchises, such as the Reds, remained holdouts for years, banning facial hair.

JOE RUDI: We sort of broke the ice. I spent six years in the Marine Corps Reserves, got out in fall of 1971. The Marine Corps, you didn't mess around. I missed 40, 50 games a year. [Rick] Monday, myself, and [Dave] Duncan all were in the Marine Reserves. Duncan and I went for part of a year without getting a haircut. We almost had hair down to our shoulders.

Charlie had his promotional nights—bald-headed day, halter-top days, hot-pants day, then a mustache day. He offered to pay any players $300 to grow a mustache by Father's Day. That sort of set the character of our ball club. It was a lot of money. I was one of those guys who struggled to grow it. You had to get up close to see I actually had one. Everyone grew them. We ended up keeping the mustaches. The headline in the [1972] World Series was "Long Hairs vs. the Squares." They [Reds] were all clean-cut with low socks, didn't wear the high stirrups.

I've never shaved it. My wife won't let me shave it. I've tried to shave it off many, many times over the years, and she throws a fit.

It was just baseball [the previous ban on facial hair]. People that ran the game were still ex-players and people in the game for years. The traditions were pretty strong. One of them was being clean-cut with no facial hair.

The more liberal teams also allowed their African-American and Latin players to grow out their Afro hairstyles. Some huge 'fros sprouted by 1973–74, some so big it was hard to understand how their bearers kept their hats on. Dusty Baker, Bake McBride, Oscar Gamble, and Jose Cardenal were just a few of the prominent players to cultivate luxuriant Afros. Amazingly, when outfielder Doug Glanville joined the Cubs for a second time in early August 2003, a by-then crew-cut manager Dusty Baker ordered Glanville to "clean up" his unkempt Afro. Baker, like Rudi and others, had a Marine background.

DUSTY BAKER: My problem was I couldn't grow an Afro during the height of the Afro era because once a month I had to cut it to be a Marine [reservist]. When I grew it, I got a bigger hat. I had two or three hats, depending on whether I had a fresh cut or an Afro cut. I was trying to be me. Jose Cardenal, Reggie Smith, Oscar Gamble, it was easier for them to have an Afro because they had a finer texture of hair than I had. It was hard for me to grow a beard because I'm not hairy. I didn't shave much till I was 35. There is Indian blood in my family. Now the Afro's coming back. Everything's revolved. At the time leisure suits were cool. Everything has its time and place.

Baker was right. Ballplayer haircuts starting in the 1990s totally wiped out the long-hair days and even undercut the classic 1950s crew cut. Chrome domes and whitewalled sides were common, while the Tim Lincecums and Jeff Samardzijas sporting long, flowing locks were the exceptions. No doubt styles will come around again.

LADIES' DAY IN MORE WAYS THAN ONE

Baseball was and still is a "boys club," with locker-room humor and macho-man posturing. But starting in the True Golden Age, a bit of room was made for women on baseball's periphery, be it the person who guides you to your seat or the broadcaster or writer who takes the fans inside the clubhouse.

Difficult to believe, but at one time they did not hire female ushers. Wrigley Field held out till Memorial Day weekend in 1970—and then the Andy Frain ushering company couldn't satisfy the fans' requests for women.

Two years later, Joanne Budka, from Chicago's Southwest Side, joined the Frain ushering crew, working both of the city's ballparks. As part of the job, she met outfielder Gene Clines when he came through town with the Pirates, then got closer when Clines became a Cub. They eventually married.

JOANNE BUDKA-CLINES: They selected fairly attractive people to work at the ballpark. I had a fairly regular spot in the aisle leading down to the [Wrigley Field] visiting team's bullpen. So I used to have to walk up and down that aisle, with that gold-and-blue uniform. The pitchers used to hit on me all the time. I'd rest myself against the wall, put my arms up against the railing. The guys would be there making comments, how are you, what are you doing after the game? They were really flattering, it really boosted my ego. They used to stay at the Executive House and they asked if I wanted to meet them later, hook up with me. I had this job at 16, my sophomore year of high school. It didn't matter I was that young. There was a core group of women working as usherettes.

The uniforms were wool. Around 1978 it changed from wool to polyester. You had to wear nylons and navy blue pumps [even on hot days]. The women's washroom was the only place you could cool off. They didn't have a changing room for the female ushers. We had to dress at the ballpark and change going home—you couldn't wear your uniforms outside. So we had to change in the women's washroom. We could leave our garment bag in the usher's room.

I did doubleheaders or a day game at Wrigley, take the L, and work a night game at Comiskey. It was a totally different crowd. A lot of times you didn't have as large of a crowd. I worked a lot of weekends at Comiskey. We were paid like $3 an hour. We had to be there three hours before the gates open and they'd do these briefings about the game. You could sit there and watch batting practice. The players used to visit us. Geno [Clines] used to come into the stands and talk to you. They were so much more accessible. An usherette named Cheryl Newman—she was gorgeous—married Sox catcher Brian Downing. She worked behind home plate at Comiskey Park. Blonde hair, blue eyes. They connected somehow.

I believe that's true [people slipping in by sometimes bribing ushers or other means]. They had the group gate on Waveland Avenue. They used to require one adult to 10 children, and it was real easy to get more people in there. You could let people slide.

Women could work as ushers through most of the 1970s, but baseball at first resisted their entrée into the locker rooms as legitimate journalists. Melissa Ludtke of *Sports Illustrated* was barred by commissioner Bowie Kuhn from doing locker-room interviews during the 1977 World Series. *SI* parent Time Inc. took the case to court. A year later a federal judge ruled that both genders must have equal access to clubhouses. But like school integration a generation earlier, changes did not take place immediately after a court ruling. Karen Chaderjian, then a young sports staffer for the *Joliet Herald-News*, found that out firsthand when she tried to work the Cubs locker room in 1979. Cubs GM Bob Kennedy and media-relations director Buck

Peden blocked her path. Chaderjian survived the episode to go on to become an editor at the *Los Angeles Times,* but remembers her travails as a kind of lesson that the clubhouses then, and now, are very much a domain of ultimate macho men. The gruff Kennedy, a World War II marine aviator colleague of Ted Williams, supposedly said, "Grow a beard or take the club to court."

KAREN CHADERJIAN: That incident began after I was trying to do my job, getting interviews with players after the game, despite being confined to the manager's office. Kennedy then made my job more difficult by ordering me out of even the manager's office. I heard Kennedy's order, but I just stood there, stunned really, and didn't do anything, neither complaining nor moving nor making a scene. He didn't force me to leave, and I pursued the discussion by following him into an office, where he began to shave. Joe Goddard, longtime baseball writer [for the *Chicago Sun-Times*] listened in, unbeknownst to me, and, to my surprise, wrote about the conversation. I was not looking for headlines or court cases or the limelight. I just wanted to do my job quietly.

I got nowhere with Kennedy, although he did call me later and ask to have a meeting to discuss the locker-room access. I went to the meeting without a supervisor, and we settled on no access to the locker room but an opportunity to stand on the field after the game, near the tunnel that led to the locker room. There I was supposed to get to talk to players. But without the backing of my paper, I made little progress in my effort to get access with the Cubs.

Instead, I pressed my case with Bill Veeck of the Chicago White Sox, and although he said he did not want women to have access to the locker room—because he felt it was like inviting women into the men's bathroom—he said he wanted to be fair, and he was true to his word.

He was also very generous with his time, giving me the "standard" Veeck three-hour interview on an off day, where we talked baseball-baseball-baseball. What fun it was, and what a kick for a young sportswriter to have that kind of access, wit, and wisdom from a baseball treasure. He was a significant contrast to Kennedy.

Kennedy was not alone in thinking that female reporters did not belong in the locker room. He was simply louder and more rigid in expressing his opinion. His son, Terry Kennedy, was helpful in answering questions as a player. I remember a game early in the season when Bobby Murcer hit a home run to win. I had negotiated with Bob Kennedy to get access to the front of the tunnel that led off the field. Murcer ran by me, saying, "I hit a curveball," and ducked into the tunnel to avoid further questions. It wasn't until the day after that I knew the journalistic cost of not getting access to the locker room. While I wrote about the pitch Murcer hit, others told about an anecdote regarding Murcer's infamous rocking chair in the clubhouse. I had no idea about that because I hadn't been allowed in the locker room. I had tried to talk with other reporters, and I sometimes even had help from a male colleague at the *Herald-News,* who would go into the locker room to encourage players to walk out of the locker room and talk with me in the manager's office, but it wasn't the same.

Kennedy still made the unevolved comment: "If it was just you, I would let you have access, but a lot of these other women just want to get in the locker room." I did not take his divide-and-conquer bait. Eventually, Buck Peden, who had continued to place stumbling blocks in front of me, made the situation much worse. He called the *Herald-News* managing editor, Reynold Hertel, who subsequently called me into his office and told me that if I made "any more trouble" in reporting the Cubs, he would not allow me to cover any more games. I continued to try to negotiate better access on my own, but the point quickly became moot because, at the time, the *Herald-News* gave up on major-league coverage the moment that either team showed it wasn't going to be a pennant contender. In the Cubs' case that didn't take long.

"I was allowed in the Chicago White Sox locker room during the same year. It was the only locker room where I got access. . . . My career soon moved on to California, where I eventually became a sports editor and worked primarily on the desk.

THE $250 HOT DOG

Sneaking food into the bullpen is an honored baseball tradition. But players have to be careful in modern times with TV cameras poking their nosy lenses into every corner of ballparks. Astros reliever Charlie Kerfeld was caught munching on a hot dog by the cameras in the Shea Stadium bullpen. Moral of the story is just don't get caught by the manager like one Pirates pitcher did, who apparently did not care that he purchased the most expensive hot dog in history by the resulting fine.

> **CHUCK TANNER:** [John] Candelaria said to this kid, here's five bucks, get me a hot dog. I'm on the bench with the other guys. Candelaria's going to the bullpen. The kid comes and says I have a hot dog here, it's for John Candelaria. I said to the kid, I'll give it to John. I said, "Hey, Candy, come here." He says, "Yeah, skip." I tell Candy: "Here's your $250 hot dog." He took it and ate it. For $250, I'm eatin' it. Those guys were just hilarious.

The thrill is not in eating the hot dog, but getting away with obtaining that and other munchies along with other high jinks. Future Hall of Famer Fergie Jenkins was a little more crafty than Candelaria at Wrigley Field, where he found a place to watch the game and have lunch while not being spotted by his manager.

> **FERGIE JENKINS:** In the second or third inning, we'd order some hot dogs. Ray Jr. [Meyer] would bring it over in a bag [from the nearby Ray's Bleachers tavern, now Murphy's Bleachers]. Milt Pappas and I, or whomever else was in the bullpen, would have an opportunity to have some lunch. We generally walked up into the [left-field] catwalk. There'd be a couple of Andy Frain or Burns guys who would stop the fans from trying to get autographs. We'd sit there and peek through the fence and watch the game, eat some hot dogs, and then go back to the bullpen. Generally it was Milt Pappas, Kenny Holtzman, and myself. Not the relief pitchers.
>
> To get beverages, you'd trade a baseball for a Coke, or a Cracker Jack. I know a lot of single guys used to try to get dates by writing their phone number on a ball or a girl would write her number on a ball. That was considered a "bomb." They'd arrange a meeting place like Ray's or the Cottage. There was always something to do out in the bullpen. It was always active.
>
> Bullpens in Philly, Cincy, Pittsburgh, even San Diego, you could take a newspaper out there. Guys would play cards out there. Guys would do a lot of different things. Some of them can't be mentioned. If they were out late the night before, they might get a catnap for two innings. I sometimes took a nap.

RELIEVERS WORK ON THEIR SHORT GAME

A lot of ballplayers can't get enough of golf—even mixing their day (or night) jobs with their passion for the links, as a curveball specialist then with the Pirates recalled.

BERT BLYLEVEN: We were in New York and we decided we were going to work on our golf game a little bit. We started putting. We took balls and bats out in the bullpen and before batting practice made about nine holes with flags. While the game was going on, Ed Ott and I were putting, not knowing they could show it on the Jumbotron.

Ed and I were working on our putting stances when all of a sudden the bullpen phone rang. It was Chuck [Tanner]. He basically had some good words for the bullpen coach to get our asses back to the dugout. We were like little kids being scolded. We never did finish our game. We were doing it for the first three or four innings till they caught us on the Jumbotron. We were having a great time out there. He didn't really say anything [when they returned to the dugout]. He didn't have to say anything. We were trying to have a good time during the ball game and we got caught.

TICK . . . TICK . . . TICK . . . TICK

Pranks are as common to baseball as chewin' or spittin'. Players know immediately who will play the best straight men for pranks. Ron Santo's teammates realized early on they easily could get a rise out of the emotional Cubs third baseman.

FERGIE JENKINS: He was getting these hate letters that they were going to shoot him in New York [near the end of the 1970 season] and bomb his car. They figured they would put the timer in the trainer's room in a box, send it to Ronnie, have it delivered to his locker. Ronnie would pick it up and hear it ticking. They did this. Ronnie grabbed it, threw it out over the wall onto Waveland Avenue, and broke the clock, which was the trainer's. The box was wrapped up by either Glenn Beckert or Billy Williams. We had to buy a new timer for the trainer.

Once you move your equipment in the trainer's room, it automatically moves into the ice bucket or refrigerator.

Kenny Holtzman once put all left shoes in my equipment bag. Every player has at least two or three pairs of shoes. I'm beating everyone up to find my right shoe, because I'm pitching that night. Fortunately, it showed up about 10 minutes before game time. I knew I packed my own bag so that [the right] shoe was packed.

The "smiley-face" button soon came into vogue. It could have been symbol for the most entertaining parts of the True Golden Age.

15

1979 and Beyond

Baseball has not further tinkered with the strike zone or mound height since 1968. Jumps in home-run production, such as a big surge in 1987, were thought to be due to a "juiced" baseball. Credence to such speculation was given by the late Cubs infielder Woody English, who recalled how owners deadened the baseball after the hits-filled 1930 season to keep down salaries during the Great Depression—a decade earlier the ball was made more lively just in time for Babe Ruth. However, the amazing increase in homers as the 1990s progressed is now attributed to another kind of "juice"—baseball's biggest scandal since the Black Sox.

"We Are Family" also split apart sooner than later. The 1979 Pirates group of championship players never really contended again in Pittsburgh. Worse yet, hero Dave Parker soon turned to villain.

Parker signed the team's first $1 million annual contract. When his production declined he was the object of verbal abuse and objects thrown at him at Three Rivers Stadium. Worse yet, Parker got enmeshed in the "Pittsburgh Drug Trial," which implicated players and drug dealers in 1985. Parker departed to play for his hometown Cincinnati Reds, then the Oakland Athletics. Later he coached for the Los Angeles Angels of Anaheim.

He was estranged from the Pirates for nearly 20 years.

"For one, I told the media I wouldn't do anything with the Pirates till they gave Willie [Stargell] a job," he said. "Willie played 21 years in Pittsburgh and after his career had to go to Atlanta for employment. I thought that was low. Here was a guy who represented the Pirates as the face of the organization and the city of Pittsburgh, and he couldn't find employment.

Kevin McClatchy [hired Stargell] and that kind of healed some wounds. I kept my promise. I made amends with the Pirates."

Parker could not believe the Pirates suffered through 18 consecutive losing seasons starting in 1993.

"It's kind of sad to see Pittsburgh be near the bottom every year," he said. "The city of champions carries on. You've got the Steelers and Penguins. Pitt is on the rebound. You hate to see the Pirates as the missing link in the city of champions. What they need to do is bring back some of those guys involved in the championship season. We were taught to win, people who were part of that winning tradition."

Ted Williams had no official ties to baseball after he left as Rangers manager in 1972. But he was in the middle of one of the most touching scenes in baseball history before the 1999 All-Star Game at Fenway Park. Driven to the mound in a cart, Williams greeted the entire All-Star roster, the players mobbing him like little kids, taping him with camcorders for their own archives. He died in 2002.

Meanwhile, Joe DiMaggio first became Mr. Coffee's spokesman, then king of the card shows as he played himself in public appearances until his death in 1999, when his last words reportedly were, "I'll finally get to see Marilyn again," meaning Marilyn Monroe, the love of his life. In 1991 a statue of DiMaggio was dedicated at the Italian-American Sports Hall of Fame in Arlington Heights, Illinois. First DiMaggio shooed away TV production people bugging him for a taping because he had made a commitment to an interview with writers. Then, when asked what he thought of fans putting him on the same pedestal as Babe Ruth, DiMaggio looked skyward and expressed gratitude for being spoken of in the same breath as the Sultan of Swat.

Magic Johnson made his NBA debut in 1979 and Michael Jordan five years later. Meanwhile, Southern state football programs that had previously barred black players now had an open-door policy as the 1970s turned into another decade. The combination of superstar role models in basketball and increased opportunities in football detoured many black athletes who previously would have chosen baseball. A quicker financial payoff than the long, laborious apprenticeship through the minor leagues was now more readily available. Some 30 percent of NFL rosters were African-American in the 1970s, but that number more than doubled to 66 percent in 2006.

The end result for baseball? Just 8.4 percent of big leaguers were black in 2006, compared to more than 12 percent of the U.S. population. The Houston Astros played in the 2005 World Series without a single African-American player.

College baseball would not be the means by which more black players would be developed. Gender equity rules mandated by Title IX cut the number of baseball scholarships to 13 in 1979, and down to 11½ two decades later. The rosters of college programs became predominately white.

Meanwhile, baseball now had a heavily south-of-the-border tint. In 2006 29.4 percent of major leaguers were Latin. Pacific Rim scouting also started to bear fruit. Some 2.4 percent were Asian.

Baseball's minimum salary was $10,000 at the start of the True Golden Age. Contrast that with Nolan Ryan attaining the first $1 million annual contract, granted by the Astros, at the very end of the decade in November 1979. Mark Grace remembered making $68,000 as a rookie in 1988. Now the minimum is $330,000—more money than home-run king Henry Aaron ever made in one season.

The Cubs' curse was commercialized, with a billy goat used as the star of a beer commercial, and got further traction from playoff collapses in 2003 and 2007–8. Some Chicago media, look-ing for a clever line or whimsy, still reference the curse rather than Cubs front-office shortcomings as a reason for the team's championship drought. But the supposed Red Sox curse came out of nowhere. *Boston Globe* columnist Dan Shaughnessy penned a 1990 book, *Curse of the Bambino,* about the Red Sox's bad luck pursuing a World Series title. Previously, there had never been talk of a curse connected with Babe Ruth's sale to the Yankees back in 1920. Once again, many media types took the easy way out to focus on otherworldly explanations rather than the deeds of mortal men in the front office and on the field. When the Red Sox came back from an 0–3 deficit against the Yankees and went on to win the World Series in 2004, one curse was retired.

Luis Tiant, who endured the sleights of Jim Crow, then the sus-picions of Joe Adcock, has been paid back with interest. He is mobbed at his Cuban sandwich shop outside Fenway Park. He also sells his line of cigars. El Tiante is a folk hero.

Roger Bossard, who had the unenviable task of repair-ing the Comiskey field after Disco Demolition Night in 1979, is now regarded as the "Sodfather"—baseball's most renowned groundskeeper. Still holding forth for the White Sox, he was put in charge of redoing Wrigley Field's surface in 2007, works for other teams, and has installed fields as far away as Saudi Arabia.

Harry Caray became bigger than ever when he defected to the Cubs late in 1981. However, he was hired with a caveat—knock off the hypercritical remarks about players that marked his White Sox broadcast tenure. Cubs GM Dallas Green and Tribune Co. VP Jim Dowdle laid down the law with Caray as a condition of employment. His image hardly suffered. Caray became more popular than most players and overshadowed the team itself, while his seventh-inning sing-along mushroomed into the highlight event of many games. Sox broadcast partner

Jimmy Piersall sought to be reunited on the North Side with Caray, but was deemed too radical by Dowdle and Co.

The seventh-inning crooning survived Caray's 1998 death with guest singers who were worse than Caray. Worst of the worst: Ozzy Osbourne, Mike Ditka, and Jeff Gordon. Ex-Bears lineman Steve McMichael was ejected from Wrigley Field by plate umpire Angel Hernandez in 2001 for ripping one of the ump's calls to the crowd right after McMichael sang.

Having sold the Oakland Athletics, Charlie Finley tried to team with *Chicago Sun-Times* columnist Mike Royko and publisher Marshall Field to buy the Cubs in 1981. But like fouling off a fastball down the middle, their timing was just off. The meeting to finalize the sale bid was scheduled for two days after Tribune Co. announced its purchase of the Cubs in a kind of insider transaction as owner Bill Wrigley got out from under a $40 million inheritance-tax burden.

The same Oakland franchise for which Bowie Kuhn barred Finley from dismantling for millions of dollars in 1976 constantly dumped its high-salaried homegrown players without interference from another commissioner in the last decade under Billy Beane. The boyish GM also was front and center in the popular *Moneyball* book. Finley would have understood.

On November 1, 1999, watching Don Baylor conduct his introductory press conference as Cubs manager was wife Becky. No one made a fuss that Becky Baylor was white. The scene would have been unfathomable at Wrigley Field just 20 years earlier. In 1997 , however, Cubs' African-American outfielder Doug Glanville was cautioned to be careful about interracial relationships by Hall of Famer Billy Williams and teammate Lance Johnson.

Progress was quantifiable, but baseball still has not moved into a postracial mode just yet.

Female journalists had to struggle to enter baseball locker rooms in the 1970s. Thirty years later, Suzyn Waldman teamed with John Sterling on the Yankees' radio broadcasts. Waldman's breathless description of Roger Clemens sitting in George Steinbrenner's Yankee Stadium private box prior to Clemens's comeback is parodied on sports-talk stations all over the country.

The interleague play that owners threw back in Bowie Kuhn's face in August 1973 is, in its second decade, an established part of baseball's midsummer schedule. Although some critics suggest many of the matchups are ho-hum, Cubs vs. White Sox, Mets vs. Yankees, and Dodgers vs. Angels are popular. New ideas are considered too radical just because they haven't been tried before.

Kicking dirt on third-base ump Mark Wegner's pants on June 2, 2007, was Lou Piniella's professed last-ever on-field eruption. Well, fudge a bit into the dugout tunnel. On June 27, 2009, Piniella confronted recalcitrant outfielder Milton Bradley in the tunnel to the clubhouse at U.S Cellular Field, called him a "piece of shit," and sent him home in midgame for busting up the dugout in the same manner Piniella did in the 1970s.

In a new century you can find a way to go back to the future, back to baseball's True Golden Age.

Acknowledgments

In an era when cell phones and e-mail should logically make personal contact much easier, it's actually much more difficult than in the 1970s when the only way to stop a ringing phone was to answer it.

Folks can literally tune out and shut down if they choose. So here is great appreciation to team officials and publicists for their contact information and persuasive powers to get some of our oral-history participants to call this author. It was interesting to pick up the phone to take the call of Dave Parker. "The Cobra" is not as renowned as the most famous person ever to phone here—a guy named O. J. back in 1984—but he ranks high nevertheless.

We start with two of the finest team alumni-relations officials around—Dick Bresciani, assisted by Rod Oreste, of the Red Sox, and Sally O'Leary of the Pirates. Both Bresciani and O'Leary were on duty on the front lines of media relations for their respective teams in the '70s, and the end product here displays the results of their long-standing relationships with players. Bresciani and I were both in Milwaukee County Stadium on July 2, 1975, when the Red Sox's Rick Wise came within an out of no-hitting the Brewers. Little did we realize we'd collaborate nearly 35 years later to help relive that moment.

Other team officials receiving plaudits are Gene Dias—who watched the Wise near-gem on TV—and Sally Gunter of the Astros, Peter Chase of the Cubs, Adam Liberman of the Braves, Warren Miller of the Padres, Bob Rose of the Athletics, Jim Trdinich of the Pirates, and Bill Stetka of the Orioles. Also meriting thanks are personal publicists Diane Hock and Dick Gordon.

Photo archivists in two contrasting locales get their plaudits. Pat Kelly always comes through from the Hall of Fame in Cooperstown when called upon. And memorabilia collector Leo

Bauby of Wilmette, Illinois, tapped into his collection of tens of thousands of baseball images originally shot by newspaper photographers back in the day.

The oral histories featured here were gathered as far back as 1994 via the *Diamond Gems* radio show, other phone interviews, and one-on-one sessions at Chicago's ballparks. Gratitude thus goes out for access at the stadiums to Chase predecessor Sharon Pannozzo and her long line of assistants led by Katelyn Thrall, and the White Sox's Scott Reifert, Bob Beghtol, and Vivian Jones.

Some of the vintage tapes featuring Harry Caray's 1972 interviews with the likes of Steve Carlton, Dick Allen, Johnny Bench, and others had been discovered by Scott Nelson, a longtime top Cubs front-office official, at a collectors' show in the 1990s. Nelson turned those tapes over to me—they were Caray's original cassettes used to distribute the interviews to radio affiliates across the country. So thanks to Nelson, with whom I have lively political discussions as we're on opposite sides of the fence, but we're on the same side of the aisle with our lifelong affection for baseball.

In memoriam goes out to Caleb "Chet" Chestnut and "Papa Carl" Leone, regal sages of Wrigley Field's right-field bleachers, for establishing a soundtrack of their own oral history and ongoing commentary back in the 1970s. "Papa Carl," who roped off bleacher benches and bought tickets when the gates opened so we wouldn't have to wait in line, is now asked to reserve some seats in the next life. Also may they rest in peace after conducting such supportive play-by-play and reporting of the True Golden Age while it was transpiring are broadcasters whom I ended up calling dear friends: Red Mottlow and Vince Lloyd.

Kudos go out to production wizards "Sweet Lou" Carlozo and Steve Leventhal, who helped shuffle some of these recorded oral histories to CDs that I could easily transcribe. This hamhanded electronics and computer Neanderthal could never have done it on his own. As usual, thanks for bailing me out to the acrobatic Ozzie Smith of book editors, Keith Wallman, he of soft hands and gentle Exacto knife in the trimming of an always too-long manuscript. Sorry for educating you about Red Sox collapses you were too young to experience. And to agent Frank Scatoni, a Marine Corps drill instructor in disguise who pushes you beyond your limits to craft book proposals that sell.

Finally, to my family—wife Nina and daughter Laura—who did big and little things to help while an author could not be distracted from his rounds. When my adeptness at handling 21st-century tasks that help produce a book ground to a halt, Laura expertly took over. Plus golden retriever Polly and basset hound Abby, angels even when they are devils, keeping an author company through the long, lonely hours of writing.

Index

Aaron, Henry "Hank," 35, 36, 37, 38, 40, 41, 54, 55, 64, 70, 71, 72, 124–29, 231, 238, 315
Adcock, Joe, 229, 316
Agee, Tommie, 24, 84
Aguirre, Hank, 201
Albert, Jeff, 251
Allen, Dick, 36–37, 51–57, 97, 107, 211, 295
Allyn, John, 216, 295, 296
Alomar, Sandy, Sr., 93
Alou, Matty, 47, 160, 233, 243, 244
Alston, Walter, 38, 116, 120
Altman, George, 249
Alyea, Brant, 28
American League (AL), 7, 8, 9, 10, 72, 89, 98
Amoros, Sandy, 226
Anderson, Sparky, 37, 153, 154–55, 157
Andrews, Mike, 148
Anixter, Jim, 197
Aparicio, Luis, 37
Armas, Tony, 243
Ashby, Alan, 239–40, 288–89

Baker, Dusty, 38, 71, 125–26, 128, 209, 230–31, 237, 278–79, 304
Baker, Gene, 226, 235, 246
Baltimore Orioles, 7, 141, 142, 144, 173–78
Bando, Sal, 142, 144–45, 146, 149, 216
Banks, Ernie, 35, 36, 37, 75, 226, 235–36, 246, 247, 285
Bannister, Alan, 204, 296
Bartirome, Tony, 169
baseball, popularity of, 3–10
basketball, 1, 315
Baylor, Don, 151, 317
Belanger, Mark, 93, 138, 139
Bench, Johnny, 37, 71, 112, 138, 139, 154, 155, 156, 157, 158, 159
Berle, Milton, 19–20
Berra, Yogi, 26, 195, 269
Berry, Ken, 92
Billingham, Jack, 127, 132, 155
Blair, Paul, 136, 176
Blass, Steve, 167–68
Blomberg, Ron, 71–72
Blue, Vida, 37, 58, 94–95, 145, 146, 150, 152, 194
Blyleven, Bert, 38, 43–44, 56–57, 100–101, 166, 170–71, 172, 216, 217–19, 254–55, 256, 301, 311
Bonda, Ted, 241, 287
Bonds, Barry, 129
Bonds, Bobby, 205–6

Bonham, Bill, 200, 201
Bossard, Roger, 293, 316
Boston Red Sox, 132–37, 182, 184–95, 316
Boswell, Ken, 24
Boudreau, Lou, 19–20, 183, 249
Bowa, Larry, 84–85, 123
Bowman, Bob, 107
Bradley, Milton, 318
Brennaman, Marty, 132
Brett, George, 38, 43–44, 179, 180
Brewers, Jim, 112
Brickhouse, Jack, 104
Brinkman, Eddie, 28
Bristol, Dave, 280
Brock, Lou, 37, 75, 209, 212, 233, 247
Brooklyn Dodgers, 4, 7–8, 13, 16
Brown, Gates, 226
Brown, Joe L., 160, 168, 242, 243
Buckner, Bill, 119, 123, 185, 203, 278
Budka-Clines, Joanne, 250–51, 305–6
Buford, Don, 175–76
bullpens and food, 309–10
bullpen system, 120–22
Bunning, Jim, 37
Burleson, Rick, 60–61, 69, 103, 135–36, 185, 187–89, 222–24
Burns, Ken, 129
Burrell, Stanley (M. C. Hammer), 148
Burris, Ray, 201–2, 250
Burroughs, Jeff, 287, 288–89
Burton, Jim, 131
Busby, Steve, 179
Busch, Gussie, 84, 209, 211, 220
Busch Stadium, 209, 210–11
Busse, Ray, 213

Camden Yards, 178
Campanella, Roy, 226
Campaneris, Bert "Campy," 146
Campbell, Bill, 120, 192
Candlestick Park, 207–9
Capps, Bill, 154
Caray, Harry, 6, 51, 84, 290, 291, 294–99, 316–17
Carbo, Bernie, 130, 154, 189
Cardenal, Jose, 275, 304
Carew, Rod, 37
Carlozo, Louis R. "Sweet Lou," 176–78
Carlton, Steve "Lefty," 37, 65, 83–87, 99, 209, 211, 219–20
Carroll, Clay, 101, 102
Carter, Joe, 247
Casanova, Paul, 28, 126
Cash, Dave, 160, 163, 243, 244, 245, 252
Cashen, Frank, 175

Cater, Danny, 8
Cepeda, Orlando, 37, 38, 206, 228
Chaderjian, Karen, 306–9
Chambliss, Chris, 136, 179, 286
Chaney, Darrel, 154
Charles, Ed, 24
Chestnut, Caleb "Chet," 152–53, 283
Chicago Cubs, 7, 12, 13–26, 182–83, 185, 195–203, 245–52, 315–16, 317
Chicago White Sox, 7, 8, 36–37, 51, 53, 204–5
Cincinnati Reds "Big Red Machine," 12, 36, 141, 152–60
Clemens, Roger, 318
Clemente, Roberto, 35–36, 37, 39, 42, 44–50, 70, 160, 162, 163, 165, 167, 173, 176, 225–26, 238, 243, 244
Clendenon, Donn, 24
Cleveland Indians, 8, 286–87
Clines, Gene, 146, 160, 163, 166, 230, 237–38, 243, 244, 250–51, 252, 305, 306
closers. *See* relief pitching and closers
Colborn, Jim, 17–18, 201
Coleman, Joe, 158
Comiskey Park, 36, 289–93, 294
Concepcion, Dave, 154
Condon, David, 198–99
contracts. *See* salaries and contracts
Cooper, Cecil, 133, 186, 237
Corbett, Brad, 219
Cosell, Howard, 2, 6
Cowens, Al, 72, 179
Craig, Roger, 113, 118, 209
Crow, Jim, 228, 316
Cruz, Jose, 50, 233–34, 301
Cuellar, Mike, 138, 139, 173, 177
Cullen, Blake, 23
Culp, Ray, 18
Curse of the Bambino (Shaughnessy), 316

Dahl, Steve, 290, 291
Dalton, Harry, 90, 174, 175
Darcy, Pat, 129, 131
Dark, Alvin, 147, 229, 261
Darwin, Bobby, 56–57, 103
Davis, Ron, 121–22
Davis, Tommy, 200, 206
Dean, Dizzy, 4, 111
Decker, Joe, 201
Dent, Bucky, 135, 185
designated hitters, 10, 71–73
DiMaggio, Joe "Joltin' Joe," 13, 26, 32–34, 314
Disco Demolition Night, 289–93, 298, 316
Dobson, Pat, 173, 177
Doby, Larry, 226, 235, 242
Donatelli, Augie, 89
Dowdle, Jim, 316
Downing, Al, 127

Dozer, Richard, 24, 87
Drake, Solly, 226
Driessen, Dan, 159
drugs and steroids, 1, 2, 313
Drysdale, Don, 90, 91, 215, 260–61
Duncan, Dave, 289, 303
Durocher, Leo "the Lip," 12, 13–26, 38, 75, 111–12, 145, 201, 249, 250, 271
Durocher, Lynn Walker Goldblatt, 14, 18, 24

Eckersley, Dennis, 38
Eckert, William, 9, 10
Ellis, Dock, 169, 244
English, Woody, 313
Enright, James, 22
Evans, Dwight, 47, 131, 185, 186

Face, Roy, 112
facial hair and hairstyles, 302–4
Feller, Bob, 88
Felske, John, 18
Fenway Park, 191–95
Fetzer, John, 1
Fidrych, Mark "the Bird," 257–59
Figueroa, Ed, 50
Fingers, Rollie, 37, 112, 113, 146, 150, 151, 194, 303
Finley, Charlie, 32, 142, 143, 144, 145, 146, 147–49, 150, 151–52, 199, 302, 303, 317
Fisk, Carlton "Pudge," 37–38, 129–33, 154, 182, 185, 187, 223, 224
Fitzpatrick, Tom, 19
Flood, Curt, 30, 215, 221
Foli, Tim, 170
football, 1, 2–3, 5–6, 10, 315
Ford, Vice President Gerald, 127
Fosse, Ray, 58–59
Foster, George, 40, 130, 154, 156–57, 159
Franks, Herman, 22, 120, 203, 265–66
free agency, 150, 217–19, 221, 222–23
Fregosi, Jim, 88, 89–90
Froemming, Bruce, 104, 105
Fryman, Woodie, 244
Fuentes, Tito, 297

Gamble, Oscar, 204, 247, 249–50, 304
Garcia, Dave, 240
Garman, Mike, 65
Garner, Phil, 169, 170, 172
Garr, Ralph, 71, 126
Garrett, Adrian, 200
Garrett, Wayne, 24
Geronimo, Cesar, 155
Gibson, Bob, 8, 37, 75–83, 234, 263
Gilliam, Jim, 206, 226, 235, 246
Giusti, Dave, 112, 203
Glanville, Doug, 66–67, 304, 317–18
Goddard, Joe, 307
Gonder, Jessie, 244

Gonzales, Mark, 207–8
Gonzalez, Julio, 117
Gossage, Goose, 38, 55, 112, 121, 136
Gowdy, Curt, 127, 142, 174
Grace, Mark, 315
Grammas, Alex, 292
Granger, Wayne, 113
Green, Dallas, 316
Green, Pumpsie, 226
Griffey, Ken, Sr., 154, 158
Griffith, Calvin, 216, 217–19, 275
Grimsley, Ross, 101
Grissom, Marv, 101, 201
Grobstein, Les, 258–59
Grote, Jerry, 24–25
Guidry, Ron, 135
Gullett, Don, 132, 154
Gura, Larry, 201

Haak, Howie, 163–64, 242
Haddix, Harvey, 240
Hairston, John, 236
Halas, George, 197
Hamilton, Milo, 127–28
Hands, Bill, 23, 198, 249
Harrah, Toby, 31
Harrelson, Bud, 154
Hebner, Richie, 160, 161
Hegan, Mike, 103
Helms, Tommy, 155
Hemond, Roland, 51, 204, 216, 294–95
Hendrick, George, 119
Hernandez, Angel, 317
Hernandez, Jackie, 244
Hernandez, Keith, 210
Hernandez, Willie, 120, 266
Hertel, Reynold, 308
Herzog, Whitey, 31, 179
Hickman, Jim, 21
Hilgendorf, Tom, 289
Hobbie, Glen, 111
Hodges, Gil, 13, 20–21, 24, 25–26, 88, 276
Holland, John, 15, 200, 246, 247–50
Holtzman, Jerome, 3, 7, 111
Holtzman, Ken, 35, 101, 145–46, 149, 150, 151, 200, 201, 247, 285, 310, 312
Hooton, Burt, 36, 201
Hornsby, Rogers, 225
Horton, Willie, 226
Howard, Elston, 235, 270
Howard, Frank, 165
Howsam, Bob, 156–57
Hrabosky, Al "Mad Hungarian," 212–13, 261–64
Hudson, Sid, 27, 30
Hundley, Randy, 25, 42, 105, 285
Hunter, Catfish, 37, 145, 146, 256
Hustle, Charlie, 36, 43

injuries and surgeries, 106–10
instant replay, 2
interracial relationships, 248–50, 317–18
Irsay, Robert, 178
Irvin, Monte, 226

Jackson, Reggie "Mr. October," 12, 37, 44, 57–62, 136, 141, 142, 146, 150, 151, 184, 188, 222, 232, 269–70, 302–3
Jansen, Larry, 201, 235–36
Jenkins, Fergie, 8, 19, 35, 37, 40–43, 63, 75–83, 99, 141, 164–65, 189–90, 247, 248, 271–72, 287–88, 309–10, 311–12
Jestadt, Garry, 104, 105
Jeter, John, 104, 243
Jobe, Frank, 106–10
John, Tommy, 8, 9, 38–39, 51, 106–10, 194, 195, 220–21, 222–23
Johnson, Alex, 43, 154–55
Johnson, Darrell, 151, 270
Johnson, Lamar, 204
Johnson, Lance, 317
Johnson, Lou, 227, 230
Johnson, Randy, 122
Jones, Randy, 196, 259, 301–2
Jones, Sam, 226

Kaat, Jim, 97–98
Kahn, Roger, 14
Kaline, Al, 37, 39
Kansas City Royals, 141, 179–81
Kapstein, Jerry, 151, 223
Kasko, Eddie, 191
Kauffman, Ewing, 179
Kendall, Fred, 104
Kennedy, Bob, 32–33, 200, 252, 306–7, 308
Kennedy, Terry, 308
Kessinger, Don, 103
Killebrew, Harmon, 37, 95, 217, 218
Kiner, Ralph, 83
kinesiology, 113–16
Kingman, Dave, 123, 264–67
Kison, Bruce, 48
Knowles, Darold, 27–28, 66, 118, 121, 158
Koosman, Jerry, 20, 88, 89
Koufax, Sandy, 7–8, 88, 90, 91, 92, 93, 94, 106–7, 215
Kranepool, Ed, 24
Kravec, Ken, 291–93, 300
Kroc, Ray, 196
Krukow, Mike, 65, 201, 202, 203, 266–67
Kubiak, Ted, 147
Kuhn, Bowie, 1, 12, 44, 72, 127, 150, 151, 152, 184, 194, 236, 279–80, 306, 318
Kusnyer, Art, 93

LaCock, Pete, 82, 197–98, 200
Lamp, Dennis, 123, 201
Larsen, Don, 104
La Russa, Tony, 152
Lasorda, Tommy, 208, 277–79
Lee, Bill, 187, 189, 193, 268
Lemon, Bob, 38, 269
Leonard, Dennis, 179
Leone, Carl "Papa Carl," 283–84
Lerch, Randy, 123
Liriano, Nelson, 109
Lloyd, Vince, 4, 11, 19, 20, 225
Locker, Bob, 200
Lockman, Whitey, 235, 275
Lolich, Mickey, 98
Lombardi, Vince, 3, 5
Lonnett, Joe, 52
Lucas, Bill, 242, 281
Lucchesi, Frank, 102
Ludtke, Melissa, 306
Lyle, Sparky, 120, 136
Lynn, Fred, 47–48, 69, 130–32, 157–58, 186–87, 194, 223, 224

M. C. Hammer (Stanley Burrell), 148
Maddox, Gary, 231
Maddux, Greg, 62, 122
Madlock, Bill, 169, 171–73, 251, 262, 284
Malzone, Frank, 186
Mangual, Angel, 243
Marichal, Juan, 37, 78, 206
Marshall, Jim, 158, 200
Marshall, Mike, 112, 113–17
Martin, Billy, 31, 58, 59, 61, 141, 152, 184, 267–72, 287
Martin, Fred, 117
Martinez, Pedro, 96
Mason, Jim, 31
Mathews, Denny, 254
Matlack, Jon, 44–45
Matsuzaka, Daisuke, 95–96
Matthews, Gary, 252, 280
Matthews, Wid, 246
Mauch, Gene, 114, 115, 116–17, 121, 274–77, 302
Mauer, Joe, 256
May, Lee, 43, 138, 139, 154, 155
Mayberry, John, 179, 300
Mays, Willie, 35, 36, 37, 38, 40, 41, 64, 70, 205–6, 231, 236
Mazeroski, Bill, 130, 243
McBride, Bake, 304
McCarver, Tim, 97
McCovey, Willie, 37, 38, 41–42, 165, 206, 207, 231
McCoy, Hal, 132–33
McCraw, Tommy, 240
McDaniel, Lindy, 51, 117
McGraw, Tug, 25
McKeon, Jack, 92
McLain, Denny, 30–31

McNally, Dave, 138, 173, 177, 221, 222
McRae, Brian, 73
McRae, Hal, 72–73, 154, 180–81
Me and the Spitter (Perry), 260
Mejias, Sam, 252
Melton, Bill, 53–55, 216–17, 294–95
Memorial Stadium, 176, 177–78
Menke, Denis, 33, 155
Meoli, Rudy, 93
Messersmith, Andy, 221, 222
Middleman, I. C., 107
Miller, Dick, 93
Miller, Marvin, 10, 215, 220–22
Milner, John, 171
minority players and managers, 7, 225–52
Mitchell, Dale, 104
Molitor, Paul, 38
Monday, Rick, 142, 145, 303
Money, Don, 103
Montanez, Willie, 50, 233
Montreal Expos, 12, 18
Moore, Donnie, 123, 201
Morabito, Mickey, 256
Morales, Jerry, 50, 203
Moreland, Keith, 63–64
Morgan, Joe, 37, 43, 131, 153, 155–56, 157, 158, 159
Morgan, Tom, 91
Morris, Jack, 61, 118, 296
Mota, Manny, 244
mound heights, 9, 313
Munson, Thurman, 38, 67–70, 93
Murcer, Bobby, 251, 283–84, 308
Murphy, Dale, 85–86, 118–19
Murtaugh, Danny, 168, 244, 245

National League (NL), 6–7, 8, 9, 12, 72, 89, 98
Neal, Charlie, 226
Nelson, Davey, 28–29, 30
Newcombe, Don, 226, 227
New York Giants, 13, 16, 205–9
New York Mets, 7, 12–13, 16, 24, 25–26
New York Yankees, 4, 7, 67–69, 141, 187–89
Nicholson, Gary, 200
Nicoscia, Steve, 169
Niekro, Joe, 18, 201
Niekro, Phil, 18, 37, 98, 99–100, 126–27, 128–29, 215–16, 238, 280–82
Nixon, President Richard M., 11, 12
no-hitters, 101–5
Norman, Fred, 105
North, Bill, 58, 59, 104, 146–48, 152, 200, 231–32, 248, 249, 250

Oakland A's (Athletics), 13, 26, 32–34, 94, 98, 141, 142–52
Oakland Coliseum, 149–50
O'Connell, Dick, 270
Oglivie, Ben, 186

Oliva, Tony, 38
Oliver, Al, 45–47, 48–49, 80, 86, 160,
  161–62, 164–65, 244, 245
O'Neil, Buck, 235, 246, 247
Orta, Jorge, 55, 204
Osney, Rick, 105
Otis, Amos, 72, 92, 179
Ott, Ed, 170, 172–73, 311

Paciorek, Tom, 223
Pagan, Joe, 244
Page, Mitchell, 243
Palmer, Jim, 37, 173, 177, 256–57
Pappas, Arthur, 222–23
Pappas, Milt, 103–5, 275, 310
Parker, Dave, 63, 160, 164, 165, 166–
  67, 169–70, 172, 243, 301, 313–14
Peden, Buck, 306–7, 308
Peña, Orlando, 229, 233
Perez, Tony, 37, 138, 154, 155, 157,
  158, 159, 181
Perry, Gaylord, 78, 100, 113, 206,
  259–61
Peter Magowan and Co., 207–8
Peters, Hank, 175
Phillips, Adolfo, 15, 18
Piersall, Jimmy, 296, 297, 298, 316–17
Piniella, Lou "Sweet Lou," 60, 68, 136–
  37, 160, 187, 253–57, 268–69, 318
Pinson, Vida, 237–38
Pittsburgh Drug Trial, 313
Pittsburgh Pirates, 7, 16, 48, 160–73,
  242–45, 313–14
Pizarro, Juan, 50
Players Association, 10, 215, 219, 220
Plaza, Ron, 233
Popovich, Paul, 23–24
Poquette, Tom, 72
Porter, Darrell, 103
Powell, Boog, 138, 139
Power, Vic, 50, 233
pranks, 311–12
Pujols, Albert, 44, 181

Quinn, John, 220
Quirk, Jamie, 179

Race Relations Information Center,
  236
Randle, Lenny, 29, 30–31, 289
Randolph, Willie, 243
Reese, Rich, 94
Regan, Phil "the Vulture," 111–12, 113
relief pitching and closers, 111–22
Remy, Jerry, 136
Rettenmund, Merv, 176
Reuschel, Paul, 66
Reuschel, Rick, 65, 124, 158–59, 201,
  202, 203
Reuss, Jerry, 211
RFK Stadium, 286
Rice, Jim, 131–32, 151, 186, 193

Richard, Bee Bee, 87
Richards, Paul, 174
Rickey, Branch, 242, 246
Ripken, Cal, 217
Rivers, Mickey, 136, 187, 256
Rizzuto, Phil, 6
Roarke, Mike, 201
Roberts, Curt, 242
Robertson, Bob, 46–47, 160, 244, 245
Robinson, Brooks, 36, 37, 137–40, 154,
  174, 176, 177, 216, 271, 273–74
Robinson, Donnie, 170, 171
Robinson, Frank, 39, 43, 72, 107, 174,
  175, 176, 177, 236–42
Robinson, Jackie, 4, 125, 126, 221,
  225, 226, 227, 229, 234–35, 236
Rodgers, Andre, 244
Rojas, Cookie, 179
Rose, Pete, 36, 38, 42–43, 70, 138, 154,
  155, 157
Roseboro, John, 91
Rosello, Dave, 248
Rosen, Al, 223
Ross, Gary, 18
Royko, Mike, 199–200, 266, 317
Rudi, Joe, 32–34, 146, 148–49, 150–51,
  152, 194, 303–4
Ruth, Babe, 313, 316
Ryan, Nolan, 37, 87–94, 164, 204, 315
Ryan, Terry, 109
Rygelski, Jim, 210–11

salaries and contracts, 214–24, 315
Saltwell, Salty, 198, 200
San Diego Padres, 12, 16
Sanguillen, Manny, 50, 160, 244
Santo, Ron, 15, 35, 38, 75, 105, 225,
  275, 276, 311
Schmidt, Mike, 36, 38, 62–67, 117, 123,
  124
Schoendienst, Red, 38, 75
Schueler, Ron, 291–92
Schultz, Barney, 201
Scott, George "Boomer," 102, 103
Scott, Mike, 118
Scott, Rodney, 251–52
Scully, Vin, 128
Seaver, Tom "Terrific," 20, 36, 37,
  88–89, 99, 153, 302
Seghi, Phil, 241
Segui, Diego, 233
Seitz, Peter, 222
Selig, Bud, 1–2
Selma, Dick, 21
Shaer, Tom, 58, 190–94, 195, 269–70
Shamsky, Art, 24
Sharp, Bill, 101–2, 103
Shea Stadium, 286
Short, Bob, 30
Shriver, Chuck, 246–47, 248–50
Sianis, Sam, 199
Sianis, William, 199

Sisler, George, 163
Smith, Lee, 120, 247
Smith, Reggie, 208, 304
Smith, Tal, 233–34
Smith, Willie, 16, 285
Sotomayor, Sonia, 1
Spencer, Jim, 204
St. Louis Cardinals, 6, 9, 14, 16, 209–13
Stahl, Larry, 104
Stanley, Bob, 136, 185
Stargell, Willie, 37, 41, 42, 80, 85–86, 160, 162, 163, 165, 166, 169–70, 171, 173, 243, 244, 263, 301, 313–14
Stark, Herb, 108
Staub, Rusty, 41, 234
Steinbrenner, George, 59, 60, 141, 184, 187, 223, 318
Stennett, Rennie, 160, 168, 243, 244
Sterling, John, 318
Stewart, Dave, 118
Stone, Steve, 153, 204–5, 296
Stoneman, Bill, 18, 201
strike zones, 7, 9, 313
Suker, Jacob, 22
Sullivan, Haywood, 195, 224
Sullivan, Paul, 292
Sutter, Bruce, 38, 112, 117–20, 122, 124, 159, 201, 203
Sutton, Don, 37
Swisher, Steve, 66
Swoboda, Ron, 16, 20–22, 24, 25, 83–84, 89, 234, 276

Tanner, Chuck, 55–56, 149, 151, 170, 171–72, 294–96, 309, 311
Taylor, Ron, 25
Templeton, Gary, 209–10
Tenace, Gene, 143–44, 146
10-Cent Beer Night, 286–89
Terwilliger, Wayne, 27
Thome, Jim, 267
Thomson, Bobby, 134
Thornton, Andre, 232, 239
Tiant, Luis, 8, 60, 68–69, 95–96, 133–34, 137, 228–29, 316
Tidrow, Dick "Dirt," 120
Tiger Stadium, 37, 58
Todd, Jim, 200
Tolan, Bobby, 205
Torborg, Jeff, 90–94, 240–42
Torre, Joe, 38, 75, 233
Torrez, Mike, 135, 136, 151
Trammell, Alan, 61–62, 257–58, 290, 292
Tribune Co., 197, 317
Trillo, Manny, 200, 203
Trout, Steve, 290–91
True Golden Age, 73, 161, 181
Turner, Ted, 279–82
TV and radio, 3–6
Tyson, Mike "Rocky," 213

uniforms, 299–302

Van Horne, Dave, 276–77, 302
Veale, Bob, 8, 244, 245
Veeck, Bill, 197, 199, 204, 205, 242, 286, 289–90, 292, 296, 298–99, 302, 307–8
Veeck, Mike, 298–99, 300
Verdi, Bob, 153
Virdon, Bill, 163
Virgil, Ozzie, Sr., 226

Waldman, Suzyn, 318
Walker, Harry "the Hat," 243–44
Wardlow, Calvin, 126
Washington Senators, 13, 26–31
Weaver, Earl, 37, 93, 139–40, 141, 175, 177, 272–74
Weis, Al, 21, 107
White, Bill, 210
White, Frank, 179–80
White, Jerry, 252
White, Roy, 136
Wilhelm, Hoyt, 112
Williams, Billy "Sweet Swinger," 15–16, 35, 36, 37, 70–71, 75, 76, 79–80, 104, 112, 225, 227, 231, 235, 247, 317
Williams, Dick, 147
Williams, Ted "Splendid Splinter," 13, 26–31, 38, 314
Willoughby, Jim, 189
Wills, Maury, 206, 236, 240, 244
Wilson, Earl, 226
Wilson, Willie, 179
Winfield, Dave, 38, 187
Wise, Rick, 84, 85, 101–3, 189, 190, 219, 220, 255
women and the baseball field environment, 305–9
Wood, Wilbur, 56, 96–97, 98
Woodward, Woody, 138
Wrigley, Phil, 4, 13, 22, 35–36, 63, 195–96, 197–98, 199, 200, 203, 246, 247, 251, 317
Wrigley, William, Jr., 195, 203
Wrigley Field, 124, 200, 285

Yankee Stadium, 61, 187
Yastrzemski, Carl, 8, 26–27, 37, 38, 44, 151, 191
Yawkey, Tom, 151, 191–92, 193
Yocum, Lewis, 108
Yount, Robin, 38

Zimmer, Don, 69, 120, 189, 190–91
Zisk, Richie, 160, 163, 204

About the Author

George Castle has covered Major League Baseball and the Chicago Cubs since 1980 for a variety of newspapers and magazines, and for the *Times of Northwest Indiana,* the Chicago area's fourth-largest daily newspaper. He hosts and produces a weekly syndicated baseball show, *Diamond Gems,* which is broadcast on 35 affiliates, a national sports radio Internet network, and the NWI.com/baseball/sports Web site.

Castle has become a multimedia purveyor of baseball's inside information and analysis, using a network of close clubhouse and front-office relationships to continually produce scoops and informative pieces that outflank other media. He has gotten to know—and gain the trust of—almost all the important figures in Chicago and general baseball history. Castle has also appeared on a wide variety of network radio—including ESPN, Sporting News, and Sirius—and local sports-talk radio programs. He was tapped by producers as one of the historical experts on the Cubs for *Wait 'Til Next Year: The Saga of the Chicago Cubs,* the 2006 HBO special on the team. He lives in Chicago.

Also by George Castle
Sweet Lou and the Cubs: A Year Inside the Dugout (Lyons Press)
Entangled in Ivy: Inside the Cubs' Quest for October
The Million-to-One Team: Why the Chicago Cubs Haven't Won a Pennant Since 1945
Baseball and the Media: How Fans Lose in Today's Coverage of the Game
Throwbacks: Old-School Baseball Players in Today's Game
Where Have All Our Cubs Gone?
The I-55 Series Cubs Vs. Cardinals

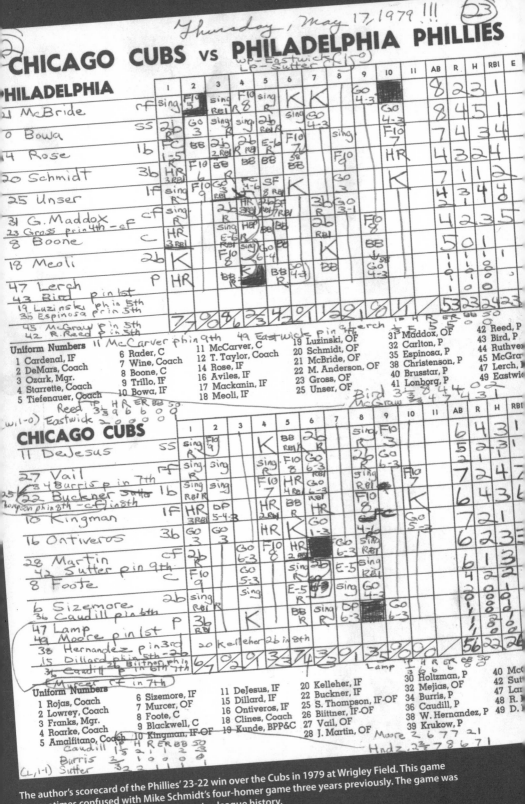

The author's scorecard of the Phillies' 23–22 win over the Cubs in 1979 at Wrigley Field. This game is sometimes confused with Mike Schmidt's four-homer game three years previously. The game was the second-highest scoring contest in major-league history.